EXTRAORDINARY RECIPES FROM

HUDSON VALLEY CHEF'S TABLE

JULIA SEXTON

Photography by Andre Baranowski

WESTCHESTER TO COLUMBIA COUNTY

Globe Pequot

Guilford, Connecticut

The culinary community is always growing and changing. Chef's move on, while restaurants come and go. This book celebrates the chef's and dishes that have given each city or region its unique flavor. We hope you will try these recipes at home and allow their legacy to live on for years to come.

Globe Pequot

An imprint of The Rowman & Littlefield Publishing Group, Inc.
4501 Forbes Blvd., Ste. 200
Lanham, MD 20706
www.rowman.com

Distributed by NATIONAL BOOK NETWORK

British Library Cataloguing in Publication Information available

Library of Congress Cataloging-in-Publication Data available

ISBN 978-1-4930-4708-6 (paperback)
ISBN 978-1-4930-1059-2 (e-book)

 The paper used in this publication meets the minimum requirements of American National Standard for Information Sciences— Permanence of Paper for Printed Library Materials, ANSI/NISO Z39.48-1992

For James, my sainted husband,
and Olivia, my delicious daughter.

CONTENTS

Acknowledgments

Even though I am a restaurant critic, I know, without the slimmest doubt, that even a middle-of-the-road chef knows more about food than the greatest critic. More succinctly put by Oscar Wilde (who, admittedly, came to a bad end), "The critic has to educate the public; the artist has to educate the critic." In my working life as a restaurant critic, I've tried to keep my eyes on the artists as I juggled my paltry quiver of words. Chefs will always have better weapons than writers, and that's why I'll always have my eyes trained on chefs.

I give my heartfelt thanks to Hudson Valley chefs who stole time from their unforgiving schedules to talk with me and contribute recipes to this book. Clearly, it is their book—I was just the one taking notes.

Thanks to the peerless photographer, Andre Baranowski, for embarking on this giant project—against, one must note, all practical sense. Andre's hard work and stunning artistry give beauty to the document in your hands and I have been incredibly blessed by his collaboration. Andre, I owe you forever.

My deepest appreciation goes to Amy Lyons of Globe Pequot press for reaching out from the blue and taking a chance on a writer whose work is sometimes strewn with F-bombs and is often followed by nasty website comments. I'm grateful to Amy for inviting me on this adventure and, also, for her patience when it finally came to an end. Thanks to Janet Crawshaw, publisher of the excellent *Valley Table Magazine,* for her gracious advice. Thanks to Esther Davidowitz for her timely encouragement and thanks to Nancy Claus for her empathy. Thanks to *Westchester Magazine* for indulging me these many years.

Thanks to Chef Peter Kelly for his unerring wisdom and kindness when I needed it most, at the beginning of my career. I know that I am not the only person in this book who has benefited from his quiet advocacy. Not only has Chef Kelly nurtured many of the voices in these pages, but, in his own pioneering restaurants in the Hudson Valley, Kelly foretold what our dining scene would become. Chef Peter Kelly is McArthur and Patton rolled into one; it is said that some call him "The Pope" (but that's never to his face).

Heartfelt thanks to Chef David DiBari for his blazing artistry, humor, and unshakable decency. Thanks to Stephen Paul Mancini and Chef Eric Gabrynowicz for effortless excellence irresistibly paired with elite intoxicants.Thanks to Chef Matt Hutchins for his Beacon insights and thanks to Chef Chris Vergara for his ability to cheerfully overlook my insanity. Thanks to Chef Christian Petroni, Rob Krauss, Coby Blount, and John T. Nealon for making me laugh until I cried. Thanks to Baron Ambrosia for enriching my life with preposterousness. Thanks to Chef Dan Barber and to Chef Zak Pelaccio for their generosity during long, often rambling, interviews.

This book could not have been written without the support of my husband, James Sexton, who has eaten with me and argued with me for the length of my career. Not only does he have one of the keenest minds that I've ever encountered, but, when the day-to-night demands of my profession overwhelm our little family, he gamely steps up. Thanks from the bottom of my heart.

Introduction

New York has closed itself off to the young and the struggling. But there are other cities. Detroit. Poughkeepsie. New York City has been taken away from you. So my advice is: Find a new city.

—PATTI SMITH

The Hudson River Valley had always been colonized by peoples hunting for a new city. In the seventeenth century, they were the Dutch, who sailed up the Hudson to find a fertile land that supplied what their land-poor nation could not. Then they were the English, who found an easily defended and navigable river that led to vast and untapped resources in its upper reaches. Then they were urban refugees who fled an inhumane city for a more healthful life in the bucolic north.

But those are only the broad strokes that have defined the Hudson River Valley since the seventeenth century. What really formed the Valley happened before the

Europeans were even conscious of a land beyond the sea. Thousands of years before Henry Hudson sailed his *Half Moon* up to modern day Albany in 1609, the glaciers that once blanketed the Hudson Valley retreated to the Arctic. What the ice left in its wake was a soil so rich that, in global satellite images taken today, the trench of its path still shows up as a jet-black streak. Lured by this soil's fertility came the family farmers of the Hudson Valley, who, over time, learned to glean the finest products that the land could provide. It was a profitable business. The ports along the river quickly moved Hudson Valley goods into booming eighteenth and nineteenth century cities, fueling the nation's new metropolises with New York State–raised meat, grain, and milk. Then, in a feat of hyper-modern engineering (for the first quarter of the nineteenth century, anyway), the Erie Canal connected the Hudson River to the Great Lakes and the spreading railroads beyond; this turned the greatest river of the East into an artery that fed the West.

While the River was the main conduit of goods within the Hudson River Valley, it was the commuter rail lines that ushered in the bulk of its populace. By the mid-nineteenth century, the Hudson, Harlem and New Haven lines had begun to spread their fingers into Westchester County and beyond. The commuter lines made it possible for the leafy triangle of Westchester—

much of which had been carved by millionaires into their rolling country estates—to also become a healthful and pleasant home for a growing middle class that worked by day in Gotham.

Finally, when Manhattan was filled to bursting and suburban sprawl had mostly edged the picturesque farms from the southern Hudson Valley, the New York State Thruway and the parkway system paved the way for a new kind of refugee. Some city and suburb dwellers, lured by the promise of bucolic retreats near the farms of the Hudson Valley, bought second homes in the horse country of Columbia and Ulster counties. There were others—most notably, counter-culture heroes like Timothy Leary and Bob Dylan, who looked to the open spaces of the Hudson Valley as sites for bohemian utopias. Ultimately, the presence of these and other counter-culture figures led the Woodstock nation northward—but, of course, ever since the days of Henry Hudson, this land had seduced pioneers.

As Patti Smith notes, that beacon still shines in the Hudson River Valley today. Every year, it leads more artists, restaurateurs, craftsmen, urban dropouts, distillers, farmers, brewers, chefs, and barmen to retreat northward. They're looking to create new utopias in a land where such dreams are still possible. This book is about them and the wonderful work that they do.

COLUMBIA
COUNTY

Cafe le Perche

230 Warren Street
Hudson, NY 12534
(518) 822-1850
CAFELEPERCHE.COM
Owner: Allan Chapin; General Manager: Jennifer Houle;
Bakers: Nichole Lasky and Robert Pecorino

Even the smallest sparks can trigger great fires. At Cafe le Perche, that spark was bread—in fact, one particular baguette. This baguette was baked in La Perche, a town almost smack in the geographical center of France; it was so delicious, so haunting, and so poetic that it inspired Allan Chapin to try to re-create it. To that end he disassembled an eleven-inch, seventeen-ton wood-fired oven (complete with a manually rotated baking stone) and had it shipped from France to Hudson, New York, where it was mortared into a basement of a former bank on Warren Street. The American bakers that Chapin hired to man this oven didn't exactly know what they were getting into.

Traditionally, the kitchen-classrooms in culinary schools feature the sort of steely equipment that comes to life when you press a red button. According to Cafe le Perche's GM, Jennifer Houle, the morning routine at Cafe le Perche is far different. "It's purely rustic. You have to load the fire and then manually vent it to get it to the right temperature.

There are so many factors that not only affect the bread-baking but also affect the oven: the humidity, the wind, the temperature inside, the type of wood that we're getting delivered. There's a learning curve to working with this oven." Faced with a toolbox of rocks, fire, and wood, Cafe le Perche's bakers found themselves working, essentially, in the Stone Age.

Then there was the challenge of re-creating the unique flours of France in the Hudson Valley. To help, Chapin imported Daniel Lambert, who baked the original baguette in Le Perche that inspired Chapin's Hudson homage. Armed with a sack of flour that he smuggled from France, Lambert consulted with Wild Hive Farm in Clinton Corners, New York. The result is Cafe le Perche's proprietary blend of locally milled soft white pastry flour and hard red wheat flour.

Meanwhile, there was Cafe Le Perche's Warren Street building's potential to exploit. Built in the 1830s, a time when bank deposits were not insured, the Hudson River Savings Bank relied on impressive architecture to instill faith. According to Houle, "The original concept was just to open a bakery. But when I saw the bones of the building, I thought, 'This is just stunning, we need to do something more with this.'" The remodeling was peppered with happy discoveries. Says Houle, "We found that grille behind the bar in the carriage house. It was the old teller cage from the time when the building was a bank. We used whatever we could find that was original."

Consistent with Chapin's commitment to locally milled flour, Cafe le Perche's sourcing is hyper-local. Says Houle, "The original chef and I were at International Culinary Institute together, and the farm-to-table movement was huge. It was just a no-brainer to source our eggs, flour, milk, vegetables, and the proteins in the Hudson Valley." The kitchen at Cafe le Perche works in conjunction with Blue Spruce Farm in Ghent, New York. According to Houle, "It's not a commercial farm—they primarily work with us. What we do is send them a list in the spring of what we would like to use for our menu and they plant the seeds. And we go out there and pick whenever we want—it's been a partnership for the last two years. As the farm is growing, we're growing with it, and using more of its stuff. We have plans to use more land for things like herbs, berries, apples, and peaches."

Cafe le Perche Roast Pork Sandwich

(SERVES 4)

For the onion jam:

6 large yellow onions
4 tablespoons canola oil
2 teaspoons ground coriander
2 teaspoons ground cumin
1 teaspoon cayenne pepper
1 cup apple cider
1 cup apple cider vinegar
1 cup water
2 tablespoons salt
4 tablespoons granulated sugar

For the house-made mustard:

2 cups yellow mustard seed
1 teaspoon crushed red pepper flakes
½ cup ground mustard
1 teaspoon ground cumin
1 teaspoon salt
½ teaspoon ground white pepper
1 tablespoon honey
1 cup dry white wine (e.g., Pinot Grigio or
   Sauvignon Blanc)
½ cup rice wine vinegar

For the braised kale:

2½ pounds kale
5 teaspoons canola oil
1½ teaspoons minced garlic
1 teaspoon crushed red pepper flakes
¾ cup dry white wine (e.g., Pinot Grigio or
   Sauvignon Blanc)
2 quarts chicken stock
2 tablespoons salt
1 tablespoon ground white pepper

For the pork tenderloin:

1 (1–1½ pounds) pork tenderloin
¾ teaspoon salt
½ teaspoon ground black pepper
½ cup Dijon mustard
2¼ teaspoons minced rosemary
2¼ teaspoons minced garlic
1 tablespoon olive oil

For the assembled roast pork sandwiches:

8 tablespoons unsalted butter
8 half-inch-thick slices Cafe Le Perche rustic bread
12 ounces roast pork tenderloin, sliced thick
16 slices gruyère
8 ounces braised kale
4 tablespoons onion jam
4 tablespoons house-made mustard
16 slices Roma tomato, thinly sliced

To make the jam: Halve the onions and slice them thin. Heat a large pan over medium heat and pour in the canola oil. Add the sliced onions to the oil and sauté over medium heat until the onions are tinged with gold. Add the coriander, cumin, and cayenne and sauté for 3–5 more minutes, or until the onions are caramelized. Add the cider, cider vinegar, water, salt, and sugar and cook this mixture until the liquid is reduced to a thick syrup and the onions have a jamlike consistency. Remove from heat and reserve.

To make the mustard: In a mortar and pestle (or using a spice grinder), grind the mustard seed and crushed red pepper together until it is a coarse powder. Pour the mixture into a small bowl and then add the ground mustard, cumin, salt, and white pepper. In a separate small bowl, combine the honey, white wine, and rice wine

vinegar. Slowly whisk the wet ingredients into the dry ingredients and continue to whisk until the mixture is fully incorporated. Refrigerate the mustard for at least 24 hours prior to use.

To braise the kale: Rinse the kale and trim the thick center stem from each leaf. Heat a large pan over medium heat and pour in the canola oil. Add the garlic and crushed red pepper to the oil and sauté for 2 minutes. Pour in the white wine and continue to cook until the liquid is reduced by half. Add the kale, chicken stock, salt, and pepper. Cover and cook for 10 minutes, or until kale is just tender; do not overcook.

To roast the pork loin: Preheat oven to 350°F. Place the pork tenderloin on a metal rack and then set the rack on a large, foil-lined sheet tray. Rub the pork with half the salt and half the pepper, then spread Dijon mustard over the entire tenderloin. Sprinkle rosemary evenly over the mustard, then season the pork again with the remaining salt and pepper. Spread the minced garlic along the top of the loin and drizzle with olive oil.

Place the pork in the oven and roast it until a thermometer inserted into the center reads 140°F (about 12–15 minutes). Remove the loin from the oven and allow it to cool for at least 1 hour.

To assemble the sandwich: Heat a frying pan over medium-low heat. Butter one side of each bread slice and place the slices, butter side down, in the pan. Fry the slices until they are crisp and golden on one side. Remove. Meanwhile, on an oven-safe pan, place the sliced pork in a single layer topped with eight slices of gruyère. Next to the pork, lay the braised kale. Top with eight slices of gruyère. Broil until the cheese is melted and bubbling.

On four of the untoasted sides of the bread, generously spread the warm onion jam. Onto the untoasted sides of the other slices, spread the house-made mustard. Layer the sliced tomato over the onion jam, then divide the kale and gruyère onto the tomato. Top this with the roasted pork and gruyère. Close the sandwiches, cut them on a bias, and serve with salad.

CLUB HELSINKI

405 COLUMBIA STREET
HUDSON, NY 12534
(518) 828-4800
HELSINKIHUDSON.COM
OWNERS: DEBORAH McDOWELL, MARC SCHLAFLER,
AND CAMERON MELVILLE; EXECUTIVE CHEF: HUGH HORNER

While Club Helsinki's 1995 origins are in the Berkshires, it didn't really get its funk until it settled in a glorious nineteenth-century factory in the center of Hudson. While much of Club Helsinki's draw comes from the artists that perform there—Shawn Colvin, Matisyahu, Ralph Stanley, Levon Helm, Norah Jones—a lot of the club's innate charm comes from Hudson itself. According to Chef Hugh Horner, who speaks in the honeyed cadences of his Low Country roots, "If you ask me, any city that has some sad hanging around it is a place where you'll have a good time. Historically, look at all the towns that rock and roll. I mean, you have New York—obviously—New Orleans, Houston,

Charleston, Atlanta. All of those cities have an underbelly and a dark side to 'em, and that's why they're intriguing. And there, they'd welcome if you were an artist or were gay or were biracial or were slightly different. That's why New Orleans, Savannah, and Charleston were wonderful—they didn't give a shit." Just like Hudson.

It wasn't easy for Helsinki's trio of owners (Deborah McDowell, Marc Schlafler, and Cameron Melville) to transform a decrepit, one hundred-plus-year-old factory into what would become a large restaurant, two performance spaces, a recording studio, and an art gallery. Says Horner, "They came over from the Berkshires without a general contractor. It was just Marc [Schlafler] and four other guys, so it's really a work of art. They didn't pay some huge thirty-man crew to finish it in six months—they handcrafted it. Also, they used recycled, green products and restored whatever they could that was here. Marc used only local construction workers. Marc's a cool guy. Actually, Deborah, Marc, and Cameron are all really cool people, and I'm blessed to work for 'em."

Horner came to Hudson after a stint at the now closed Williamsburg Cafe in Brooklyn. "Brooklyn was cool. I liked Brooklyn a lot. We were in Williamsburg early on when it was really the wild, wild west. We could do whatever we wanted with food and it was fun." He laughs, "Talk about industrial and 'hood! I mean, in Williamsburg back then, you stayed in the Bedford area and maybe you touched a little bit on Metropolitan. Now everyone is all over the place. But it was cool. You know, everyone got together; there was a real sense of community among the chefs. Everyone was helping each other out and sending diners to other restaurants."

Amazingly, Horner's transition to the Hudson Valley from New Orleans, Charleston, and the hipster heydays of Williamsburg was effortless. "The people up here are very friendly. A lot of them grew up on farms. I think part of the reason I love it here so much is because, on some of my days off when I was still living in the city, I'd come up here and it was like the first time I'd seen nature in a long time." He laughs, "I also love the fact that Hudson's a left-brain town: It's an artistic town."

LOW COUNTRY SHRIMP & GRITS

(SERVES 4)

For the grits:

6 cups milk

2 teaspoons salt

1 teaspoon freshly ground white pepper

4 tablespoons unsalted butter

1½ cups yellow Anson Mills grits (not instant
    or quick cooking)

Grated white cheddar cheese to taste

For the shrimp:

½ cup butter

¼ cup minced red bell peppers

¼ cup minced green bell peppers

½ cup minced celery

½ cup minced Vidalia onions

1 tablespoon minced garlic

½ cup Andouille sausage

¼ cup flour

4 cups shrimp stock

½ cup heavy cream

2 dozen (21–25 count) Gulf shrimp, peeled
    and deveined

Salt and black pepper to taste

To make the grits: In a large saucepan placed over medium heat, combine the milk, salt, pepper, and 2 tablespoons of the butter. Bring the liquid to a gentle boil and then stir in the grits. Cook for 1 hour and 15 minutes, stirring occasionally. The grits will stick to the bottom of the pan, so make sure not to scrape the bottom of the pan because they will be scorched and might taste bad—they wash away easily—but will make the presentation flecked and chunky if scraped). If the grits absorb all the liquid, add a little hot water to thin them out. Remove the pan from heat and stir in the remaining 2 tablespoons of butter and cheese. Reserve while you finish the recipe.

To prepare the shrimp: In a large skillet melt butter over medium-high heat. Add the peppers, celery, onion, garlic, and the diced Andouille. Sauté for 3–5 minutes, stirring occasionally. Sprinkle in flour, stirring constantly for 3–5 minutes, or until slightly golden. Slowly add shrimp stock, 1 cup at a time, stirring until a saucelike consistency is achieved. Additional stock may be added if necessary. Blend in cream, bring to a low boil, and then add shrimp. Cook for 3–5 minutes, or until shrimp curl and turn pink. Season with salt and pepper. Serve with grits on the side.

THE CRIMSON SPARROW

746 WARREN STREET
HUDSON, NY 12534
(518) 671-6565
THECRIMSONSPARROW.COM
CO-CHEF/OWNERS: JOHN MCCARTHY AND BENJAMIN FREEMOLE

It takes commitment for two talented young chefs to leave Manhattan and set up shop together in Hudson, New York. In this case that commitment is not just toward a new project but also to each other. Says Chef John McCarthy of Crimson Sparrow, which he opened with co-chef/owner Benjamin Freemole, "Frankly, there's not a large culinary community around here. It's not like you can go to a bar and see, like, fifteen other cooks from the neighborhood. You grow to rely on your partner and that person relies on you. You are, for lack of a better term, on your own."

McCarthy met Freemole in the most cosmopolitan of circumstances. They were both working under Chef Wylie Dufresne at the molecular gastronomy landmark, WD-50. Although, as McCarthy says, they don't "put it in your face" at Crimson Sparrow, the futuristic precepts that McCarthy and Freemole learned under Dufresne come into play in their Hudson kitchen. Having been asked a hundred times about molecular gastronomy, McCarthy is bored by the notion that modern techniques are separate from the traditional repertoire. "Almost every single kitchen in the United States uses xanthan gum, uses gelling gum, uses emulsifiers and modified starches to create textures. And that's the true legacy of the Wylie Dufresnes of the world: They've made these advances in the culinary word that everyone takes for granted."

As at WD-50, Crimson Sparrow is devoted to the narrative arc of tasting menus. "We opened with a menu that had close to twenty-two different things on it. We were really just stretching our legs and doing dishes that we wanted to do. On the one-year anniversary of the restaurant, we decided to do a tasting menu of dishes that we thought would be really good in the context of five or six courses. At the time, we were giving folks the option of the tasting menu versus the a la carte menu. That first week, I'm not exaggerating, we had only two diners who came in and didn't order the tasting menu. Naturally, we just moved to a tasting menu format, and we change that every week."

While McCarthy already had a house in Claverack before he and Freemole joined forces, the city of Hudson has an energy that is alluring to both chefs. "It's an incredibly historical looking and feeling town. By the same token it's got artistic vibes to it. You

only need to know what's going on in Hudson to know that it's a magnet of culture—and that's not only for the people in it, but for the people who come to visit. As cooks, we press ourselves to be creative, and I think the Hudson environment is conducive to the artistic energy that we all try to tap into. Hudson is a special place; I mean, artist Marina Abramović will be building a fifteen million dollar performance space and cultural center here within a year or so. Obviously, we weren't thinking of Marina Abramović when we opened, but we saw something in Hudson that other people are seeing as well."

But don't worry. Success won't spoil Hudson, whose grittiness gives this town what McCarthy calls "an edge." The notion of turning Warren Street into a status label shopping mall actively disgusts this chef. "I'll be honest with you. I'm with 99 percent of the people here who, when they hear that Hudson is the 'Hamptons of the Hudson Valley,' get kinda [moaning] 'Oh, no!' It's a sickening thought."

Beef with Avocado, Cauliflower, Radish & Potato

(SERVES 8)

For the shallot confit:

8–10 shallots, peeled and minced
Grapeseed oil to cover
Salt and pepper to taste

For the avocados:

4 ripe avocados
¼ cup Greek yogurt, strained
1 tablespoon strained shallot confit
Salt to taste

For the beef tendon:

2 pounds beef tendons
1 head garlic, halved
Sake to cover

For the cauliflower and radish:

1 head cauliflower, cut into small florets
2 bunches English breakfast radishes, tops removed
   (reserve these), cut into pieces the size of
   cauliflower florets
2 tablespoons strained shallot confit
1 tablespoon whole unsalted butter
2 tablespoons lemon vinegar
Water, as needed
Salt to taste
1 tablespoon julienned beef tendon

For the radishes:

1 bunch English breakfast radishes, sliced as thin as
   possible lengthwise, placed in ice water
¼ cup reserved radish tops, cleaned, sliced on a bias,
   placed in ice water
¼ cup red-veined sorrel, sliced on a bias
¼ cup minced chives
¼ cup micro radish greens or your favorite petite
   greens from the farmers' market
2 teaspoons lemon vinegar
2 teaspoons shallot confit oil
Salt to taste

For the potatoes:

6 Yukon Gold potatoes, peeled and cleaned, cut into
   uniform pieces
2 heads garlic, cut in half
1 bunch thyme
2 bay leaves
Salt to taste
Oil for frying, as needed

For the beef:

4 pounds beef (flap, tri-tip, hanger, skirt, or
   flank steak will all work)
4 shallots, peeled and sliced thin
8 sprigs thyme
2 tablespoons extra-virgin olive oil
Salt and cracked pepper to taste
2 tablespoons whole unsalted butter, cubed

To confit the shallots: In a small, heavy-bottomed pot over low heat, place the shallots. Add enough grapeseed oil to the shallots to barely cover them. Cook the shallots until tender. Make sure to keep the heat very low so that they don't burn. When the shallots are very tender, remove from heat. Once cool, season the confit to taste. Store them in the oil and refrigerate until use.

To prepare the avocados: In a blender place avocados, yogurt, and shallot confit and puree the mixture until smooth. Season to taste with salt and reserve.

To cook the beef tendons: In a pressure cooker place beef tendons. Add one head of garlic, halved. Cover with sake and cook for 1 hour. Remove from heat and allow pressure to subside. Remove the tendons from the cooking liquid and allow them to rest for 10 minutes. Place the tendons between two cookie sheets or trays and press with about 15 pounds of weight on top. (Sacks of flour and sugar work nicely here.) Press the tendons in the refrigerator until cooled. Reserve.

To prepare the cauliflower and radish: Into a large sauté pan, place cauliflower, radishes, shallot confit, butter, and vinegar. Add just enough water to cover the bottom of the pan. Place over high heat and cook until water is almost evaporated. Season very lightly with salt and deglaze with more water. Continue this process until the vegetables are tender but still maintain a little crunch. Add beef tendon and stir to coat.

To prepare the radishes: Just before service, combine all ingredients in a bowl and toss gently.

To cook the potatoes: Several hours before you intend to serve the dish, place potatoes in a medium-size pot, cover with water, and add garlic, thyme, bay leaves, and salt. Simmer until very tender. Make sure not to boil the potatoes or they will break. Carefully remove the potatoes from the water, place them on a parchment paper–lined sheet tray, and freeze. When they are frozen, heat the oil in a pot large enough to fry the potatoes. When the oil reaches 275°F, remove the potatoes from the freezer and fry for 5–7 minutes, or until a crust forms. Remove the potatoes from the oil and place them back in the freezer for 1-2 hours Turn off the heat under the oil. Once the potatoes are fully frozen, turn the heat back on under the oil and raise it to 375°F. Remove the potatoes from the freezer. Place in the fryer and fry until golden and warmed through. Season with salt.

To prepare the beef: Place the beef in a zip bag with the shallots, thyme, olive oil, cracked pepper, and salt. Allow to sit at room temperature for at least 30 minutes and up to 4 hours before cooking. Remove the beef from the bag and discard excess marinade. Re-season lightly with salt and cracked pepper. In a pan over medium-high heat, sear the steak to desired doneness. Remove from heat, top with butter, and allow meat to rest for 5–10 minutes before slicing.

To plate: Onto eight plates, arrange cauliflower and radish salad, radishes, potatoes, and sliced steak. Using a pastry bag, pipe avocado puree onto plates. Serve.

Fish & Game

13 South 3rd Street
Hudson, NY 12534
(518) 822-1500
FISHANDGAMEHUDSON.COM
Owning Partners: Zak Pelaccio, Jori Jayne Emde,
and Patrick Milling Smith; Co-Chefs: Zak Pelaccio
and Kevin Pomplun

On the face of it, Fish & Game in Hudson could not be further from Zak Pelaccio's introduction to the spotlight (in 2003) at Chickenbone Cafe in South Williamsburg, Brooklyn. At Chickenbone, where Pelaccio landed after stints at the French Laundry and Restaurant Daniel, the young chef was required to cook without using actual fire. Zoned as an "assembly kitchen," Chickenbone Cafe's kitchen was—in essence—a few plug-in crockpots and panini presses. Pelaccio's remarkable artistry shone through, and within a decade Pelaccio was steering an international brand with his landmark restaurants, Fatty Crab and Fatty 'Cue. At Fish & Game, Pelaccio's current *batterie de cuisine* reflects his stature. His kitchen bears a nearly pornographic wealth of wood-fetishizing grills, smokers, and rotisseries.

Still, Fish & Game shares key characteristics with Pelaccio's launching pad. First, there's its size. At only thirty-six seats Fish & Game is more minuscule than even Chickenbone, which had forty. But more striking, both restaurants were opened on bohemian frontiers. In 2003, when Chickenbone opened, Williamsburg was as yet undominated by youthful trust fund recipients; it was a gritty, ethnic nowhere on the wrong side of the river. As in Hudson, artists and musicians could actually afford to live and work in Williamsburg. Says Pelaccio, "What is interesting to a lot of people coming up from the city is that they feel the same way about Hudson as they did about Brooklyn or parts of Brooklyn at the time I was opening Chickenbone Cafe. There was still potential. You could still do things in Brooklyn because the cost of getting in was not that high. People felt that they could try things out and take a risk. It wasn't such a huge investment—and if they failed, so what?"

Though some found Pelaccio's defection from New York City and the Fatty juggernaut shocking, the transition for Pelaccio and his life and business partner, Jori Emde, could not have been more natural. "Jori and I have been coming out here since 2005. We have a place in Old Chatham, and we fell in love with the place—we got hooked. We'd been gardening for a couple of years, and we'd built relationships with the people and the farmers. We were thinking the same way about committing to the area and having the products be a focus of a new restaurant."

Located two hours north of Manhattan, Hudson is a tricky proposition. It is a town with many past lives, and not all of them have been glamorous. Settled in the nineteenth century by Nantucket whalers—when a sandbar made access to Nantucket harbor difficult for increasingly large whaling ships—Hudson offered a deep harbor and access, via river and rail, to the lucrative markets of the west.

But unlike Nantucket, whose post-whaling lull was eventually followed by a prosperous tourism boom, Hudson has struggled through multiple booms and busts. Warren Street's historic eighteenth- and nineteenth-century architecture might rival that on Nantucket's Main Street, but you won't find Warren colonized by Murrays Toggery or a Ralph Lauren store. Instead, Hudson (along with Brooklyn) is home to an outpost of Etsy, the cultish hipster shopping website. When musician Melissa Auf der Maur and filmmaker Tony Stone debuted The Basilica, Hudson's art/event/performance space housed in a former factory, proto-punk poet Patti Smith herself gave her blessing. Just try to catch Smith on Nantucket.

Urbanity will always be a part of Hudson's charm. Says Pelaccio, "It's got an edge and a diversity, and that's healthy. There's no white picket fence that you have to get behind before you unveil the underbelly that exists in everything. Nothing is totally whitewashed in Hudson. It all takes place before your eyes."

For increasing numbers of city dwellers, Hudson is the anti-Berkshires or anti-Hamptons. "People need a place to go," says Pelaccio. "And people of my generation are not buying out in the Hamptons. So where are they going to go? Here, there's affordable land. You can get something opulent or you can get something modest and spend, like, two hundred thousand dollars. Those deals are still around. And here, there are fields and woods and rivers, and, obviously, towns. It's accessible and it's easy. It's still agricultural,

too—and that resonates with people, especially nowadays." He continues, "People are more into their lifestyle. I mean, people were always into their lifestyle, but now it's about food and green, organic wholesomeness. Everything from using green laundry soaps to eating from farmers' markets, that's just living well, right? The valley is the closest place to New York City where you can live that way."

For Pelaccio, the move to Hudson was not about bugging out; it was about tuning in. "We were looking inward. And it was where we wanted to be right now. It wasn't like we wanted this gigantic career and we wanted to open a ton of restaurants in cities all over the world. Instead, we really looked at the valley and looked for a good place to showcase what we love about the Hudson Valley. Doing what we do here just dovetails with what we are doing with our lives at this time. It's about expressing how we feel right now in our careers and where we are in the world.

"The restaurants in the city have their own built-in infrastructure, and slowly, over time, my role had been marginalized. They had more and more structure and a way of doing things. I'm a creative guy, and, for me, I need to roll onto something new. So putting my talents to use up here seemed to make more sense. But it's also just where my life is headed right now. It been over two and a half years now, and I owe it to Jori and to Kevin and to Patrick to be here and to be focused and to be dedicated. And I owe it to myself, of course. It's not much fun to spread yourself too thin." Cooking in restaurants is "brutal. And you can either become more involved in management or keep cooking on the line from day to day. And I realized that I was doing more management than the thing I was interested in. I like to be immersed in it."

ROTISSERIE ROASTED PORK SHOULDER WITH FRESH CURRANTS & RADISHES

(SERVES 6)

For the pork brine:

3 quarts water

1 quart white wine

7 tablespoons salt

1 cup maple syrup

3 onions, sliced

1 bulb fennel, sliced

2 heads garlic, crushed

2½ teaspoons toasted white peppercorns

5 tablespoons toasted coriander seeds

2 tablespoons plus 1½ teaspoons toasted fennel seeds

4 fresh cayenne chiles

3 bay leaves

1 pork shoulder

For the basting mixture:

2 cups sunflower oil

¼ cup salt

¼ cup maple syrup

1 clove garlic, peeled

3 pickled jalapeños

For the pork loin:

1 (5-plus pounds) pork loin

For the pork sausage:

2 tablespoons plus 2 teaspoons salt

1 tablespoon black pepper

1½ teaspoons granulated sugar

1½ teaspoons red pepper flakes

1 tablespoon ground cumin

1 tablespoon whole cumin

1½ teaspoons ground coriander

1½ teaspoons fennel seeds

5 pounds pork

1½ pounds fatback

Hog casing

For the sauce:

Pig skin, reserved from shoulder and loin (above)

Bones from shoulder and loin (see above)

A few whole heads garlic

1 quart fresh currants

Maple syrup, to taste

Fish sauce, to taste

For the radishes:

A selection of radishes: Pelaccio recommends
    Red Globe, Golden & Breakfast, and Rat Tail,
    which, according to Pelaccio, "is actually a bean
    that has a spiciness similar to the flavor of radishes."

A few tablespoons of homemade fennel vinegar or white
    wine vinegar, or just enough to dress the radishes

For the congee:

2 cups high-quality short grain rice

Skin stock

A few cloves of thinly shaved garlic

Salt to taste

Fish sauce to taste

For the finished dish:

Anise hyssop

To prepare the brine: Pour everything except the pork into a large pot and bring to a simmer. Leave at a low simmer for 30 minutes, then remove from heat and allow it to cool to room temperature. Meanwhile, remove the skin from the pork shoulder and reserve it for the sauce, below. Place the shoulder in the prepared brine. Be sure that the meat is fully submerged (place a plate over the shoulder to weight it down in the brine, if necessary). Brine the shoulder in the refrigerator for 4 days before proceeding with the recipe.

To make the basting liquid and roast the pork: Heat a fire under a rotisserie large enough to hold the pork roast. In a blender or food processor (Pelaccio uses a Vitamix), puree the basting mixture ingredients together. Reserve. After the pork has brined, thread it onto a rotisserie rod and roast it, turning constantly, over a medium-hot wood fire for about 7–8 hours, or until a thermometer inserted into the meat's center reads 150°F. Remove the pork from the rotisserie and remove the rod from the roast.

To prepare the pork loin: Two days before you plan to smoke the loin, remove the belly from the loin, cutting through the ribs with a bone saw. Remove the skin from the loin, leaving the fatback on. Brine the loin for 2 days using another batch of the brine. Smoke the loin over a wood fire until it has reached an internal temperature of 130°F. Remove the loin from the smoking shelf and allow it to return to room temperature. Once it's cool, remove the loin from the bone, wrap it in plastic, and chill in the refrigerator.

To make the pork sausage: According to Pelaccio, it's critical to keep your equipment cold during this process. "When making any sausage, fresh or cured, you need to make sure that all your equipment is very clean, dry, and extremely cold. You can achieve this by storing the grinder equipment in the freezer. Have your mise en place portioned and ready to go before setting up any equipment. When using the grinder, have

your 'catch pan' sitting in another pan of ice water to keep the meat very cold during the whole process." He also suggests that you wear rubber gloves while mixing the seasoning through the meat. "Aside from this practice just being cleaner, it helps to create a barrier between the heat of your hands and the fat in the grind. This prevents the sausage mixture from breaking down too quickly, especially when incorporating the spices. If at any point the meat becomes warm or the fat starts to render from exposure to heat, take a break from the mixing process and place everything in the refrigerator or freezer to tighten it up and avoid further breakdown. This shouldn't ever happen, but just in case."

To begin, toast the seasonings in a dry pan until they are lightly colored and fragrant. Transfer the spices to a spice grinder or a mortar and pestle and grind them coarsely. Mix just enough water into the spice mixture to make a stiff paste. Set aside. Set up a "catch pan" that rests in another pan filled with ice. Using a meat grinder fitted with chilled parts, grind the pork and fatback together and extrude it into the prepared "catch pan."

When the meat is ground and resting in the prepared pan, add the spice paste. Mix the spices and meat together and knead until the mixture is tacky. Allow the sausage mixture to chill in the fridge for 2–4 hours so that the flavors meld and the mixture becomes firm. Meanwhile, rinse and soak the hog casings well. When the sausage mixture is cool and set, pass the mixture through a medium tube into the hog casing. Twist each link off at 6 inches. When all the sausages have been extruded, make tiny holes in the links so that they don't burst while you cook them. Hang them in the refrigerator for 1–2 days to dry and set.

To make the sauce: Take the skin from the pig, remove the fat, then put the skin in a pot and cover with cold water. Bring this to a boil, then pour off the liquid, reserving the skin. Return the skin to the pot, cover again with cold water, and

bring to a boil. Immediately turn the heat down to a simmer and simmer the skin in the water for 5 hours. Strain and discard the skin, reserving the liquid. Meanwhile, place the bones from the pig on a shelf above a wood-fired grill and grill the bones over direct heat. Let them smoke for 3 hours. After 3 hours place the smoked bones in a stockpot and cover with water, adding a few heads of garlic. Bring the bone stock to a boil, then reduce the heat to a simmer and simmer for 5 hours. After 5 hours strain the stock, reserving the liquid. Discard the bones. Return the bone stock to a saucepan and cook until it is reduced by three-quarters. Add enough skin stock to the bone stock to reach a lipsmacking, gelatinous consistency. Whatever skin stock you don't use at this point, reserve; you will need it for the congee below.

Using a juicer, juice the currants. Carefully season the skin and bone stock reduction using the currant juice, maple syrup, and fish sauce.

To prepare the radishes: Slice the radishes very thin on a mandoline and toss with the vinegar.

To make the congee: In a medium-size pot cook the short grain rice according to package directions, Strain, then transfer the cooked rice back to the pot and cover with a 50/50 blend of water and skin stock. Cook the rice in the water/ skin stock blend until it has absorbed all the liquid. Cover the rice once more with just water and continue to cook until the rice has absorbed all the water. Repeat the process with water one more time. Season the rice with thinly shaved garlic, salt, and fish sauce to taste.

To plate the dish: On a wood-fueled grill, grill the sausage until fully cooked. Remove. Slice the pork loin very thin on a slicing machine. Cut a few slices from the pork shoulder. Warm the sauce and drop in a handful of currants. Plate the cuts of pork, along with the radishes, on top of a small scoop of congee. Season with salt and finish with the sauce and currants and small leaves of anise hyssop.

LOCAL 111

111 MAIN STREET
PHILMONT, NY 12565
(508) 672-7801
LOCAL111.COM
OWNER/EXECUTIVE CHEF: JOSEPHINE PROUL

Josephine Proul comes to Philmont after a heavy-duty internship in the trenches of the Hamptons. "I'd done a couple of seasons after coming out of Seattle, and I didn't like the way the restaurant where I was working [in the Hamptons] was going. I just didn't like prepackaged things. What happened was the restaurant hired a new chef who said that he wanted the food to be consistent. But I was looking at stuff like box tempura and thinking, I don't want anything to do with this." In 2009 Proul returned to Philmont, where her mother owned a pub in town, and she took the job of sous-chef at Local 111.

From the outset Local 111 was a peculiar enterprise. Open since 2004 the restaurant offers only thirty-eight seats in a former filling station whose three original bays remain intact. The space's garage doors have been replaced by square glass panels that open to the small-town street life of the Hudson Valley. Given Proul's passion for cooking clean, locally sourced food, the then twenty-three-year-old chef says the decision was a "no-brainer" when Local 111's original owners, Linda Gatter and Max Dannis, approached her to become executive chef.

"Over the last ten years of living in the Hudson Valley on and off, I've seen this region come into its own when it comes to farm networks and the cultivation of realistic relationships. I've been working hard at this for the last six years at Local 111." Proul explains, "In the past I'd get a root storage crop from a farm in Miller's Crossing. Now they deliver—I don't actually have to go there with a truck."

While Proul admits that culinary hotspots like Hudson have their attractions, she doesn't feel particularly hampered by Local 111's Philmont location. "We're a restaurant that thrives on our food, and not our foot traffic." She continues, "People get in their cars to come here, and once they've eaten, they tend to come back."

CHILLED GOAT CHEESE & HERB CREAM WITH ARUGULA, CRISPY KIELBASA, DILL VINAIGRETTE & TOASTED ALMONDS

(SERVES 8)

For the goat cheese and herb cream:

2 tablespoons thyme
2 tablespoons dill
2 tablespoons oregano
2 tablespoons mint
3 cloves garlic
1 shallot
Juice of ½ lemon
1 tablespoon extra-virgin olive oil
Salt and pepper to taste
1 cup fresh, room temperature chèvre
3 cups heavy cream

For the dill vinaigrette:

¼ bunch dill
Heavy pinch of fresh parsley
2 cloves garlic
1 shallot
1 teaspoon buckwheat honey
1½ tablespoons Dijon mustard
Salt and pepper to taste
¼ cup Champagne vinegar
¾–1 cup extra-virgin olive oil

For the finished dish:

1 cup kielbasa, chopped into a small dice
⅓ cup sliced almonds
Salt to taste
1 pound arugula
¼ cup chèvre
Pepper to taste
8 sprigs dill

To make the goat cheese cream: In a blender place the herbs, garlic, shallot, lemon, oil, salt, and pepper. Pulse until well combined. Add the chèvre to the blender and mix well on high speed. Pour the cream into the blender and mix slowly until it reaches a texture that Proul calls "fluffy milk." Adjust the seasoning with salt and pepper and chill while you prepare the rest of the dish.

To make the vinaigrette: In a blender place all the ingredients except the olive oil. Puree. With the blender running, slowly add the oil to make an emulsion. Taste and adjust seasoning as you go; reserve.

To assemble the dish: In a pan placed over medium heat, render the kielbasa until crispy. Drain off the fat and allow the kielbasa to cool at room temperature. In a dry pan placed over medium heat, toast the almonds until golden, then toss with salt. Allow the almonds to cool to room temperature. In a bowl toss together arugula, kielbasa, fresh chèvre with the vinaigrette. Taste and adjust seasoning with salt and pepper, if needed. To serve, ladle ½ cup of goat cheese cream into each of eight bowls. Place the salad onto the goat cheese cream, top with almonds and dill, and serve.

Swoon Kitchenbar

340 WARREN STREET
HUDSON, NY 12534
(518) 822-8938
SWOONKITCHENBAR.COM
CHEF/OWNERS: NINA BACHINSKY GIMMEL AND JEFF GIMMEL

While Nina Bachinsky Gimmel and Jeff Gimmel opened Swoon in 2004, they'd already been visiting Hudson for at least four years (Nina's parents were artists with studios in town). Swoon predates Fish & Game, the Crimson Sparrow, and Cafe le Perche by nearly a decade. Having been in town so long, the Gimmels remember Hudson's really tough times. Says Jeff Gimmel, "We were living in what used to be my wife's parents' art studio, which was on the corner of Third and Union, the big house right next to where Fish & Game is now.

"And so one night we were watching TV, and all of a sudden we heard gunshots. Just pop-pop-pop-pop-pop-pop. And I look out the window, and right across the street from us at the Boy's Club there was a drive-by shooting. And right around the corner from there on Third and Warren was one of the heaviest drug corners I'd ever seen—and that's after living in New York for ten years." He concludes, "Just in 2000, Warren Street was pretty rough."

Undeterred, the Gimmels returned to Hudson to open Swoon in 2004. "There was a real energy in town with a lot of new people showing up and starting new things." But the Gimmels, who both came out of high-profile kitchens in Manhattan, also noticed, "There wasn't a lot of good food. Even the number of farms now has greatly increased from what there was then. I mean, there were definitely farmers around—and some that we knew for years before we opened—but now you see this influx of younger farmers starting up these smaller farms that are geared to supplying restaurants and the new foodie markets. The farmers that were here before were the generational farmers that were still farming the same land that their grandparents had farmed before them.

"My wife and I [both chefs] were working in Manhattan for ten years before leaving, but she grew up around here, so we knew this area well. We were regular shoppers, both

for work and for home, at the Union Square Greenmarket. So, when we first moved to the Hudson Valley and started driving around, we realized that these were the farms that we saw at the Union Square Greenmarket. To be here in the Hudson Valley among these farmers—and to walk their land and talk to them about their day-to-day lives—gave me a really personal connection to the food. It wasn't just about a stand in Union Square; it was about the people and their livelihood."

Their connection, through Nina's parents, to the art community in Hudson gives the Gimmels some perspective about the way the town has changed. Says Gimmel, "Hudson is really unique from the Berkshires or even Rhinebeck in that it offers a level of sophistication that you really don't find in small towns. Its culture and sophistication are equal to a large city—a Manhattan or a Boston—and you can just see that in the storefronts on Warren. You know, when the Internet came on big for antiques shopping, the dealers and the designers from the city could go online to buy things instead of having to come up to Hudson. That started the end of Hudson's identity as an "antiques only" town. Correspond this with the real estate boom of 2004–2006, and these antiques dealers who bought their properties in the late 1980s or 1990s for $20,000 and $30,000 could sell them in 2004 and 2005 for $200,000. They cashed out. And so that was what brought a greater diversity to Hudson." He concludes, "But I think that because the architecture is so unique and beautiful and old, it attracted a certain type of person that wanted to be part of a beautiful, but still kinda bohemian, place."

The Gimmels fell in love with 340 Warren Street, a spot that had been a restaurant since it was built in the late nineteenth century. Though its upper floors had been damaged in an arson fire, the street-level restaurant remained mostly intact. "We always loved the bones of the place with the high tin ceilings and the tile floors. It just had a really great feel to it. The fire started on the second floor, so a lot of the first floor is original—of our tin ceilings, about 70 to 75 percent are original.

"For the first year that we were open, someone—and I still don't know who—would come by in the morning and slide Xeroxed copies of old local newspapers under our front door. These said things like 'Brandow's at 340 Warren Street: The First Restaurant in Hudson to Have an Electric Icebox!' They were just these old, weird clippings about the history of the space and of the building from somebody in town."

More bizarrely: "And my next-door neighbor where I live here in town is a retired Hudson police officer, and he said that when he was a cop in the 1960s, my restaurant was a bookie's shop. You could come in here and make a bet on anything, from baseball to horses. You could bet against the lottery and they'd take your money. So my neighbor used to run a wiretap from his basement next door to where I live now to the basement at the restaurant where I'm sitting right now!" Gimmel sighs. "It's just kind of funny, the long connected history of the place."

LOCAL ASPARAGUS SALAD

(SERVES 4)

1 clove garlic

1 day-old baguette

High-quality extra-virgin olive oil

Salt

3 bunches good-quality asparagus: 2 bunches for cooking, 1 for shaving

As many fresh, tender herbs as you can get. Gimmel recommends parsley, tarragon, chervil, basil, celery leaves, lovage, mint, and chives, but warns against cilantro, sage, or lavender.

3 lemons

Fleur de sel

Freshly ground black pepper

½ pound sliced, high-quality cured meats, such as prosciutto, speck, lomo, bresaola, etc. (Gimmel cures his own meats, but he recommends that you substitute cured meats from artisanal producers)

The day before you plan to serve the salad, peel the garlic clove. Cut off the root end, and rub the baguette all over with the cut side of the garlic. Slice the baguette into thin rounds and lay them in a single layer on a cookie sheet(s). Air dry the bread for 1 day, then, using a food processor, grind it into crumbs. Season with a touch of olive oil and salt and reserve.

Free the asparagus of all rubber bands, then, taking each stalk between forefinger and thumb, snap off each stalk, Gimmel says, "at the point at which they would like to be snapped." Discard the snapped ends and reserve the stalks. Separate approximately one-third of the asparagus stalks and reserve for shaving.

Fill a large pot with cold water and salt the water heavily. Bring to a boil. Meanwhile, prepare an ice bath and salt the ice water, too. When the water reaches a full rolling boil, blanch two-thirds of the

asparagus in small batches, trying not to let the water cool between each addition of vegetables. When you remove each batch of asparagus, shock it immediately in the ice bath to halt its cooking.

Drain the blanched asparagus and prepare it for grilling by dressing it in a bit of olive oil and salt. Heat a grill pan. Meanwhile, cut the reserved raw asparagus into manageable lengths. Prepare a small ice bath and shave the asparagus using a mandoline. The slices can't be too wispy because the asparagus won't crunch, and they can't be too thick or it will be tough. Gimmel suggests trying a couple of thicknesses to see where you like it. When you finish, refresh the shaved asparagus in the ice water. Drain after 5 minutes; it should still be crunchy and appealing.

Take all the herbs that you have assembled, and pick the leaves off the stems. Clean in an ice bath and drain after 10 minutes. Lay out four plates. Grill the asparagus in the pan, turning the slices often to get an even char on all sides, being careful not to burn. When you have finished grilling, dress the asparagus with a healthy squeeze of lemon juice, olive oil, a pinch of fleur de sel, and pepper. Gimmel says, "If you want to go all out, hit it with some lemon zest as well."

In a large mixing bowl, place the herbs, shaved asparagus, and some slices of cured meat. Dress with salt, pepper, olive oil, and lemon juice. Gimmel says, "Consider some zest. It is up to you." Mound the grilled asparagus on the plates, says Gimmel, "in a fashionable way," and sprinkle with a healthy dose of the reserved bread crumbs. Dress with the shaved asparagus, herb, and meat salad. Finish with more slices of cured meats and bread crumbs.

DUTCHESS
COUNTY

Another Fork in the Road

1215 Route 199
Milan, NY 12571
(845) 758-6676
Owner/Chef: Jamie Parry

Coming to Milan, New York, Chef Jamie Parry was the classic fish out of water. Having grown up in Manhattan and worked through some of the city's finest restaurants—Montrachet and Tribeca Grill—Parry arrived in Milan and literally could not drive a car. Says Parry, "I'm like a real Manhattan kid. I met my wife and she has an established

business up here, and so this is where we wanted to be. I mean, we live in the woods!" The move continues to be a bit of a culture clash: "The first thing I do when I go home—and by 'home' I mean New York City—is walk. Like, I walk down Columbus Avenue for twenty blocks or something. I can't walk by the side of the roads up here. It's really different; there are no locks on the doors." He admits, "But I love it; it's a wonderful life."

Another Fork in the Road is an offbeat restaurant that serves high-toned, locavorian cuisine in simple digs. Parry describes his forty-six-seat restaurant thus: "It's an old diner. Sadly, the original diner fixtures have been taken out, so it's just a comfortable, small little rectangle. The walls have been very eclectically decorated with all of the stuff that I've accumulated over the years—movie posters and strange drawings made by my daughter." Parry's menu is also eclectic and includes dishes that might be equally at home at Tribeca Grill or a roadside food stand. Says Parry, "That's how I cook—it draws on growing up in New York City and my love of ethnic food and fine dining, plus my experiences at Swoon [in Hudson, where Parry was chef de cuisine]."

The eclecticism and quality of Another Fork in the Road's menu is a daring feat to pull off in Milan, where there are no throngs of foodies daily walking by the door. When he opened, Parry admits that he "was terrified." He adds, "But I also knew that this was my first restaurant. I wanted to cook

what I wanted to cook." Parry's personal crusade has softened, and now he draws from the talents of his staff. "It's a group effort among all my cooks. Everyone has a say and everyone can put up a dish. We talk about what's working and what's not working. We constantly strive to put out the best food that we can."

Like many other Hudson Valley chefs, Parry cites the quality of local ingredients as his inspiration. "The pure bounty—I mean, the vegetables! It's unbelievable what we have available to us. I mean, *especially* the vegetables and the sheer amount of stuff that we have. Tiny growers like Common Hand Farm in Hudson or Starling Yards Farm in Red Hook. They made our entire year just by bringing in fun things that we could give our customers."

PASTA WITH RABBIT & SPRING VEGETABLES

(SERVES 4–5)

1 Red Hook Farms rabbit split

Salt and cracked black pepper to taste

4 tablespoons oil

3 cloves garlic, shaved thinly

1 carrot, peeled and sliced thinly on a bias

1 onion, peeled, split, and sliced thinly

½ cup sliced morels

2 bay leaves

1 cup white wine

2 cups vegetable stock

¼ cup fava beans, blanched

¼ cup fiddleheads, blanched

1 pound fresh pappardelle

1 tablespoon loosely torn Red Hook Farms lovage

2 tablespoons grated Coach Farms Goat Stick

Preheat oven to 350°F. Using paper towels, pat the rabbit pieces dry and season with salt and pepper. In a skillet over medium-high, heat 2 tablespoons of the oil until hot but not smoking, then add the rabbit, browning it, turning over once. Allow it to cook about 4 minutes per side. When all sides of the rabbit are golden brown, transfer the pieces to a plate.

Reduce the skillet's heat to medium and add the remaining 2 tablespoons oil, garlic, carrot, onion, mushrooms, and bay leaves. Cook, stirring frequently, for about 4–5 minutes, or until the vegetables begin to brown. Add the wine and deglaze the skillet by boiling, stirring, and scraping up any brown bits, then cook until the wine is reduced by about half, about 2 minutes. Add the vegetable stock, salt, and black pepper. Return the rabbit pieces to the pan and bring up to a simmer. Cover with a tight-fitting lid and place in the preheated oven for 1 hour. Remove from oven and discard bay leaves.

Set a large pot of salted water on high heat. Meanwhile, take the rabbit from the pan and pull the meat from the bones. Return the meat to the sauce and add the fava beans and fiddleheads. Season with salt and pepper.

Cook the pasta in the salted boiling water, drain well, and transfer to serving platter. Spoon rabbit and sauce over pasta and garnish with lovage and grated goat cheese. Serve.

Beekman Arms

6387 Mill Street
Rhinebeck, NY 12572
(845) 876-7077
beekmandelamaterinn.com
Owner: The Banta Family; Executive Chef: R. Preston Faust

While the Rhinebeck's Beekman Arms is the oldest, continually operated hotel in the US (and dates from the pre-Revolutionary period), it wasn't until the 1990's that its cozy, hearth warmed restaurant really hit its stride. When Chef Larry Forgione took on the kitchen of the restaurant—then called the 1776 Tavern—this "godfather of American food" introduced a locavorian, New American menu that drew critical praise and helped to pin the Hudson Valley to the national dining map.

Though Forgione has since sold his interests in the restaurant, his successor at the Beekman, Chef Preston Faust, continues the tradition Forgione began back in the 'Nineties. "I started with Larry and Tony Novales, who was his Executive Chef. I was in the area: I graduated from the Culinary Institute in 2000, and just stayed." Faust cites the innate beauty of riverside Rhinebeck for his choice to remain in the Hudson Valley. "Especially in the fall; it's just amazing. We get a lot of 'leaf-peepers' here."

The storied inn, which is said to have sheltered George Washington, Philip Schuyler, Benedict Arnold, and Alexander Hamilton, became a refuge for patriots in 1777 when the British burned New York's state capital, then just across the River in Kingston. The weathered boards of Beekman Arms now welcome travelers to Rhinebeck who come to visit the Culinary Institute of America or the Dutchess County Fairgrounds and linger to enjoy the picturesque town's many restaurants and shops.

Linguine & Shrimp Sauté with Ramps

(SERVES 6)

For the linguine:

1 pound linguine

2 tablespoons extra virgin olive oil

2 shallots, diced

2 garlic cloves, minced

2 pounds jumbo shrimp, peeled and deveined

1 lemon, zested

¼ cup lemon juice (about 2 lemons)

1 teaspoon kosher salt

½ teaspoon freshly ground black pepper

1 pound fresh ramps (if not in season,
    Faust recommends using fresh arugula)

In a large pot of water, add salt and bring to a boil. Cook the linguine in boiling water until it's a firm al dente. Drain the pasta in a colander and reserve.

Meanwhile, place a sauté pan over high heat until it's very hot. Add a little olive oil, and then immediately add the shallots and garlic. Cook for about a minute until they are just starting to brown. Add the shrimp, and cook them on both sides until they start turning pink. Turn the heat down to medium and continue to cook until the shrimp are nearly cooked through.

When the shrimp are just about done, sprinkle lightly with salt, and grind some pepper over the pan. Add the lemon zest and the lemon juice, then remove the shrimp to a separate plate.

Place the ramps in the pan, and raise the heat. Cover and cook until wilted. Add the linguine and toss well, cooking until the pasta has reached your desired degree of tenderness, adding a

scoop of pasta water if the pan becomes dry. When cooked, transfer the linguine into a large serving plate or platter. Arrange the shrimp over the linguine, and add some lemon slices and chopped parsley to garnish. Serve immediately.

Brasserie 292

292 Main Street
Poughkeepsie, NY 12601
(845) 473-0292
brasserie292.com
Owners: Mark Margiotta, Stephen Gruberg, and Alex
Serroukas; Executive Chef: Mark Margiotta

It's an arguable assertion to say that the Hudson Valley is the breeding ground for global restaurant culture; after all, graduates from Hyde Park's Culinary Institute of America go on to create menus in kitchens all over the world. This geographic oddity means that there is a distinct foodie bubble in the towns that surround the Institute—the streets are filled with passionate diners who are both informed and discerning about food.

Brasserie 292 steps in to satisfy this region's basic need for craveable French standards, the kind of dishes that give the national cuisine its earthy soul. Here, in a long menu, you'll find brimming shellfish plateaux, house-made charcuterie, and the ultimate

in carnal: steak tartare with capers, white anchovies, and sticky, golden egg yolk. Says Brasserie's Executive Chef, Mark Margiotta, "Being a French brasserie, we're casual—almost like a French diner, in a way." He continues, "But we don't limit ourselves to French cuisine, as you can tell with the tortelloni [included below]. My own heritage is Italian, so we joke with customers who come in and think I'm French. It's especially funny when they think I speak the language," Margiotta laughs. "I mean, I've been to France, but . . . "

Margiotta's Italian-American background has not been a hindrance. "French cooking shares basic techniques with of a lot of cuisines. So, at that point, we just try to make really good food that our local clientele will come in for." When it comes to local clientele, Brasserie 292 is blessed. "We're right next to the Culinary, so we have a lot of culinary students and a lot of chef instructors coming in. We also have people who are visiting the Culinary, say, the families of the students or chefs at the Culinary. They, in particular, can appreciate what it takes to make time-consuming dishes like our house-made charcuterie. Also, they're more geared to the steak tartare or an oddball special." Is it easy for Margiotta to find customers among the students at the Culinary? "Yes and no—when I was in the Culinary, I was eating a lot pizza just trying to keep it cheap!"

CRAB TORTELLONI WITH YELLOW TOMATO BRODO & RICOTTA CHEESE

(SERVES 5)

For the tortelloni:

2¼ cups OO flour (all-purpose flour can be substituted) plus more if needed

3 large eggs, at room temperature

3 tablespoons vegetable oil

2 tablespoons unsalted butter

2 cups yellow tomatoes, medium diced (red can be substituted)

1 cup thinly sliced leeks, white and light green parts only

1 shallot, minced

1 clove garlic, minced

Kosher salt and fresh ground pepper

1 cup vegetable stock

4 ounces extra virgin olive oil

8 ounces fresh crabmeat, picked over for shells and cartilage

8 ounces mascarpone cheese

2 tablespoons scallions, chopped

1 teaspoon mint, chopped

Pinch of grated nutmeg

Butter

1 cup ricotta cheese

To make the tortelloni: Mound 2¼ cups of flour on a wooden cutting board. Make a well in the middle of the flour and add the eggs. Using a fork, beat together the eggs, then begin to incorporate the flour, starting with the inner rim of the well. As the well expands, push the flour up from the base to keep the well shape. When the dough starts to form, start kneading the dough with the heel of your hand. Once the mass has come together, lightly flour it and knead the mass for 6 more minutes. The dough should be a little sticky and elastic. Wrap the dough in plastic wrap and allow it to rest for 30 minutes.

Meanwhile, heat a medium-heavy pot over medium heat. Add 3 tablespoons of vegetable oil and the unsalted butter. When the butter has melted, add the tomato, leek, shallot, and garlic and sweat the vegetables until they are soft but not brown, stirring occasionally. Season with salt and pepper, then add the vegetable stock and bring up to a simmer. Simmer on low for about 4 minutes, stirring occasionally.

Pour tomato mixture into a blender and blend on high until the brodo is smooth. Slowly add the extra virgin olive oil to the blender while it is running, allowing the sauce to emulsify. Strain the brodo through a fine-mesh strainer. Season with salt and pepper and reserve.

Cut the dough into 4 equal portions and, using a pasta machine, roll each section out to the thinnest setting on the pasta machine. Lay each piece on a lightly floured work surface and keep hydrated under a damp kitchen towel. Put the crabmeat, mascarpone, scallion, mint, and nutmeg in a medium bowl and gently mix until

incorporated. Season with salt and pepper. Line a rimmed baking sheet with parchment paper and lightly dust with flour. Lightly dust a work surface with all-purpose flour and lay the pasta sheets on it. Using a 4-inch cookie cutter, cut out 20 circles, keeping the circles hydrated under a damp kitchen towel. Fill each circle with about 2 teaspoons of filling. Use a pastry brush to lightly brush the rim of each circle with water.

Working with one at a time, fold circle in half, being sure to push all the air out and use your fingers to seal the edges. Hold the half-moon with the straight edge facing up and bend the two corners around, overlapping the ends by a ¼ inch and pressing the edges together. After each is done, arrange it on the floured baking sheet. (The tortelloni may be refrigerated for up to 1 day or frozen for up to 2 months.)

When ready to cook the tortoloni, fill a large pot two-thirds of the way with water, salt it liberally, and bring to a boil over medium high heat. Meanwhile, in a medium saucepot, heat the tomato brodo.

Add the tortelloni to the boiling water and cook until they float to the surface, 2 to 3 minutes (if fresh), or 4 to 5 minutes (if frozen). Carefully drain the tortelloni, return them to the pot, and coat them in butter.

In 5 shallow bowls, place a scoop of the ricotta and spread it out with the back of a spoon. Ladle in 4 ounces of tomato brodo. Divide the tortelloni between the bowls. Garnish with fresh tomatoes extra virgin olive oil, basil, and mint.

NURSERY OF ICONS

What if only 3 or 4 universities drew half of the intellectuals on the planet? This is the sort of math that represents the power of The Culinary Institute of America. With its nearly hundred million dollar endowment and rolling, 170-acre campus, "the Culinary" is—for chefs—Yale, Harvard, Princeton, and MIT rolled into one. Since 1946, CIA has been the entity that shaped the most prominent American culinary minds that range, on one hand, from superstar graduates like Michael Ruhlman and Grant Achatz to, on the other hand, dastardly provocateurs like Anthony Bourdain.

While an education at CIA is expensive and, by all report, prone to cause lasting emotional scars, visiting its hallowed campus is a pain-free way to share in its glamor. Walk among the check-trousered students and enjoy the campus's stellar river views, or drop into any the four inexpensive, student-run restaurants that are open to the public.

The restaurants, which provide practical, real-life training in every aspect of the restaurant business (from cookery to service and management) are overseen by the CIA's esteemed Chef/Instructors. In each, you'll find a restaurant that almost perfectly exemplifies its chosen dining genre. Happily, visitors can choose among them to hit any price and degree of elegance on the spectrum. Culinary Institute in Hyde Park, 1946 Campus Drive, Hyde Park, NY 12538, (845) 452-9600; ciarestaurants.com.

The Bocuse Restaurant

(845) 471-6608; bocuserestaurant.com

While its predecessor in this spot was known as The Escoffier and was marked by eccht-formal (and, some might say, outdated) tableside service, the CIA's newest take on haute cuisine offers feats of molecular gastronomy in the place of silvery chafing dishes. Look for a stylish, modern dining room and excellent, Hudson Valley ingredients transformed by CIA students into spectacular triumphs of cooking wizardry. Best of all, dining at The Bocuse is a steal compared to non-student-run restaurants of its ilk.

Ristorante Caterina de' Medici

(845) 471-6608; ristorantecaterina
demedici.com

Originated to celebrate the many regional cuisines of Italy, the soaring, all-but-Tuscan dining room of Ristorante Caterina de' Medici is centered on a fully-scaled olive tree. Here, diners can expect everything from textbook salumi and crudo to perfect pastas and wood-fired pizzas, all paired with carefully-chosen Italian wines. As at The Bocuse, Ristorante Caterina de' Medici offers stunning bargains and prix fixe menus.

American Bounty Restaurant

(845) 471-6608; americanbountyrestaurant.com

Europe might be the bedrock of a classical restaurant education, but, at American Bounty, the CIA celebrates the land beneath its students' feet. Look for perfect Hudson Valley ingredients sourced from the fertile region surrounding its Hyde Park campus. The seasonal, a la carte, and prix fixe menus at American Bounty are served by students and paired with an all-American beer and wine list.

Apple Pie Bakery and Cafe

(845) 905-4500; ciarestaurants.com/dining
atthecia/applepie-bakery-cafe

Expect this strictly diurnal cafe to feature a casual menu of soups, salads, and sandwiches with Hudson Valley cheeses, beers, wines, and meats taking center stage. CIA bakers-in-training craft all the breads, pastries, and desserts served at Apple Pie Bakery and Cafe; its easy price point means that students are also most likely to join visitors here as diners.

PHOTOS © THE CULINARY INSTITUTE OF AMERICA

CRAVE RESTAURANT & LOUNGE

129 WASHINGTON STREET
POUGHKEEPSIE, NY 12601
(845) 452-3501
CRAVERESTAURANTANDLOUNGE.COM
CHEF/OWNER: ED KOWALSKI

Poughkeepsie holds a position in the Hudson Valley that's unlike the vacationlands of the north and the bedroom suburbs to the south. Though a stately city sited on a picturesque bluff over the Hudson, it's also a bustling metropolis with an independent source of life. But as urban as Poughkeepsie can seem, it is also clearly tied to the natural beauty that surrounds it. For evidence, take a look at the Walkway over the Hudson, the mile-long footbridge that soars over a majestic stretch of the river and connects Poughkeepsie with rural Ulster County.

Crave, a stylish restaurant snuggled at the foot of the Walkway in Poughkeepsie, was not debuted by some Manhattan expatriate looking to cash in on the Hudson Valley's new cool. Says Chef/Owner Ed Kowalski, "I was actually born and raised here. I'm a local guy." He continues, "I was married young —at 21, to a girl who was also from this area, my high school sweetheart—and I started cooking out of necessity, basically, because we didn't know what we were doing." He laughs. "I had to learn quickly because my wife really *does not* cook. So, I started playing around with recipes from some old books that I found from the Culinary." Soon, Kowalski's adventures in emergency cooking evolved into something like a career. "I began working as a grill cook here and there and that's when I discovered that this is what I wanted to do for a living.

"Yeah, I was tempted to go to the city. I had two or three good job offers in Manhattan when I graduated from CIA and the money was good. But the hours were a little weird because, basically, I had to add four hours of commute time." Kowalski sighs. "It's a hard enough profession to begin with, but, then, to add on a four-hour commute. I figured I'd never be around, and my kids were *young*."

The city might have been unworkable for this young chef, but it turns out that

Poughkeepsie was on the verge of regeneration. "I actually worked in both of these two buildings that I currently lease back when I was in high school. The spaces used to be an Italian restaurant and an old-world Italian deli. I had worked in both of them—I grew up four blocks away—and so I was familiar with the area. There was a fire, and the buildings' owners boarded up the ground floors." In the restaurant business, one owner's loss is another's opportunity. "I figured that I wanted to try something and that this would be a perfect location." Kowalski took on the space, and transformed it with a minimal budget and a lot of his own labor. In 2005, he debuted Lola's Cafe and Catering, which he calls a "fast casual" breakfast and lunch restaurant that left him with time in the evenings to spend with his young kids. "I started out as an owner/operator; I had no other employees in the kitchen. Lola's ended up doing very well, so we kept adding staff, adding staff, and adding staff. That's how we ended up taking over the space next door."

At Crave, which he debuted in 2010, Kowalski gave the burnt shell a stylish revamp with a flickering, candle-lit brick wall and a copper, faux-finished ceiling. There, Kowalski is finally able to return to the elegant cooking that left him dreaming of culinary school while he was still trying to figure out an emergency family dinner. Look for stylish New American cuisine with occasional feats of molecular techniques, all at the foot of the Walkway over the Hudson.

Pan Seared Duck Breast with Heirloom Baby Carrots, Rainbow Swiss Chard, Farro & Caramel-Orange-Tamarind Sauce

(SERVES 2)

For the farro:

3 ounces of Spanish onion
1 tablespoon of chopped garlic, chopped
½ cup farro
2 cups of vegetable or duck stock

For the caramel-orange-tamarind sauce:

¼ cup sugar
Juice from half a lemon
1 cup orange juice fresh squeezed
¼ cup soy sauce
¼ cup tamarind paste

For the carrots and chard:

1 bunch of baby heirloom carrots: orange, yellow, and purple (if possible)
3 leaves of rainbow Swiss chard, de-stemmed
Corn kernels cut from 1 sweet corn cob
4 halved cherry tomatoes

To finish the dish:

2 duck breasts
¼ cup kosher salt
1 star anise pod, ground in a spice grinder
Rind from 1 orange, microplaned
2 tablespoons cracked coriander seed
Lemon juice

To prepare the farro: In a small pot placed over medium heat, sweat the onion in the olive oil until it is translucent. Add the garlic and sauté on low heat until it's fragrant. Add the raw farro and cook, toasting the raw grain until it smells slightly nutty. Pour in the stock and bring the mixture to a boil. Reduce the heat to a rapid simmer, and cook the farro until it is tender and slightly chewy, approximately 20-22 minutes.

To make the caramel: Fill a small bowl with water and set out a pastry brush. Set aside. In a medium, heavy-bottomed pot, place the sugar and lemon. Cook the mixture over low heat to melt the sugar. Continue to cook the sugar mixture until it reaches a rich amber caramel color, occasionally brushing down the sides of the pot with the water to prevent crystals.

When the caramel is amber, remove the pot from the heat and slowly add the orange juice and soy. The caramel will bubble up. After the bubbling has subsided, add the tamarind paste and return the pot to the heat. Cook until the liquid is reduced by half. Taste and adjust the seasoning with salt, making sure that there is a balance of sweet, sour, salty in final product. Reserve.

To prepare the vegetables: Prepare an ice bath. In a medium pot filled with boiling water, blanch the carrots until they are just tender. Remove and immediately plunge the carrots into the ice bath to halt them from further cooking. Reserve the carrots with the chard, corn, and tomatoes as you finish the dish.

To prepare the duck breast: Preheat oven to 350°. Place duck breast in a non-reactive container and season it liberally with the salt and spice mixture. Refrigerate for two and a half hours to cure, then rinse the cure mix off and pat the duck dry with paper towels.

Using a sharp knife, score the skin of the duck in a shallow grid, being careful not to cut into the meat. This will help to render its fat. In a cool, oven-safe pan, place the duck skin side down. Turn the heat under the pan to medium and begin to render the fat from the duck breast. When the duck skin is crisp and chestnut brown, flip the breasts over and place the pan in the preheated oven for about 4 minutes or until the breast is cooked to medium-rare. Remove duck from the pan, retaining the duck fat in the pan, and allow the breasts to rest on a plate for 2–3 minutes before slicing. While it rests, sauté the blanched heirloom carrots, corn, Swiss chard, and the farro in the duck fat until they are warm. Season with a pinch of salt and a squeeze of lemon juice. To plate, arrange the farro and vegetables on two plates. Slice the duck breast across the grain, place on farro and serve.

Ella's Bellas

418 Main Street
Beacon, NY 12508
(845) 765-8502
facebook.com/ellasbellasbeacon
Owners: Jason and Carley Hughes; Baker: Carley Hughes

It's unusual for bakeries, which are generally places of indulgence, to be defined by what they do *not* do. Nevertheless, Ella's Bellas in Beacon is a vegetarian, vegan-friendly bakery/cafe that also happens to be 100 percent gluten free.

Says owner/baker Carley Hughes, "Ella's Bellas is a gluten-free restaurant because I have a special place in my heart for people who have this disability. Being gluten intolerant dictates your entire life; you don't have a place where you can feel comfortable." Exclusively catering to the dietary needs of a small section of the populace wasn't in Hughes's original business plan. The idea came when Hughes realized the impact she could have with something as basic as a pan of brownies. "I used to do cake both ways, and then I just kept leaning toward gluten free. Finally, I had a close friend's

niece over, and because she had celiac disease, we made gluten-free brownies and chocolate chip cookies together. She was so happy." Hughes continues, "It made me think of when I was little and I used to go on Saturdays to the bakery with my mom, and how this girl could never do that. And then I thought, 'I have to do this.' And it turns out that I have a gluten intolerance. I just didn't realize it at the time, but gluten is a migraine trigger for me. I haven't had a migraine since I gave it up."

Hughes came to baking as a bit of an escape hatch. "I started out of my house, because I couldn't just be a stay-at-home mom. I tried it and it didn't work for me. Food is my passion, especially when it's locally sourced—and I also want to be sure that everyone has food that they can eat.

"Then we decided that we wanted a storefront. We wanted to start small, so we opened [in 2011] at about half

of our current size. And then, as things were building up, we realized that wholesale wasn't the way to go; retail was smarter. The person next door was leaving, so we broke through the wall in spring 2013." They decorated their new cafe with wainscoting made from chalkboards and the old windows of their house. Carley's husband and business partner, Jason Hughes—who has a background in theater—executed Carley's idea of repurposing giant Hobart mixer whisks as light fixtures. The couple also hit the Internet and found things on Craigslist. What is now Ella's Bellas came from here, there, and everywhere.

Finally, Ella's Bellas added a tiny micro-roasting machine not much bigger than a home stand mixer. "Yeah, that's from Tas Kafe, which was down the street when I was building the business. When I was doing the Beacon Farmer's Market, he was the stall across from me." When you visit, look for sweet and savory goods baked with ingredients sourced in the Hudson Valley and, soon, from the owners themselves: "My husband and I just bought a couple of acres, and we're in the process of putting in a little mini-farm for the shop."

APPLE CHEDDAR SCONES

(MAKES 8 SCONES)

½ cup good-quality buttermilk (Hughes uses
Hawthorne Valley Farms brand)

½ cup heavy cream (Hughes uses Hudson Valley
Fresh brand)

8 tablespoons unsalted butter

1 teaspoon salt

1 teaspoon baking soda

¾ teaspoon xanthan gum

1 cup sorghum flour

½ cup teff flour

½ cup tapioca starch

½ cup potato starch

¼ sweet rice flour

¼ cup stone-ground rice flour

1 cup shredded sharp cheddar (preferably local), plus
additional for topping scones before baking

1¼ cups shredded apple, about 2 medium-to-large
apples (see Chef's Note)

1 sliced apple for topping

Local honey (optional)

Whisk together the buttermilk and cream until the
mixture is frothy, then chill in the refrigerator while
you continue making the scones. Cut the butter
into tablespoon-size cubes and chill. Preheat
oven to 425°F.

In a medium bowl combine the dry ingredients
and whisk them together well. Using a pastry
blender, cut the butter into the dry ingredients
until the butter is reduced to pea-size lumps.
Using a fork, toss the cheddar and shredded
apple into the flour-butter mixture until they are
well coated.

Create a well in the middle of the mixture and, still
using the fork, toss in all but 2 tablespoons of the
buttermilk-cream mixture (reserve the remainder
for brushing the tops before baking). Continue
to toss the mixture with the fork until it starts to
pull together into a dough. Turn the dough onto
a floured surface and gently knead it until dough
comes together but is still a bit crumbly. Form the
dough into a circle about 9 inches in diameter
and 1½ inches thick. Cut into eight wedges. Brush
with remaining buttermilk-cream mixture and
top with cheddar and apple slices. Bake for 12–14
minutes.

Drizzle scones with honey, if desired, as soon as
they are removed from the oven. Serve.

Chef's Note: Hughes recommends not peeling
the apples: "I leave the skins on because I like the
flecks of color. Red Delicious is my first choice of
apple."

Homespun Foods

232 Main Street
Beacon, NY 12508
(845) 831-5096
HOMESPUNFOODS.COM
Chef/Owner: Jessica Reisman

Like many of the chefs that ultimately settle in the Hudson Valley, Homespun's chef/owner, Jessica Reisman, was a New York City transplant. "I moved to Beacon but I was still commuting into the city for work, and I certainly didn't want to continue doing that. Basically I moved up here knowing that Dia: Beacon had opened up." The stunning riverside museum, which opened in 2003, houses the Dia Art Foundation's collection of modern and contemporary art. Looking around town, Reisman sensed an opportunity. "There just seemed to be an overabundance of Italian restaurants. There was nothing that you would want to eat on a daily basis. There was not the kind of food that I ate, anyway, or any of the food that I was interested in eating." Reisman concludes, "Beacon was underserved by fresh, basic, healthy food."

At the time, Reisman was working in Whole Foods, but she was coming off a long career in the industry. In the 1980s and 1990s, Reisman owned McGraw Street Bakery in Seattle; she also owned a commercial bakery there called Homespun. During her

long commutes to Manhattan, Reisman had time to think. "Beacon is full of artists, and I thought, 'This is where I could fit in.' And so, I decided to do it one more time."

Homespun is part breakfast/lunch cafe and part bakery with a long vintage counter and exposed brick walls. Some of its eclectic mix of chairs and tables are wobbly, but if you're lucky, you'll sit down to the previous diner's newspaper. Says Reisman about the spot, "It was a fairly empty space when we opened. There was half an exposed brick wall and there was wainscoting going up it. The person before me had considered opening up a restaurant; they'd built a big box and put the triple sink in. So I outfitted the kitchen, and everything else is just my taste."

Reisman, who recently took over the cafe at Dia: Beacon, is happy with her decision to go north. "There's a sense of community in Beacon that I haven't felt since the 1970s. Now we have all these Brooklynites—people starting families but who can't afford the room they need at city prices. For a small town we have a lot going on."

Homespun Harvest Salad

(SERVES 6–8)

For the pomegranate dressing:

¼ of one shallot, peeled and minced

3 tablespoons pomegranate molasses

6 tablespoon sherry vinegar

1½ teaspoons Dijon mustard

¾ teaspoon salt

¼ teaspoon pepper

1 cup olive oil

For the salad:

2 medium Hudson Valley red beets

½ small butternut squash

1–2 tablespoons olive oil

Salt and pepper to taste

⅓–½ cup pepitas

1 firm, tart apple (preferably local)

1 head romaine lettuce, washed and chopped

6 cups mesclun

⅓ cup dried cranberries

½ cup Coach Farm goat cheese

To make the pomegranate dressing: In a bowl whisk all the ingredients except the olive oil. Add the oil, still whisking, until the vinaigrette is emulsified. Reserve.

To make the salad: Preheat oven to 425°F. Rinse the beets and wrap them in foil. Bake for 45 minutes, or until a knife can pass easily through them. Allow to cool, then peel and chop into ½-inch cubes. Set aside. Peel the butternut squash. Chop into ½-inch cubes and toss with 1–2 tablespoons olive oil. Season with salt and pepper. Bake until the squash cubes are golden brown on the edges. Remove squash from the oven, cool, and set aside. On a sheet pan toast the pepitas for 4–5 minutes, or until they look swollen and are slightly brown on edges. In a large bowl slice the apple and toss with the roasted butternut, beets, pepitas, and lettuces. Toss all ingredients with pomegranate dressing. Garnish with cranberries and goat cheese. Serve.

The Hop Beacon

458 Main Street
Beacon, NY 12508
(845) 440-8676
THEHOPBEACON.COM
Owners: Matt Hutchins, John Kavanagh, and John Kelly;
Executive Chef: Matt Hutchins

When Chef Matt Hutchins first popped up on our radar, he was the opening chef at Peekskill's Birdsall House, who—when the kitchen closed—moonlighted on Birdsall's decks as "DJ Mood Swing." I remember Hutchins standing near the ladies room with his crates of vinyl, playing an unending lineup of The Coolest Music Ever. I picked out The Smiths, Fugazi, Television, and Patsy Cline, but a lot of the music was more obscure. Periodically I'd see diners holding up their phones (with beers gripped in their other hands), trying to identify the songs that Hutchins was spinning. If only these diners knew that the chef who'd just seduced them with locally sourced, pork-centric comfort food was also the guy responsible for Birdsall's amazing sounds.

In September 2011 Hutchins decamped from Peekskill's Birdsall House to pursue his own venture, which was rumored to be located somewhere farther north. Hutchins took his sweet time before announcing what that project was to be. In lieu of news, his fans were teased by Hutchins's Facebook reports of nearly supernatural foraging hauls of morels and hen-of-the-woods mushrooms. Had Hutchins gone feral?

Finally, in March 2012 Hutchins debuted The Hop Beacon, a hybrid beer store/bar/restaurant that slings more than 150 retail craft beers alongside a geeky draft list for growler fills and drinking on-site. To complement the beers, Hutchins is spinning a menu that offers locally made artisanal cheeses, handcrafted pickles, and all those house-made sausages, terrines, and pâtés that earned him his rep. Still staunchly locavorian, all of The Hop's meats are locally sourced and butchered in-house. It's also a nose-to-tail restaurant: Very little precious protein is wasted.

And DJ Mood Swing? He's morphed into the singer/bass player of the temporarily named Marquee Mooners, a band that covers the music of proto-punk icons Television. Hutchins's next project is rumored to be a tribute to Fugazi. Meanwhile, you'll find him at The Hop, generally with a beer.

Rabbit & Raisin Terrine
with Champagne-Pickled Vegetables, Frisée, Crostini, Lemon-Saison Vinaigrette & Berkshire Blue Cheese

(SERVES 6)

For the forcemeat:

1 (2-pound) rabbit
¼ pound fatback or fatty pork
Pinch of ground cloves
2 teaspoons ground coriander
3 dried bay leaves, ground in a spice grinder
¾ teaspoon cinnamon
1 teaspoon ground ginger
1 teaspoon ground red pepper flakes
2 teaspoons onion powder
½ teaspoon garlic powder
¾ teaspoon salt
½ teaspoon freshly ground black pepper
1 teaspoon brown sugar
2 teaspoons granulated sugar
1 teaspoon ground nutmeg
1 tablespoon white wine
2 teaspoons minced parsley
⅓ cup Thompson raisins
⅔ cup toasted pistachios

For the terrine:

Caul fat (as needed), soaked in brine, then rinsed
Thompson raisins (as needed)
2 reserved rabbit loins

For the lemon-saison vinaigrette:

¼ cup extra-virgin olive oil
¼ cup olive oil
¼ cup Saison beer or Biere de Garde, a strong
    ale originated from the Nord-Pad-De-Calais
    region of France

1 tablespoon minced shallots
2 tablespoons Champagne vinegar
2 teaspoons whole grain mustard
2 tablespoons honey
Juice of ½ lemon
½ Meyer lemon, seeds removed, minced
1 teaspoon parsley
Pinch of cayenne
2 teaspoons salt
Ground black pepper to taste

For the Champagne-pickled vegetables:

Enough assorted vegetables (baby carrots, cauliflower,
    green beans, radishes, turnips, beets, garlic scapes,
    squash, etc.) to fill a lidded 1-quart container
½ cup water
½ cup granulated sugar
1 cup Champagne vinegar

For the finished dish:

½ baguette
Several leaves of frisée, washed and dried
1 cup Berkshire Blue from Berkshire Cheese Company

To butcher the rabbit and prepare the forcemeat:
Using a boning knife, remove the legs from the
rabbit. For the forelegs, slide the blade behind
the shoulder blades and pull the knife up toward
the neck until they break free. For the hind legs,
wrap the blade around the pelvic bone from the
belly to the spine, drawing the cut toward the tail.
Bend the legs back until they break a little from

the spine. Run the knife through to complete their removal. If the sternum has not already been split, do so by laying the rabbit on its side and cutting through the center of the sternum with the knife, cutting away from you to avoid any accidents. Lay the rabbit on its belly and pull back on the ribs with your fingertips while applying pressure on the spine with your thumbs until they break from the spine and the chest cavity is open and facing downward. Make a cut with the tip of the knife down either side of the spine, directly against the bumps on the spine. Then, fillet the loins off, simultaneously removing the belly flap. Roll the loins off the belly flap with your fingers and reserve, covered, in refrigerator. Flip the carcass and remove the small tenderloins under the belly region of the spine. Debone all the legs and cut the meat into 1-inch cubes. Cube the tenderloins and belly flap meat, add to the rest of the cubed meat, and reserve.

Note 1: Hutchins recommends roasting the rabbit bones, then simmering them with water into a stock for another use. When the rabbit is especially large, he confits their forelegs, and makes a sauce with the reduced rabbit stock.

Place the cubed rabbit and fatback (or fatty pork) into a large mixing bowl. Fold in ground cloves, coriander, ground bay leaves, cinnamon, ginger, red pepper flakes, onion powder, garlic powder, salt, pepper, brown sugar, and nutmeg and mix thoroughly with your hands until evenly incorporated. Refrigerate mixture for at least 1 hour, covered. When thoroughly chilled, remove the mixture and grind it once through a meat grinder fitted with a medium die. Then fit the meat grinder with a small die. Remove half of the meat mixture and grind this once more through the small die. Combine the finely ground meat with the more coarsely ground meat. Add all remaining ingredients and toss the mixture thoroughly by hand until everything is evenly dispersed and the liquids have been incorporated.

To assemble the terrines: Line two 2½-cup, lidded stainless steel terrines with plastic wrap, leaving an overhang on all sides. Squeeze the excess liquid from the caul fat, then line the terrines with caul fat, ensuring that it covers the entire inner walls of the terrines with about 2 inches to spare, left overhanging on the outside. Trim whatever exceeds the overhanging 2 inches with a small knife or shears. Fill the bottom of the terrines to one-third full with raisins, packing them down tightly. Layer the next one-third of the terrines with about ½ pound of the forcemeat. Lay one rabbit loin in the center of each terrine, trimming them if they are too wide. Be sure the loins do not touch the edges of the terrines. Cover the loin, filling the last one-third of the terrines with another ½ pound of the forcemeat. Pack down the terrine with your hands. Fold the caul fat over to completely cover the top of the terrines. Trim excess. Fold the plastic wrap back over the caul fat and trim the excess. Cover the terrine with its lid, tying it down tightly with two pieces of butcher's twine.

To cook the terrines: Preheat oven to 300°F. Place terrines in a large, deep roasting pan that is slightly taller than the terrines. Fill the baking pan with hot tap water to about ¼-inch below the lid of the terrines. Place the baking pan in the oven and bake for 45 minutes. Remove the baking dish from the oven. Remove the terrines from the water bath and refrigerate overnight.

Note 2: Hutchins will often cook just one terrine, then pack the rest of the forcemeat for freezing, pairing 1 pound of forcemeat with one loin and some caul fat. According to Hutchins, "It freezes beautifully."

To make the vinaigrette: Whisk the oils together, then add the beer slowly, whisking constantly. Whisk in the remaining ingredients. Refrigerate until needed.

To pickle the vegetables: Trim and clean the vegetables. In a large bowl prepare an ice bath. In a large pot of boiling water, cook the vegetables until they are barely tender. When vegetables are tender (but still firm), remove from boiling water and shock them in an ice bath to halt the cooking. Drain vegetables and place in a lidded container. In a medium pot heat water, sugar, and vinegar and bring mixture to a simmer, stirring to dissolve the sugar. Remove the brine from heat and cool slightly. When tepid, pour the brine over the vegetables and refrigerate overnight until needed.

To plate: Preheat oven to 400°F. Split the baguette in half lengthwise and cut the two halves into ½-inch slices. Place on a baking sheet and toast in the preheated oven for 5–7 minutes, or until the crostini are golden and crisp. Set aside. Toss the frisée with a few teaspoons of vinaigrette, being sure not to over-dress the lettuce. Season it with salt to taste. Garnish the edges of six plates with a few drops of vinaigrette. Slice terrines into ½-inch slices. Place a small bunch of frisée off center on the plates. Place a few pickled vegetables on the frisée. Onto this base, layer crostini, pickles, and slices of terrine with leaves of frisée, finishing with one slice of the terrine. On the opposite side of the plates, place a few slices of the Berkshire Blue. Garnish the plates with assorted pickles and sprinkle top of the terrine layer with a pinch of salt. Serve cold.

Red Devon

108 Hunns Lake Road
Bangall, NY 12506
(845) 868-3175
REDDEVONRESTAURANT.COM
Owners: Julia and Nigel Widdowson;
Executive Chef: Sara Lukasiewicz

Even though Red Devon is snuggled in the moneyed, horsey nook of Bangall, New York, you couldn't confuse it with, say, a restaurant in New Canaan, Connecticut. Instead of a clientele driving immaculate SUVs in costly new Barbour jackets, in the dining room of Red Devon you'll find diners clopping around in barn boots, perhaps a little damp with horse sweat.

Red Devon's rusticity is a far cry from Chef Sara Lukasiewicz's start in the business as an intern at Momofuku Noodle Bar under the notoriously gimlet eye of Chef David Chang. Admits Lukasiewicz, "David has quite the temper, but he's a great person to work for. I learned a lot—both from David and his sous-chef at the time. They introduced me to many of the local products in the Hudson Valley." She points out, "A lot of the farmers they use at Momofuku, we use here."

While her work at Red Devon ultimately snagged Lukasiewicz a James Beard Foundation nomination for Rising Star Chef of the Year in 2012, she came to the job in 2009 while still attending The Culinary Institute of America. Says Lukasiewicz, "Basically, I took the job when the owners said, 'We make all of our own charcuterie. We're buying whole animals and we're using local and sustainable products.'" Much of the grass-fed beef that Lukasiewicz uses in her kitchen comes from Temple Farm in Millbrook, which is also owned by the pair behind Red Devon, Julia and Nigel Widdowson. In fact, the restaurant's name comes from the Devon steer that the Widdowsons raise.

The commitment to using whole animals does not always come easily to Lukasiewicz, who, unluckily, is a rather petite chef. "Breaking down whole animals is kinda part of being a chef nowadays, but still, it's challenging. You know, I'm five feet tall and I'm moving this thing around that weighs 250 pounds—it can be difficult at times. But it also shows—when I have some six-foot-tall cook in here and he's watching me break down a steer or a pig into smaller pieces—that I know what I'm doing as a chef. People definitely respect it."

Sea Salt & Black Pepper Roasted Pork Tenderloin with Spring Vegetable Hash, Log Grown Shiitake Mushrooms, Sugar Snap & English Peas, PeeWee Potatoes & Sherry Vinegar Reduction

(SERVES 2)

For the sherry reduction:

½ cup sherry vinegar (Lukasiewicz recommends Our Lady of the Resurrection Monastery vinegar)

¼ cup water

½ cup granulated sugar

1 bay leaf

1 clove garlic, sliced

½ shallot, sliced

4 black peppercorns

For the finished dish:

12 ounces Red Barn Produce Pee Wee potatoes

8 ounces Migliorelli Farms sugar snap peas

8 ounces Migliorelli Farms English peas

8 ounces Mill Creek "Log Grown" shiitake mushrooms

1 Meili Farms or Northwind Farms pork tenderloin

Sea salt or kosher salt

Cracked black peppercorns

4 ounces Cabot butter

1 medium shallot, minced

1 clove garlic, sliced

To make the reduction: In a pot combine all the ingredients and bring to a simmer. Cook until the liquid is reduced to a syrup consistency. Strain, cool, and reserve.

To make the dish: In a pot of cold, salted water, place the potatoes. Place the pot over high heat and bring to a boil. Reduce the heat to a simmer and cook the potatoes until they are tender. Drain, cool, and cut the potatoes in half. Reserve.

Bring another pot of salted water to a boil. Meanwhile, in a bowl prepare an ice bath. Blanch the sugar snap peas in the boiling salted water until they are cooked through but still crisp, 1–2 minutes. Using a spider, fish out the snap peas and immediately plunge them into the ice bath. Using the same boiling water, blanch the English peas until they are almost fully cooked, about 2–3 minutes. Immediately plunge into the ice bath.

Remove the stems from the shiitakes and slice the caps into ¼-inch pieces.

Preheat oven to 425°F. Rub the pork tenderloin with sea salt and cracked black pepper. Place a large ovenproof sauté pan over medium-high heat, coat the pan with oil, and sear the tenderloin on all sides. Place the sauté pan in the oven to roast the tenderloins for 8–10 minutes to finish cooking. Remove when they reach an internal temperature of 130°F–135°F for medium rare, 140°F–145°F for medium. Rest the pork for 10 minutes as you finish the recipe.

In a sauté pan over medium-high heat, place the butter. Add the cooked potatoes and lightly sauté them in the butter until golden, 2–3 minutes. Add the shiitake mushrooms, minced shallot, and garlic and continue sautéing the mixture for about 6–8 minutes. Once the shiitakes are cooked, add both peas and sauté until warmed through. Season to taste with salt and pepper.

To serve: Divide the spring vegetable hash between two plates. Slice and arrange the pork tenderloin over the hash and drizzle with the sherry vinegar reduction. Serve.

SEREVAN

6 AUTUMN LANE
AMENIA, NY 12501
(845) 373-9800
SEREVAN.COM
CHEF/OWNER: SERGE MADIKIANS

Some of the greatest chefs come to cooking via unusual paths, and Chef Serge Madikians of Serevan is definitely one of them. Before cooking, his master's in public policy and economics took him into New York City Mayor Giuliani's administration. Says Madikians, "I went into cooking at thirty-seven. In 2002 I was a forty-year-old man. I had been cooking for just three years professionally. And I realized that I just didn't want to be a chef in New York City. I thought, 'I'll just go back to my other career.' And then I realized that some of the greatest chefs in the world do not work in cities—they work in small villages or near small villages. I thought that maybe I should try that lifestyle. And in 2002 that realization opened up a whole new world for me."

While Madikians may not have been the first New York City chef to decamp to the Hudson Valley, he was still part of the advance guard. Madikians's decision to cook farm-to-table cuisine in the Hudson Valley predates Blue Hill at Stone Barns by three years. "At that point, there were a few chefs, Jeff Gimmel at Swoon [in Hudson], who gave up their cooking lives in New York City to come up to the Hudson Valley. In the last couple of years, it has become incredibly hip for chefs to do this, but Jeff gave up his city life and moved up to Hudson a decade ago. It's the chefs like me and Jeff who showed that coming up here is doable, it's actually very enjoyable, and it's a great lifestyle."

Though Amenia is a town with somewhere around 4,500 residents, elegant Serevan does not fall into the trap that befalls other restaurants located in sparsely settled communities. In the effort to capture every potential diner, many restaurants resort to serving lowest-common-denominator menus in hopes of repelling the few and capturing the many. Instead, at Serevan, Madikians works in an innovative style that

celebrates Hudson Valley ingredients with a distinctly Persian point of view. He's infusing locally raised meats with saffron, sumac, and fragrant flower waters—you'll also find fish wrapped in kataifi pastry. This balance between Middle Eastern and Hudson Valley locavorian does not seem to perturb Madikians. "For me, as an Armenian who grew up in Iran, living here and cooking is for me very similar to living and cooking over there. I will always be an Armenian from northern Iran. So when I cook, my sensibility is always that of an Armenian who is strongly influenced by Middle Eastern flavors, specifically, Persian."

IRANIAN-ARMENIAN STYLE YOGURT SOUP

(SERVES 8)

3 large English cucumbers, peeled

2 tablespoons kosher salt

¼ cup water

1 bunch (about 8–10 sprigs) fresh dill

1 bunch (about 8–10 sprigs) fresh mint

1 bunch (about 8–10 sprigs) fresh cilantro

⅛ cup extra-virgin olive oil

3 shallots, peeled and quartered

2 cloves garlic

8 cups plain yogurt

1 lemon

1 lime

Dash cayenne pepper

To make the soup: Cut two of the cucumbers in half and then slice them into ½-inch slices. Place the sliced cucumbers with 1 tablespoon of the salt in a blender, then add the water and blend for about 2 minutes. Using a fine sieve set over a bowl, drain the cucumber pulp, reserving the water. Allow the cucumber water to drain without pressing down on it for about 30 minutes. The pulp should yield just about 4 cups of cucumber water. If not, add enough water to bring it to 4 cups.

Meanwhile, wash the herbs and remove the leaves from the stems. Set aside one-third of the herbs and discard the stems (or use them for vegetable stock). Place 1 cup of the cucumber water back in the blender. Add the olive oil, shallots, garlic, lemon, lime, cayenne pepper, and one-third of the herbs and blend for about 1 minute. Drain the cucumber-onion pulp through a fine sieve, again without pressing down on it, for about 15 minutes. Combine the onion-cucumber water with the remaining cucumber water.

Slice the third cucumber in half; remove and discard the seeds. Cut each cucumber half lengthwise into two spears and slice thin. Set aside. Combine the remaining herbs and chop into a fine chiffonade. Set aside.

To serve: In a large bowl whisk the yogurt and cucumber water mixture lightly, then add the herbs and cucumbers and mix well. Serve cold in chilled bowls and garnish with a sprig of herb.

Swift at the Roundhouse

2 East Main Street
Beacon, NY 12508
(845) 765-8369
ROUNDHOUSEBEACON.COM
Owner: Robert McAlpine; Executive Chef: Brandon Collins

When the team behind the elegant, industrial Roundhouse Hotel took on its current property in Beacon, the enterprise was not a sure bet. Though the collection of former factories has an unparalleled view of Beacon Falls, according to Chef Brandon Collins (whose restaurant Swift is located inside the Roundhouse), "They bought in total six dilapidated buildings on nine acres. And I know that the Roundhouse building had been abandoned for about fifty years. Basically, whatever they bought was rundown and overgrown. I've had numerous people come up to me and say, 'Hey, we used to sneak in here and smoke pot.' It was like a lot of old factories in a lot of old factory towns; it was an abandoned building and people exploited it."

Collins continues, "The reason why they chose Beacon is that the price was right, the location was beautiful—and there are not a lot of places that come with this kind of

view without having to alter the landscape. Basically, they just found a bunch of beautiful buildings and snagged 'em. In the past the buildings were machine shops, blacksmith shops, bleacheries—just a whole slew of stuff. The original mechanized lawnmower was built here in the Roundhouse [in the 1850s]. It was the first one in the United States, built by a man named Horatio Swift—that's where the restaurant's name comes from."

On Collins's menu (and in his recipe, which follows), you'll find touches of Korea, Vietnam, and Indonesia—yet Collins is a Midwest-born chef from Dayton, Ohio. He came to the Hudson Valley to attend The Culinary Institute of America and stayed to work under Chef Jeff Raider at the Valley Restaurant at the Garrison. The eclecticism in Collins's menu at Swift is intentional. "Basically I wanted to create food that isn't something you could make at home. And not because I don't want people to create it at home—but if you're going to come out here for dinner—I want you to enjoy something that you would not have thought of, or wouldn't have the tools to cook, at home."

John Dory with Charred Parsnip, Brown Butter, Morels & Potato

(SERVES 4)

For the parsnip puree:

3 pounds parsnips, peeled and sliced into discs
Vegetable oil to coat
1 white onion, quartered
2 cloves garlic, quartered
1 quart heavy cream
Salt and pepper to taste
2 tablespoons unsalted butter

For the brown butter:

1 pound butter
1 pint dry, nonfat milk powder

For the morel and potato hash:

½ pound morel mushrooms
Vegetable oil
4 potatoes, peeled and diced small, blanched
    until tender
2 shallots, chopped
1 clove garlic, chopped
2 tablespoons chicken stock
1 tablespoon unsalted butter
Zest of 1 lemon
Salt and pepper to taste
1 tablespoon chopped chives

For the John Dory:

2 tablespoons unsalted butter
2 tablespoons vegetable oil
4 sides John Dory, skin removed
1 cup mixed micro green lettuces

To prepare the parsnip puree: Toss the parsnips in just enough oil to coat. In a medium-size sauté pan over high heat, sear the parsnips until they are burnt on the outside. Add the onion and allow it to caramelize slightly. Add the garlic and sauté until it is translucent. Pour in the heavy cream and season with salt and pepper. Bring to a boil, reduce the heat, and simmer the parsnips in the cream until the parsnips are tender. Strain, reserving the liquid, and place in a blender. Puree until the mixture is smooth, adding enough cooking liquid to make a silky puree. Add the butter and season to taste with salt and pepper. Reserve.

To make the brown butter: In a pot melt the butter and add the powdered milk. Stir constantly over medium heat until the mixture is brown and has a slightly nutty aroma. Strain through a chinois or fine mesh sieve. Lay out on paper towels to cool; the brown butter crumbs should be crisp.

To make the hash: In a hot pan slicked with oil to coat, sauté the morels. Add the potato and cook until the potatoes are brown. Add shallots and garlic and cook until they are translucent. Add the stock and reduce the liquid until it has thickened into a glaze. Finish with butter, lemon zest, salt, pepper, and chives.

To finish the dish: Heat a nonstick sauté pan over medium heat, then add the butter and the oil. Place the fish in the pan and sauté on one side only while using a spoon to continuously flick the butter and oil over the top of the fish. Sauté until the fish is golden and cooked through. Remove from the pan and drain on a paper towel.

To plate: Spoon a pool of parsnip puree onto each of four plates and then drag your spoon through the pools. In the center of the plates, spoon some of the hash. Top the hash with John Dory and top this with a spoonful of the crispy brown butter. Garnish with a small handful of mixed micro greens and serve.

Terrapin Restaurant

6426 Montgomery Street
Rhinebeck, NY 12572
(845) 876-3330
terrapinrestaurant.com
Owner/Executive Chef: Josh Kroner

Many newcomers to the region view the Hudson Valley as a monolith, but, in fact, the towns that hug the river bear characteristics that make them quite distinct. One chef, Josh Kroner, opened his restaurant, Terrapin, in two different communities on either side of the Hudson. He's in a good position to suggest some of the differences between two popular Hudson Valley regions. "I founded Terrapin in 1998 at its original location in West Hurley." The town, just outside of Woodstock, is on the western shores of the Hudson in Ulster County. "When I came up, I was a chef in New York City and I wanted to get out of the city. I was really hopeful that I could do something in this environment."

Kroner continues, "And I knew Woodstock. I used to go up to Woodstock. And, with my first wife, I found an old restaurant that was failing; I was able to get turnkey at a very low price." Terrapin's original West Hurley iteration had challenges, and the work was exhausting. "It was in the middle of the woods. We opened up as Terrapin, and it was strictly fine dining; we were open for dinner five nights a week." He adds, "To do that, I was there almost every second that the restaurant was open. Every plate went through my hands. But I was able to build up a reputation, and I became very successful with what I do.

"I took what I had developed over the five years in West Hurley, and I was able to finance the restaurant that I have here in Rhinebeck. I mean, I had seen Rhinebeck shortly after I moved up here, and I saw that Rhinebeck was really the place to be. In fact, I had even seen this building, which was at the time a brick-oven pizza place. I thought it was incredibly underutilized, and I saw something bigger for it." Kroner had his eyes on the joyous architecture of Rhinebeck's First Baptist Church, originally built in 1825.

"I had seen a lot of things in the city, especially restaurants like Gramercy Tavern, where you had a fine dining room paired with a more casual, comfort food area. I always thought that was such a great idea, and there was really nothing like that up here at the time. My goal was to do something like Gramercy Tavern, and this space is perfect—you know, where I am now—I have the bistro and the fine dining area."

When asked why the city of Rhinebeck would be a preferable location for Terrapin to the neighboring town of Woodstock, Kroner pauses and becomes more selective with his words. "Well, certainly there is more money on this [the eastern] side of the river in general. More people have the ability to go out to eat. The number of people that I have in my restaurant here compared to over there is probably four or eight times as many. And the type of diner is different. In Woodstock people are more fickle." He continues, "It's tougher to run a restaurant in Woodstock, for sure. In West Hurley I wasn't in Woodstock—I was just outside

of Woodstock—and I did very well. In fact, I was one of the most successful restaurants in the Woodstock area." He pauses, "I just saw how, in Woodstock, if a restaurant didn't get a good footing right away, it was tough for them to get going—whereas on this side of the river, it might not be the same way.

"There is definitely some crossover between Woodstock and Rhinebeck, but the markets are very, very different. And moving over, I always figured that since I was a fine dining chef, the bistro would just be a supplement to what I did in the dining room. That really was the case in the beginning, but the interesting thing was that when the economy got bad, Terrapin's bistro business picked up. What happened was, basically, the percentages switched. It used to be that 60 percent of business came from the dining room, and now 60 percent comes from the bistro. But overall, even with the recession, my last four years have been record years."

HARDNECK GARLIC SOUP

(SERVES 8)

2 tablespoons light olive oil

½ pound Spanish onions, diced

1½ cups peeled garlic cloves

½ cup dry sherry

1½ quarts chicken stock

¾ cup heavy cream, heated

5 slices white bread, crusts removed and diced

¼ cup Italian parsley leaves, cleaned well

3 teaspoons honey

Salt, black pepper, and Sriracha to taste

Heat an 8-quart (or larger) stockpot over medium heat. Add the oil, and when it's hot, add the onions and garlic. Sweat the vegetables for about 30–40 minutes, or until the garlic is very soft and golden brown.

Turn the heat to high and add the sherry. Cook a few minutes until the sherry has almost completely evaporated. Add the stock and bring the mixture to a boil. Add the cream and simmer for 20 minutes.

Remove the soup from the heat and mix in the bread and parsley. Allow it to cool slightly. In a blender puree the soup in batches, never filling the blender more than halfway, and return the pureed soup to the pot. Add the honey and the salt, pepper, and Sriracha to taste. Reheat and serve with crusty French bread.

ROCKLAND COUNTY

Freelance Cafe

506 Piermont Avenue
Piermont, NY 10968
(845) 365-3250
xaviars.com
Executive Chef/Owner: Peter Kelly;
Chef de Cuisine: Philippe Scouernec;
Xaviar's Restaurant Group Beverage Director: Billy Rattner

Located just next door to Chef Peter X. Kelly's tiny, perfect Xaviar's, Freelance Cafe offers a casual ying to Xaviar's formal yang. Says Kelly, who owns both restaurants, "At Freelance [which opened in 1989] we predated the modern movement toward casual dining. We offered a simpler, more approachable cuisine that blended classic French with bistro, Italian trattoria, and American Cafe. Contrary to some rumors, we do maintain two separate kitchens at Xaviar's and Freelance, but we're able to consistently offer more than twenty wines by the glass because we benefit from the depth of Xaviar's cellar next door."

Like all of Kelly's restaurants, the bulk of Freelance's ingredients are sourced in the Hudson Valley; characteristically, Kelly does not blow his own locavorian horn. "Look, I started using local farmers way back at Xaviar's in Garrison because, up there, I could not get what I needed—quail, trout—through the usual channels. I'm still going to the same farms that I started with back in the '80s." Ned Kelly, Chef Peter Kelly's brother (with whom he used to play restaurant as a child), is a constant face at Freelance, where he oversees the front of the house.

Grilled Hudson Valley Quail, Doc Davies White Corn Maque Choux, Cherry Mostarda with Conklins Cherries

(SERVES 8 AS A STARTER AND 4 AS A MAIN)

For the quail:

8 boneless quail
Salt and freshly ground black pepper
6 tablespoons extra-virgin olive oil
3 tablespoons balsamic vinegar
2 cloves garlic, peeled and sliced
2 sprigs fresh rosemary
4 sprigs fresh thyme

For the maque choux:

2 tablespoons (¼ stick) unsalted butter
1 cup finely diced Spanish onion
¼ cup finely diced red bell pepper
3 cups fresh white corn kernels (cut from 4 medium
    ears of corn)
¾ cup heavy whipping cream
1 teaspoon chopped fresh thyme
¼ teaspoon cayenne pepper
2 green onions, finely sliced on a bias

Coarse kosher salt

Freshly ground black pepper

For the mostarda:

½ cup chopped shallots

4 cloves garlic, sliced

½ cup chopped red onion

1 cup granulated sugar

½ cup water

½ cup Champagne vinegar

2 tablespoons mustard seeds

1 teaspoon crushed red pepper flakes

Zest of 1 orange, removed in strips with vegetable peeler

1 bay leaf

6 (about 2 pounds) cups stemmed and pitted cherries

1 tablespoon Dijon mustard

To marinate the quail: Starting 12–48 hours before you plan to serve the dish, season the quail with salt and freshly ground black pepper. Using a sharp knife, pierce a hole along the lower left leg of each quail. Pull the right leg through this slit to cross the legs of each quail. Place the quail and the marinade ingredients in a sealable plastic bag. Place the bag in a bowl and allow the quail to marinate in the refrigerator for 12–48 hours.

To prepare the maque choux: In a large skillet over medium-high heat, melt the butter. Add the onion and sauté in the butter for about 5 minutes, or until the onion is translucent. To the onion, add the bell pepper and sauté until it begins to soften, about 3 minutes. Add the corn and sauté for 2 more minutes, then add the cream, thyme, and cayenne. Simmer all the ingredients together until the sauce thickens, about 5 minutes. Stir in the green onion. Season to taste with salt and pepper and set aside.

To make the mostarda: In a heavy-bottomed saucepan combine all the ingredients except the cherries and mustard. Over high heat bring the mixture to a boil, then reduce the heat and allow the mixture to simmer gently until it reduces to a syruplike consistency. Stir occasionally to ensure that the sugar does not burn and stick to the bottom of the pan.

Add the cherries to the mixture. Stir to combine. Cook until the cherries are soft and breaking into pieces. Remove from heat and mix in the mustard. Remove the bay leaf and cool in an ice bath before serving.

To grill the quail: Heat a griddle or griddle pan and cook the quail for 3 minutes on the breast side. Turn the quail and cook for 2 more minutes. Serve with sweet potato mousseline (recipe follows), maque choux, and cherry mostarda.

MOUSSELINE OF GINGERED SWEET POTATOES

(SERVES 8)

5 sweet potatoes, peeled and coarsely chopped
½ cup plus 1 tablespoon unsalted butter
7 cloves garlic, chopped fine
1½ ounces ginger, chopped fine
1¾ cups heavy cream
Salt
Freshly ground white pepper

Place the sweet potatoes in a large pot and cover with cold water. Place over high heat and bring the water to a boil. Cook the potatoes for 20–30 minutes, or until they are very soft. Drain sweet potatoes and transfer them to the bowl of a food processor.

While the potatoes are cooking, put a large sauté pan over moderate heat. Melt half the butter, then add the chopped garlic and ginger and sauté for 3 minutes, or until the vegetables are translucent (but not brown). Add the heavy cream, bring the mixture to a boil, and boil for about 10 minutes, or until the mixture is thick and reduced by a third. Remove the pan from the heat and pour the warm cream mixture and remaining butter into the food processor over the potatoes. Process the mixture until it is very smooth. Season to taste with salt and freshly ground white pepper. Serve immediately.

Restaurant X & Bully Boy Bar

117 North Route 303
Congers, NY 10920
(845) 268-6555
XAVIARS.COM
Executive Chef/Owner: Peter X. Kelly;
Chef de Cuisine: James Kelly;
Xaviar's Restaurant Group Beverage Director: Billy Rattner

Chef Peter X. Kelly had a prescient view of the Hudson Valley. He knew back in the 1980s, when he started opening restaurants in Garrison and Rockland County, that the Hudson Valley was poised for restaurant greatness. "People who travel to San Francisco spend a few days in Napa Valley. People who go to Florence spent time in the Tuscan hills. We knew that the Hudson Valley could attract people interested in food and wine when they traveled to New York City." With characteristic modesty, Kelly credits some of the culinary stars who migrated north from Manhattan with finally making it happen in the first decade of the twenty-first century.

In 2005 the Rockefellers and Dan, David, and Laureen Barber proved that city diners would make the trek to Blue Hill at Stone Barns and the Stone Barns Center for Food and Agriculture, but it was really the Batali/Bastianich project in Port Chester—Tarry Lodge (opened in 2008)—that proved that suburban restaurants could be profitable. In the wake of Tarry Lodge, others followed, but Kelly was first because he knew all along.

In 1997, a full sixteen years before Zak Pelaccio debuted his Fish & Game in Hudson, Kelly took on the Bully Boy in Congers. "The Bully Boy had been a well-known suburban restaurant for forty years. It was on the way to the Catskills, plus the Bully Boy was a country restaurant, with fireplaces and charm. But it was dying a slow death, so I took it on."

Upon installing his brother, Chef James Kelly, in the newly rechristened Restaurant X & Bully Boy Bar kitchen, Kelly began to serve soulful American cuisine in the landmark's intimate, clubby rooms. Kelly redesigned the space with help from another brother, Ned Kelly; many of the seats now offer views to a sylvan garden and pond. Like the restaurant's decor, Restaurant X's menu slings newly fashionable, old-school classics. Look for beef Wellington, filet mignon with foie gras, and the luscious Roast Hudson Valley Lola Duckling, below.

ROAST HUDSON VALLEY LOLA DUCKLING

(SERVES 2–4)

For the duck:

1 (4–5 pound) Lola duckling
Salt and pepper
1 teaspoon crushed juniper berries
1 orange, cut in half
1 stalk celery, coarsely chopped
1 onion, quartered
2 carrots, coarsely chopped
1 stem lemongrass, smashed to release fragrance
1 large leek, cleaned and sliced lengthwise
    (white part only)

For the sauce:

½ cup Grand Marnier
2 cups chicken stock
2 shallots, minced
2 tablespoons honey
2 tablespoons Champagne vinegar
1 pint pitted Picholine olives
1 tablespoon unsalted butter

To prepare the duck: A full 24 hours before you intend to cook the duck, rub the duck inside and out with salt, pepper, crushed juniper berries, and orange. Place the orange, celery, onion, carrots, lemongrass, and leeks inside the cavity of the duck. Prick its skin all over with a kitchen fork to allow the fat to drain as it cooks. Cover and refrigerate for 24 hours.

Preheat oven to 550°F. Place the duck, breast side up, on a rack in a large roasting pan and place it in the oven. Roast for 30 minutes at 550°F, then lower oven to 400°F and continue roasting for 15 minutes longer, basting periodically. Remove the duck from the oven and transfer it to a platter. Cover with aluminum foil and keep warm as you prepare the rest of the dish.

To make the sauce: Pour off the fat from the roasting pan. Empty the contents of the duck carcass, including its juices, into the roasting pan. Deglaze the pan over high heat by adding Grand Marnier, chicken stock, minced shallots, honey and vinegar, gently scraping up all the flavorful brown bits from the pan. Pour the liquid from the roasting pan into a saucepan and add the olives. Cook over medium-high heat until the liquid is reduced by half. Add butter and strain through a fine mesh strainer. Keep warm and serve with the duck.

Xaviar's at Piermont

506 Piermont Avenue
Piermont, NY 10968
(845) 359-7007
xaviars.com
Executive Chef/Owner: Peter X. Kelly;
Chef de Cuisine: George Demarsico;
Xaviar's Restaurant Group Beverage Director: Billy Rattner

What eventually became Chef Peter Kelly's flagship bijoux is actually his second go-round by that name. Kelly's first Xaviar's debuted in 1983 and was located at Highlands Country Club in Garrison. When he opened that Xaviar's (his first restaurant), Kelly was a superannuated twenty-three. To cover his modest start-up costs (about nine thousand dollars), Kelly had to sell his car.

"I hadn't been trained as a chef, but I knew what I wanted. I wanted dinner to be an event—six courses paired with six wines. Really, Xaviar's was a mid-1980s restaurant—like the Quilted Giraffe." The second Xaviar's in Piermont opened four years after the first and shows a chef who can—finally—indulge his taste for luxury. Xaviar's is truly tiny, a jewelbox of only forty seats, but it glitters with costly details: lavish flowers, soft candlelight, buttery linens, Baccarat crystal, Versace china. Almost instantly, this second venture by a self-taught chef who had to sell his car to enter the business snagged four stars from the *New York Times* and top ranking in the *Zagat Survey* and stole the hearts of locals. Xaviar's has been the host of hundreds of proposals and important anniversaries since it opened in 1987. When talking of Xaviar's, Kelly's voice takes on an uncharacteristic lilt of tenderness. "It's where we do our most *haute* work. We have the ability to touch each guest a little more warmly."

Black Cod with Honey & Sake Glaze, Ragout of Orzo with Morel Jus & Del Cabo Tomatoes

(SERVES 4)

For the ragout:

1 tablespoon unsalted butter
8–12 cloves garlic, roasted
1 cup mushroom stock (chicken stock may be substituted)
½ pint Del Cabo tomatoes, sliced in half (cherry tomatoes may be substituted)
8 ounces fresh morel mushrooms or 2 ounces dried morels that have been soaked in water
16 fresh shiitaki mushroom caps, quartered

1 cup cooked orzo pasta
Salt and freshly ground pepper

For the cod:

1 cup miso
½ cup mirin
½ cup sake
¾ cup honey
¼ cup soy sauce
4 (5–6 ounce) black cod fillets, boneless and skinless
1 tablespoon vegetable or olive oil

To make the ragout: Place a large sauté pan over medium-high heat. Add 1 tablespoon butter to the pan and allow it to melt without browning. Add the roasted garlic and cook about 1 minute. Pour in the stock and tomatoes. Add the morels and shiitakis and cook for 2 minutes. Stir in the cooked orzo and cook the ragout until it's heated through, about 1 minute. Season the mixture to taste with salt and freshly ground pepper. Reserve the ragout while you finish the dish.

To prepare the cod: In a nonreactive bowl whisk miso, mirin, sake, honey, and soy until fully combined and smooth. Slip the cod fillets into this mixture and marinate in the bowl, covered in plastic wrap, for at least 4 hours (or, preferably, overnight). Do not allow the cod to marinate more than 24 hours or fish will start to cure.

Preheat oven to 450°F. Remove the cod fillets from the marinade and wipe off most of the liquid, leaving just a thin film on the fish. Rub a baking sheet with 1 tablespoon vegetable or olive oil and place the cod on the baking sheet, leaving an inch or 2 between the fillets. Place the baking sheet in the preheated oven and cook for 5 minutes. Meanwhile, heat the broiler. After the fish has been in the oven for 5 minutes, remove and place under the broiler. Broil the fish for about 30 seconds. Serve with the orzo ragout.

Pan Roasted Double Veal Rib
with a Bouquet of Vegetables & Roasted
Doughnut Peaches

(SERVES 2)

For the vegetables:

4 ripe doughnut peaches

Extra-virgin olive oil to coat

Salt and pepper

1 head garlic

3–4 fingerling potatoes, scrubbed

1 baby artichoke, trimmed

10 pearl onions, peeled

¼ cup shelled fava beans

¼ cup shelled English peas

6–8 asparagus spears, cut into 2-inch lengths

¼ cup finely diced carrots

¼ cup finely diced zucchini

¼ cup finely diced yellow squash

For the veal:

1 double-cut veal rib chop (approximately 20 ounces),
    trimmed to 1 bone

Salt and pepper

¼ pound quartered mushrooms

2 sprigs each fresh thyme and sage

2 ounces Madeira

½ cup veal stock (chicken broth may be substituted)

2 tablespoons unsalted butter

To prepare the vegetables: Preheat oven to 400°F. Place the peaches on an oiled cookie sheet; rub each with olive oil and season with salt and pepper. Place the peaches in the preheated oven and roast for 15–20 minutes, or until the skin is blistered and peaches are very tender. Remove peaches from the oven and allow them to cool. When they're cool, cut the top from each peach and, using a spoon, scoop out the stones. Leave two peaches whole and cut the other two into a dice. Set aside.

Cut the stem from a head of garlic to expose the tips of its cloves. Drizzle the exposed cloves with a bit of olive oil, wrap the head of garlic in foil, and bake in the preheated oven until the head is soft when you squeeze it with tongs, 30–40 minutes. Meanwhile, prepare the potatoes (they can bake simultaneously). When the garlic is soft, allow it to cool and reserve six to eight cloves.

Place scrubbed fingerling potatoes on a baking sheet. Sprinkle them with salt and pepper and drizzle with a teaspoon of olive oil. Place them in the preheated oven and roast for 20 minutes. Remove the potatoes from the oven and allow them to cool. The potatoes will be quite firm. Cut them into a ½-inch dice and set aside.

Bring a large pot of salted water to boil. Have ready a bowl filled with ice water. For the artichoke, trim off the tough outer leaves and base. Place it in the boiling water and cook for about 10 minutes, or until tender. Remove the artichoke from the pot with tongs or a skimmer and shock it in ice water. Leave the water boiling as you prepare the rest of the vegetables. When the artichoke is cold, drain and cut it into quarters or eighths. Remove its fuzzy interior choke and reserve the rest.

Place the pearl onions in the boiling water and blanch for 3 minutes. Shock them in ice water, then drain and set aside. Drop the shelled fava beans in the boiling water and cook for 1 minute. Remove the favas from the pot and shock them in the ice water. When cold, slip off their filmy skins and set aside.

Place the shelled peas in the boiling water for 30 seconds. Remove the peas from the pot and shock them in the ice water. When cold, drain and set aside. Repeat the blanching/shocking process for the asparagus, carrots, zucchini, and yellow squash, adding ice as needed. Do not overcook the vegetables; they should be blanched until just tender. Reserve while you finish the dish.

To roast the veal: Place a 12-inch ovenproof skillet over medium heat. Season the veal chop on both sides with salt and pepper. Place the veal chop in the pan and sear over medium heat for 4 minutes. Turn the chop over and continue cooking on the other side for 4 more minutes. The meat should be well bronzed.

To the pan add the quartered mushrooms, diced peaches, artichokes, fingerling potatoes, roasted garlic, and pearl onions. Place the fresh thyme and sage on top of the chops and place the pan in the preheated oven. Roast for 12 minutes. Remove the veal from the pan and place it on a cutting board. Allow it to rest (at least for 10 minutes before slicing) while you finish the sauce.

Return the pan of vegetables and veal juice back to the stovetop over high heat and sauté for 1 minute. Add the Madeira and the veal stock (or chicken broth) and boil the mixture until the liquid is reduced by half. Add the peas, fava beans, asparagus, carrots, zucchini, and yellow squash. Add the butter (cut into small pieces) to the pan. Swirl the pan to incorporate the butter. Spoon the vegetables and sauce onto two warm dinner plates. Place one whole roasted peach on each plate; slice the veal and lay it over the vegetables. Serve.

ULSTER COUNTY

A Tavola

46 Main Street
New Paltz, NY 12561
(845) 255-1426
ATAVOLANY.COM
Co-Chef/Owners: Nathan and Bonnie Snow

Before they opened their restaurant, A Tavola, in New Paltz, Nathan and Bonnie Snow both had enviable careers as chefs in Manhattan and Brooklyn. After eight years working for JP Morgan Chase, Bonnie Snow followed her passion and attended culinary school. She became chef de cuisine at Sfoglia; meanwhile, Nathan Snow was helping Andrew Carmellini open A Voce. Nathan later hit Brooklyn to head up the kitchen at Al Di La—absolutely none of which predicts that the pair would decamp for the wilds of New Paltz.

Says Nathan Snow, "Well, there were a number of reasons for us to open in New Paltz. Number one was that we wanted to start a family, and we didn't want to do that in the city. Basically we wanted to get out and live at a slower pace of life. In the city we were working long, long hours. And another reason is that the cost of opening a

restaurant here is so much lower. Finally, a lot of the food that we were cooking in the city actually comes from here, so we were kinda thinking, 'Why don't we just move closer to the food?'"

With his experience, Snow was in a better position than most youthful first-time restaurant owners. "I was fortunate enough to have opened a bunch of restaurants in Manhattan—not my own, but working for other people who were opening restaurants. On one of them [A Voce] I was very involved, even though that was on a much larger scale than anything we were interested in doing."

Though Snow claims that the building that would eventually become A Tavola had "always been a restaurant," it's actually so old that it predates official records. Snow laughs, "It's pretty old—you know, it's got some Underground Railroad stuff in the basement. Almost every building on our block is connected. I can't even tell you how old it is because there's no record in Town Hall. We tried to find out its age and couldn't."

The stresses of working so closely together don't seem to faze the Snows, who not only have a toddler at home but also have a new restaurant, Huguenot (also in New Paltz), on the way. "It's great. If I can't be in the restaurant for some reason, Bonnie can fill my shoes. Now we have a fifteen-month-old daughter, so I'll say, 'Why don't you go to the restaurant tonight and I'll stay home?'"

Ricotta Gnocchi con Frutti di Bosco

(SERVES 4)

For the gnocchi:

1 pound fresh ricotta cheese

5 ounces all-purpose flour (plus more for dusting the table)

3 ounces grated Parmigiano Reggiano

1 teaspoon extra-virgin olive oil

1 whole egg

Pinch of salt

Cracked black pepper

For the sauce:

3 tablespoons vegetable or grapeseed oil

1 pound Hen-of-the-Woods (maitake) mushrooms

4 tablespoons unsalted butter

½ cup fresh corn kernels, removed from cob

1 clove garlic

Pinch of red pepper flakes

1 bunch basil

½ cup fresh blueberries

Salt and pepper to taste

Freshly grated Parmigiano Reggiano, for garnish

To make the gnocchi: In a large bowl mix all the ingredients by hand for several minutes. As the dough begins to form, start kneading it into a ball by folding half of the mixture over itself and pressing. Do this for several minutes. Add small amounts of flour, only as needed, to achieve a firm but still slightly tacky consistency. The final dough ball should "bounce back" when pressed but not be completely dry. Wrap in plastic and allow it to rest in the refrigerator while you prepare the other ingredients.

To prep for the sauce: Using your hands, pull the mushrooms apart into smaller, bite-size pieces. Coarsely cut the basil leaves into quarter-leaf pieces. Mince the garlic clove. Reserve.

To form the gnocchi: On a large, clean table, using a bench scraper or large chef's knife, cut the dough ball into four equal pieces. Place a small container of extra flour within reach. Dust a portion of the table surface with flour and place one of the dough quarters in the center. Gently begin rolling the ball with your hands, applying moderate (but not hard) pressure. Keep rolling the dough back and forth while moving your hands toward either side to elongate the ball. Continue this process, adding a dusting of flour as needed to prevent it from sticking to the table, until dough forms an even cord roughly ¾-inch in diameter. Once your cord is formed, use your bench scraper or knife to cut the cord into 1-inch lengths. Place the gnocchi on a floured baking tray and repeat the rolling/cutting process with the remaining three balls.

Meanwhile, bring a large pot of water to a boil. Add a hefty pinch of salt—water should taste slightly less salty than the ocean.

To make the sauce: Heat a large sauté pan over medium-high heat and add the oil. Once oil is hot, add the mushrooms and lower the heat to medium, tossing the mushrooms frequently for several minutes. The mushrooms should begin to color and become fragrant. Once the mushrooms have begun to soften, lower the heat to medium-low. Add the butter and allow it to brown and bubble with the mushrooms. Once the butter is slightly brown, add the corn, garlic, and red pepper flakes, then reduce the heat to low. Sauté everything for 2 minutes; the corn can brown and pop a little.

To cook the gnocchi: Drop the gnocchi in the boiling water and cook for about 3 minutes, or until the gnocchi float. Once they are floating, remove the gnocchi using a spider or slotted spoon and transfer them to the pan with the mushrooms and corn. Raise the heat back to medium. The gnocchi should crackle as the water combines with the hot butter. Once all the gnocchi are transferred, add a little bit of the pasta water until the mixture reaches the consistency of a sauce. Toss in the basil and blueberries and allow the gnocchi to simmer for another minute.

To finish: Season the gnocchi with salt and pepper to taste and then transfer it to four plates. Garnish with freshly grated Parmigiano Reggiano and serve.

BREAD ALONE

Main Bakery and Boiceville Cafe
3962 Route 28
Boiceville, NY 12412
(845) 657-3328

Rhinebeck Cafe
45 East Market Street
Rhinebeck, NY 12572
(845) 876-3108

Woodstock Cafe
22 Mill Hill Road
Woodstock, NY 12498
(845) 679-2108
BREADALONE.COM
Baker/Owner: Dan Leader

Bread: It seems like a perennial product, but when Dan Leader founded Bread Alone Bakery, the world of regional bread would be unrecognizable to anyone familiar with today's scene. Says Leader, "Thirty years ago there were basically all of the commercial breads and then the old-school Italian bakeries in New York like B and G and Vito's—all those old brick-oven places. I think Au Bon Pain had opened their first store in New York."

Says Leader, "I'm going to say something that's maybe unbelievable, but we didn't have a plan, initially. The plan was to make bread and then try to sell it. We were in at the beginning [of the popularity of artisanal bread], so we were able to get into a lot of farmers' markets. This helped build our wholesale business—we've been very lucky that one part of the business fed another."

Though he introduced his bread through farmers' markets, it's Leader's wholesale business that kept him afloat. "There are a very limited number of farmers' markets. So of course it's better to have the cash sales, but you can't rely on it within a fifty-two-week business model. The farmers' markets go to sleep in the wintertime; if we didn't have our wholesale business, we'd be out of business."

Leader was relentless. "I'm a very hardworking guy, and I was out constantly looking for customers. I met distributors and I met stores. Believe it or not, up until last year we never had a salesperson—*I* was the sales force. My son is now in the company and he's taking over most of the sales, but I'm a good networker. I would just go out and meet the distributors, meet the supermarket people." The big break came when Leader cracked into two major supermarket chains. "We were lucky to get in Whole Foods and Fairway."

In the thirty years of Bread Alone's lifespan, the artisanal bread market has become frighteningly competitive. "Now in every supermarket in America you can get this par-baked frozen bread—whether it's Ecce Panis or LaBrea. Every supermarket takes it out of the freezer, warms it up, and calls it artisan bread. It's changed dramatically."

While much of Bread Alone's sales are in crowded downstate markets, Leader's roots, bakery, and three restaurant/cafes are all upstate. His original bakery, located "out past Woodstock in Boiceville," is still operational, though Leader is building a much larger bakery in Lake Katrine, also in Ulster County. Leader's decision to open in the Hudson Valley, as opposed to, say, Long Island City, was about as strategic as his initial business plan. "I had a weekend house up here, and I just thought that it would be interesting to have a business in the Hudson Valley. I liked it up here; I went to school here." He adds, "I like being close to New York. I like both—being up here is a good way to have a business in New York without *living* in New York."

BRIOCHE FRENCH TOAST

(SERVES 6)

If you are adventurous, you can make the brioche at home (recipe follows). Most of us simply buy the best quality brioche loaf available.

For the French toast:

7 large eggs
½ cup sugar
4 cups milk (or milk substitute—almond milk is lovely)
1 teaspoon cinnamon
Pinch of cardamom
Pinch of salt
12 slices of 1-inch thick Brioche Slices (buy a loaf or see Brioche Dough recipe, opposite)

For cooking:

¼ cup clarified butter (or unsalted butter, see Note below)

For serving:

Confectionary sugar for dusting
Fresh fruit (blueberries, strawberries, peach slices— whatever is in season or on hand)

Place a baking pan in your oven and keep the oven warm (200°F).

Whisk together the eggs, sugar, milk, cinnamon, cardamom, and salt.

Place your brioche slices in a large shallow pan and pour the egg mixture over. Allow to soak in 3–4 minutes, then turn slices over (you will most likely have to do this in two shifts).

Heat your pan, add the clarified butter (see Note 1), and, when it is hot, add the first slices. Avoid having the slices touch each other. Once the first side is set, turn the slices over.

As the slices are finished, place them on the pan in your warming oven.

When ready to serve, dust with confectionary sugar and top with fresh fruit.

Note: The clarified butter will keep the slices from getting burned, but if you like the nutty browning flavor of full cream butter, you can add a few pats of unsalted butter as you are turning the slices (of course if you do not have clarified butter, simply use the butter you have on hand, being careful not to burn the butter—using clarified butter helps to avoid this problem).

BRIOCHE DOUGH

For the brioche dough:

1 ½ cups all-purpose flour

3 tablespoons granulated sugar

2 teaspoons dry yeast

¾ teaspoon salt

6 tablespoons cold unsalted butter,
    cut into ½-inch pieces

2 eggs

2 tablespoons milk

Butter an 8-inch loaf pan.

In the bowl of a stand mixer fitted with a dough hook, combine flour, sugar, yeast, and salt. Add the butter and blend until the butter pieces are pea size and coated with the dry mixture. Add the eggs and milk and blend on low until a dough forms. It should be cohesive and shiny.

Remove the dough from the bowl and shape it into a loaf by first rolling the dough out to a rough 8 x 11-inch rectangle and then rolling the rectangle up. Place in your buttered loaf pan. Cover with plastic and let rise at room temperature until double in volume, 1½ hours or more. When the loaf is ready to bake, it will be airy and light to the touch. Preheat oven to 350°F and bake for 35–40 minutes. To check if the loaf is fully backed, knock on the bottom of the pan––it should be hollow. Remove from the pan when just cool.

GUNK HAUS

387 SOUTH STREET
HIGHLAND, NY 12528
(845) 883-0866
GUNKHAUS.COM
OWNERS: ELIZABETH STECKEL AND DIRK SCHALLE;
EXECUTIVE CHEF: DIRK SCHALLE

It might seem oxymoronic for a restaurant to offer locally sourced German cuisine in Highland, New York, but for Elizabeth Steckel and Dirk Schalle, the Hudson Valley was an obvious choice for their venture. Laughs Steckel, "Well, my husband is from Bavaria. And we knew that we wanted our restaurant to focus on local craft brews, locally

raised meat, and local produce. We also knew that we wanted to pair food with beer the way so many restaurants pair food with wine." She continues, "It was just natural for us to look to the example of Germany for our restaurant. They've had a long tradition of farm-to-table dining and of pairing food with beer. And, in Germany the beer is often local because almost every town has its own brewery." Happily, in the Hudson Valley the pair can choose from a wealth of locally brewed craft beers.

Steckel and Schalle employ a full-time baker who only uses grains milled in New York State. Says Steckel, "It's labor intensive because it's all made from scratch. There are certainly people who come in here who don't know what we're all about. They might be disappointed that our prices are as high as they need to be. Or that they're not getting a free bread basket with every meal." She continues, "The bread basket thing is something that comes up from time to time, and it's really funny. We just don't do it for a number of reasons. One is that if a bread basket is put in front of Dirk and me, we're just going to mindlessly eat it—and we don't want to promote that sort of mindless eating. But also, we don't want to put out food that often gets thrown out." She concludes, "If people want bread, they can order it. We don't want to waste food.

"And, also, we feel very strongly at the restaurant that the price should reflect the cost—and that means the cost of what it took to produce. So, what it costs for us to have a full-time baker who earns a living wage and makes everything from scratch. What it costs the local millers in New York State to raise these grains. I would hate to give something away that's subsidized by raising the cost of something else on our menu. And our regulars all get that, and I know they support us, because we have been enormously successful."

Gunk Haus Goulash

(SERVES 15)

For the paprika sauce:

8 cloves garlic

1 bunch thyme, minced

1 bay leaf

2 quarts dry red wine

2 cups olive oil

4 tablespoons Hungarian sweet paprika

4 tablespoons Hungarian hot paprika

2 teaspoons sumac

2 teaspoons ground pepper mix (white and green peppercorns, allspice, coriander)

1 can (#10) fire-roasted red peppers

4 tablespoons Dijon mustard

4 tablespoons Sriracha

4 tablespoons brined green peppercorns

1 tablespoon hot chili oil

For the goulash:

1 pork butt (preferably a slow-growing heritage breed like a Berkshire)

2 tablespoons cumin seeds

2 tablespoons caraway seeds

1 tablespoon plus 1½ teaspoons sumac

1 tablespoon plus 1½ teaspoons ground mustard

1 tablespoon plus 1½ teaspoons ground pepper mix (white and green peppercorns, allspice, coriander)

¼ cup Hungarian sweet paprika

1 tablespoon plus 1½ teaspoons kosher salt

4 quarts white mushrooms

½ cup oil

2 tablespoons minced garlic

2 quarts red wine

2 quarts mushroom stock

2 quarts paprika sauce

1 quart caramelized onions

1 quart stout beer, such as Keegan's Mother's Milk

To make the sauce: In a saucepan combine the garlic, minced thyme, and bay leaf with the red wine. Cook until the liquid is reduced by half and the garlic is very soft.

In another pan, add olive oil and spices. Warm very gently for 1 minute, then set aside so that the spices can infuse the oil, about 1 hour.

Remove the bay leaf from the wine reduction. In a large blender, or using an immersion blender, combine the infused oil, wine reduction, and all other sauce ingredients. Blend until very smooth. Reserve.

To make the goulash: On the day before you intend to cook the goulash, trim the top fat off the pork and butcher it into ½-inch cubes. In a big bowl add the meat and toss in the cumin, caraway, sumac, ground mustard, pepper mixture, paprika, and salt and allow the mixture to marinate overnight.

When ready to cook, de-stem the mushrooms and reserve the caps. Into a pot place 2 quarts water and the mushroom stems and cook until the liquid is reduced by half. Quarter the mushroom caps and, in a saucepan, brown in ¼ cup of the oil. Reserve.

Preheat oven to 200°F. In a large pan with remaining ¼ cup oil, brown the pork, then add garlic and sauté until fragrant. Add wine, stock, paprika sauce, mushroom caps, onions, and beer. Liquid should cover pork. Cover and braise in the oven for 4–5 hours, or until very tender. Do not let liquid boil—should be at a bare simmer. Serve over mashed potatoes.

Joshua's Cafe

51 Tinker Street
Woodstock, NY 12498
(845) 679-5533
Joshuascafe.com
Chef/Owner: Stefanie Schacter

The funny thing about Woodstock and its perennial hippie associations is that the 1969 festival didn't even occur in town. Max Yasgur's 600-acre dairy farm, the site of the concert, was actually located forty-three miles from the Ulster County town of Woodstock, in the Sullivan County hamlet of White Lake.

Still, any walk through the shopping district of Woodstock will involve the sight of store windows filled with acid-hued tie dyes and hempen garments. The town is punctuated by organic and vegan-friendly restaurants—but most of these are newcomers and actually debuted long after Woodstock's hippie heyday.

Except one. Joshua's Cafe opened in 1972 and has been a landmark in the town ever since—Ruth Reichl famously raved about it in the pages of *Gourmet*. CIA-trained Chef Stefanie Schacter took over for Joshua (her father) in 1992 and continues to make a visit to Joshua's Cafe the de rigueur stop in Woodstock. While Joshua's is both vegan and vegetarian friendly—not to mention welcoming to diners with gluten intolerances—Schacter does spin Hudson Valley–raised meats into stunning Mediterranean and Middle Eastern dishes like this moussaka.

Moussaka

(SERVES 8–10)

For the sauce:

2 pounds ground lamb
1 small onion, diced
1 clove garlic, minced
1 cup sliced mushrooms
¾ cup red wine
¾ cup tomato puree
2 bay leaves
2 tablespoons dried oregano
Salt and pepper to taste

For the "mustard custard":

1 cup ricotta cheese
2 eggs
¼ cup prepared mustard
¼ teaspoon nutmeg
Pinch of cayenne
Pinch of salt
Pinch of black pepper

For assembly of the moussaka:

2 medium eggplants, peeled and sliced ¼-inch thick
Olive oil
8 ounces shredded Swiss cheese

To make the sauce: Preheat oven to 350°F. In a large sauté pan, brown the lamb and remove. Sauté the onion and garlic in the same pan until they are translucent, then add mushrooms and sauté until soft. Return lamb to the pan and add wine, tomato puree, bay leaves, and oregano. Bring to a simmer and cook until the lamb is cooked through, about 10 minutes. Add salt and pepper to taste.

To make the custard: Whisk together the ricotta, eggs, mustard, and spices until well combined. Reserve.

To assemble the moussaka: Lightly grill or sauté the eggplant slices in olive oil. In a 9 x 13-inch casserole pan, layer ingredients as follows: eggplant slices, lamb sauce, shredded Swiss cheese, "mustard custard." Bake at 350°F until well browned and bubbly, approximately 45 minutes. Serve.

Ralph Erenzo of Tuthilltown Spirits

What we're talking about when we talk about Tuthilltown whiskey is a sweet little bottle that has been variously described as chubby, cute, and the perfect stocking stuffer. But, simultaneously, we're talking about a revolution that brought the culture and craft of distilling back to its historic home in the Hudson Valley.

At the turn of the century, the Hudson River Valley—with its easy access to shipping arteries and (via the Erie Canal) the markets of the West—had been an established site for distilleries. Most notably, the vast Fleischmann Distilling Company was built on Peekskill's waterfront in 1901; this is the company that produced the first gin in the United States. Sadly, Prohibition ended American spirit production, and when it resumed in the 1930's, the industry was concentrated by the powerful distilleries in the South. Even the Fleischmann Distilling Company was eventually subsumed by Louisiana's many-armed Sazerac Company. And so things remained until the founder of Tuthilltown Spirits, Ralph Erenzio, decided to put the land that he owned in Gardiner to profitable use.

Here's what happened, in Erenzo's words:

"Oh, well—when we started there was no New York distilling scene. Tuthilltown was the first distillery to open in New York State since Prohibition. So, four generations ago, New York State had distilleries, but, when we started [in 2007], we were the first to operate in nearly 40 years.

"The fee for a permit in New York State had been $65,000. And then, in 2002, a law was passed establishing the A-1 license," Erenzo explains. "The A-1 license was sort of a mini-distillery license, like a micro-license; it capped production at 35,000 gallons per year, but it also lowered the permit fee to $1,500 dollars for three years. I was looking into distillery law, and I discovered that there was this new license that nobody seemed to know about.

"Of course, New York City is only 75 miles away, and, here in Gardiner, we're located in a large visitor area. Five hundred thousand tourists per year come through our neighborhood. And so it occurred to me: We could do what the wineries and breweries of the Hudson Valley had done, which was to create a small destination for people to go and visit—say, like the small distilleries that I'd seen while travelling through Europe. Because, although for many years people had been able to go and visit wineries and breweries and take tours, it had been eighty years since anybody had gone inside a distillery to see how it ran.

"But, really, there was no scene until 2007. Before then, we were still unable to sell our goods to visitors or offer them tastings or samples. This made tours a very high cost thing to offer because visitors would be in the way of operations and we couldn't sell them anything." Erenzo adds, pointing out the obvious: "Plus, telling them the whole story of how we made whiskey meant almost nothing if they couldn't actually taste the product at the end.

"And so I became engaged in the four-year lobbying effort to get that law changed. We got the Farm Distillery Act passed in 2007 and that allowed for the same volume of production—35,000 gallons. It also lowered the fee a little, plus it came with the ability to have a shop at the distillery and offer samples. This changed everything. In 2007, we were the only New York distillery. Since then, 38 liquor distilleries have opened in New York State and all of them are farm distilleries.

"What the Farm Distillery Act does is that it allows you to make anything you want as long as you make it with at least 75 percent New York State–grown agricultural raw materials. In exchange for using raw New York materials, you can have a shop and do tastings and sell directly to customers."

In 2007, when Tuthilltown debuted its first batch of Hudson Baby Bourbon (made from 100 percent New York State corn), it was the first New York whiskey to be produced since the fall of the Northeastern spirit industry. This liquor was big news, but bourbon is not particularly a historic Northeastern whiskey. For that, you need to look at rye, which had traditionally been distilled in the Mid-Atlantic states. "For many years, rye had been out of favor," explains Erenzo. "When whiskey production moved south, rye production fell off. It was historically a Northeastern thing: I mean, rye was a real New York spirit.

"Most of it was made with grain grown in Pennsylvania and New York; rye was a cover crop, plus, they were using it for bread. Now, rye is still

DISTILLERYMAN

© TUTHILLTOWN SPIRITS

a crop, but it's almost always plowed under—basically, it's planted to hold the ground together in bad seasons." While using the rye for spirits has the bottom line appeal of economy, Erenzo's inspiration to make rye had more to do with culture. "We wanted to have something that had a historic link to New York, and rye was it.

"For many years—well, since Prohibition—if Americans were drinking rye, it was Canadian rye, which is not made with 100 percent rye grain. It contains only a small amount of rye grain mixed with grain neutral spirit made in a big industrial plant. We thought we would start making rye in the traditional way with 100 percent rye grain. And we just happened to time it right; articles were starting to come out in the *New York Times* that discussed rye as the disappeared spirit. We could see that rye was starting to get some notice and that it was going to come back."

Erenzo's choice to use local grains and fruit in his spirits was not based in ethics; this was simply the smarter way for him to source. "It would be easier to source from outside the state, but it wouldn't necessarily be cheaper," he explains. "We pay a little more to our growers because, the way we do it, it's our crop—it's not the farmer's crop. This means that we're somewhat immune to real difficulties in the marketplace, like failed crops on a mass scale. If there is a difficult season on the commodities market, these local farmers are growing these crops for us with our seed. They're not going to sell that crop off to someone else if, by circumstance, they could get a higher price elsewhere. Also, we're willing to accept a little extra cost up front because, if we were buying corn from Iowa, we'd have to ship it here. It would cost us more to ship than for the grain itself. So it's not only for environmental and local/agricultural reasons that we use local suppliers; it's also good business sense. It saves us money."

Tuthilltown Spirits, PO Box 320, 14 Grist Mill Lane, Gardiner, NY 12525

Tours Saturdays & Sundays at 12 p.m., 2 p.m. and 4 p.m. by reservation only. Book online at tuthilltown.com or call (845) 633-8734.

Miss Lucy's Kitchen

90 Partition Street
Saugerties, NY 12477
(845) 246-9240
MISSLUCYSKITCHEN.COM
OWNERS: MARC PROPPER AND MICHELLE SILVER;
PASTRY CHEF: MICHELLE SILVER

In the sophisticated caste system that ranks towns of the Hudson Valley, Saugerties has traditionally held a position somewhere below the nearby town of Woodstock. It's a shame because Saugerties has it all: stunning nineteenth-century architecture, high-

end antiques stores, and a bourgeoning food scene. And, though Woodstock usually snags the credit, The Band's landmark album, *Music from Big Pink,* was actually composed in a Pepto-Bismol–colored house in West Saugerties that Rick Danko, Richard Manuel, and Garth Hudson shared.

Take that, Woodstock.

In fact, Saugerties is so attractive that chefs Michelle Silver and Marc Propper bought a second house in town while they were still running their primary business, the restaurant Grove in Manhattan's West Village. Says Silver, "We had a weekend house, which is now our regular house. We gave up our apartment in the city when we realized that we really wanted to open up a restaurant in town.

"For us, we have two kids—my daughter Lucy and my son Eli—and when we first opened [in 2003], they were young. We wanted a place where families could come, and the parents could have a nice bottle of wine and the kids could get a milkshake and mac and cheese and everyone could be happy. We were having a hard time finding that in Saugerties."

The space that Silver and Propper settled on couldn't have been more inauspicious. Says Silver, "It was a burnt-out shell. We'd be driving by looking at buildings, and we saw it and said, 'You know—we should find out about that space.' It has a great location, it was in our town, and the price was right." The two chefs built a restaurant whose vintage-seeming quirks are deceptively new, an effect that is aided by their repurposing of the building's original bricks, which are still charred from the fire.

All around Miss Lucy's Kitchen you'll see aprons that hearken to the (perhaps wholly fictional) days when women cooked in dresses and stiletto shoes. Says Silver, "The aprons were just an idea that I had; I had a little apron that my grandma made me, and I

hung it up in the restaurant on one of the racks. And then, on a whim, when I took down the curtains to be cleaned, I decided, 'Oh, let me just put some more aprons up in the window.'" She laughs at what would ultimately become the crowd-sourced decor of Miss Lucy's. "People just started bringing me aprons. It's like every old lady in town has a bag of aprons. A customer just came in and saw the apron that I was wearing. She said it was the apron that they sewed in the Saugerties Home Ec class—and she was like eighty!"

Silver and Propper have always been inspired by the food that grows around Saugerties. "The most fun part is being really seasonal—and not even just the four seasons, but hyper-seasonal. We're talking about the beginning of spring, then mid-spring—it really changes. In the city it's all kinda clumped together into spring, summer, fall, and winter. Here, as soon as the rhubarb pops up, then you know what's coming. It's ramps, then fiddleheads, asparagus, and peas. And then, following that, it's the next round of things. That's what we really like to do on our menu."

When asked whether her customers are mainly vacationers or live in town, Silver notes, "First of all, there are tons of New Yorkers. We rent apartments upstairs, and most of the people that rent the apartments are New Yorkers. And we can even tell from the zip codes on the restaurant's Amex reports that most of the people who dine with us are either local or from the Upper West Side or Brooklyn." She laughs, "Those are our people."

STRAWBERRY RHUBARB & PISTACHIO BRITTLE
ICE BOX CAKE

(SERVES 7–8)

For the strawberry-rhubarb compote:

10 stalks rhubarb, coarsely chopped
2½ cups orange juice
½ cup granulated sugar
6 star anise pods
6 chopped strawberries, plus extra for garnish

For the rhubarb caramel:

1¼ cups granulated sugar
½ teaspoon lemon juice
¼ cup plus 2 tablespoons water
1 cup reserved juice from strawberry-rhubarb compote

For the pistachio brittle:

1 cup granulated sugar
¼ cup water
½ cup shelled pistachios

For the strawberry parfait:

1¼ cups cream
4 egg yolks
6 tablespoons plus 2¼ teaspoons granulated sugar
⅓ cup water
⅛ teaspoon salt
¾ cup strawberry-rhubarb compote
½ cup chopped pistachio brittle

For the graham cracker crust:

1½ cups graham cracker crumbs
2 tablespoons melted unsalted butter
1 tablespoon granulated sugar

To make the compote: In a medium-size saucepan place the rhubarb, orange juice, sugar, and star anise. Bring this mixture to a boil over medium heat, then reduce to a simmer. Simmer the mixture, stirring occasionally, until the rhubarb is soft. When the rhubarb is tender, add the strawberries and cook until the strawberries have broken down. Remove the pan from heat and discard the star anise pods. Strain the compote, reserving the juice to make rhubarb caramel.

To make the caramel: In a saucepan stir the sugar with the lemon juice and water and bring this mixture to a boil. Lower the heat and continue to cook the mixture until it is golden brown. Remove the caramel from the heat and whisk in the strawberry-rhubarb juice. Return the saucepan to the burner and boil the mixture for about another minute. Remove the sauce from the heat and transfer to another container to cool. Reserve.

To make the brittle: Line a half-sheet pan with parchment paper and spray the paper with nonstick spray. In a saucepan heat the sugar and water over medium-low heat until sugar dissolves. Increase the heat under the pan to bring the mixture to a boil. Cook the mixture until it is a deep amber color. Stir in the nuts and, working quickly, pour the mixture onto the prepared parchment paper. Quickly spread into a thin layer. Let cool. Reserve.

To make the parfait: In a large bowl whip the cream until it reaches soft peaks. Set aside. In the bowl of a stand mixer fitted with the whisk attachment, beat the egg yolks on high speed until they are pale. Prepare an ice bath large enough to accommodate the mixer bowl.

Meanwhile, in a saucepan combine the sugar, water, and salt. Place over medium-high heat and bring the mixture to a boil. Cook the sugar mixture until a digital thermometer reads 230°F. Turn the stand mixer back on low speed. In a slow, steady stream, pour the sugar syrup down the side of the mixer bowl into the egg yolks. When all the syrup has been poured in, increase the mixer's speed to high and continue to beat the eggs until they are thick and cool. Place the mixer bowl into the ice bath to cool the yolk mixture completely. When cool, fold the yolk mixture into the whipped cream. Fold in the strawberry-rhubarb compote and chopped pistachio brittle. Reserve.

To make the crust: Preheat oven to 350°F. In a bowl combine graham cracker crumbs, butter, and sugar. Place eight stainless 3 x 2-inch ring molds on a parchment-lined sheet pan. Spoon 2 tablespoons graham cracker mixture into the bottom of each ring mold. Press down into an even layer to form tart crusts. Bake for 10 minutes. Remove the pan from the oven and allow the graham cracker crusts to cool.

To finish the dish: Fill the cool tart crusts with strawberry-rhubarb parfait. Freeze for at least 6 hours or overnight. When ready to serve, use a blowtorch to lightly heat the sides of the rings to loosen the cakes from the molds. Garnish with fresh strawberries, rhubarb caramel, and pistachio brittle. Serve.

Oriole9

17 Tinker Street
Woodstock, NY 12498
845-679-5763
oriole9.com
Owners: Pierre-Luc Moeys and Nina Paturel;
Chef: Pierre-Luc Moeys

Though sleek Oriole9 debuted in post-millennial 2006, it nevertheless bears a direct connection to Woodstock's 1960s heyday. The parents of one of Oriole's co-owners, Nina Paturel, once operated the town's Café Espresso, a noted haunt of the counter-cultural aristocracy, including its king and queen, Bob Dylan and Joan Baez. When Paturel met her future husband, a chef, in Amsterdam, she brought him home to Woodstock. Chef Pierre-Luc Moeys recounts the story of how the newlyweds opened Oriole9:

"I had never been to the United States before and she drove me up to Woodstock on the first day that I arrived. We went to this place called Heaven and I was, like, 'I want this to be my restaurant one day.'" Paturel and Moeys opened Oriole9 on the Tinker Street site of Heaven within a year. Though classically trained in French and Italian cuisines, Moeys hit the kitchen with the intention to "cook whatever I want." Moeys continues, "I like to say, what people bring us is basically what we cook. I guess our food is very much Mediterranean and, now—more and more—North African. We do a little bit of Asian stuff, but we also own Yum Yum Noodle Bar [with Erica A. Mahlkuch] in town." Moeys, who grew up in Holland, says, "I just grew up with the flavors of North Africa in my house. In Amsterdam, there is a large North African influence, also, of Indonesia. These flavors are like second nature." Though Moeys serves meat dishes in his restaurants, happily, the cuisines of North Africa and Indonesia are also vegan friendly. Laughs Moeys, "Well . . . we *are* in Woodstock, New York: It's the vegan capital of the world!"

PHOTOS © PIERRE-LUC MOEYS, ORIOLE9, WOODSTOCK, NY

Sunny Eggs with Sofrito & Fresh Cepes

(SERVES 4)

For the eggs:

1 pound of fresh cepes (if the season does not allow, use ⅓ pound of dried, rehydrated cepes)

1 cup Armagnac

10 ripe plum tomatoes

2 cups olive oil, plus more for frying eggs

20 peeled garlic cloves

1 tablespoon dried chili flakes

Salt and pepper

1 big bunch flat leaf parsley

Olive oil for frying

8 eggs

1 whole loaf fresh, good quality bread (says Moeys, "your choice, and make it delicious")

To prepare the sofrito: Chop the cepes and combine them with the Armagnac and set aside. Peel the tomatoes, either by using a potato peeler or by blanching in boiling for 20 seconds after making a shallow, x-shaped cut on the bottom of each tomato. After blanching, immediately shock the tomatoes in an ice bath, and, when cool, slip off their skins. Set aside.

In a stock pot, place the olive oil. Chop all the garlic cloves but one (keeping it whole) and then add the chopped garlic to the pot. Heat the mixture on low just until the garlic starts to sizzle. Once the garlic starts to brown, add the chili flakes. Crush the peeled tomatoes with your hand, then carefully add them to the pot. Once all tomatoes are added, bring the mixture to a boil. Lower the heat to a simmer and simmer the mixture on low for 4–5 hours, stirring occasionally to make sure the mixture does not scorch on the bottom.

After 4–5 hours, the oil on the mixture will start to turn red. Add the cepes and the Armagnac. Return the mixture to a boil and then lower again to a simmer. Simmer for another hour, then season with salt and pepper. Meanwhile, chop the parsley fine. Place a splash of olive oil in a frying pan and place it over low heat. Add the eggs and slowly cook until the whites are firm. Cut 4 slices of bread and toast. While the toast is still hot, rub it with the reserved whole garlic clove and set it onto four plates. Place two eggs on each toast slice, then add a heaping spoon of the *sofrito*. Sprinkle with parsley and serve.

Peekamoose Restaurant & Tap Room

8373 State Route 28
Big Indian, NY 12410
(845) 254-6500
PEEKAMOOSERESTAURANT.COM
Co-Owners: Marybeth Mills and Devin Mills;
Executive Chef: Devin Mills

While nearby Woodstock bears the tie-dyed mother lode of 1960s nostalgia, in fact, many other Hudson Valley towns have equally notable histories in 1960s counterculturalism. The Band's landmark was composed in West Saugerties in a house at 2188 Stoll Road (now 56 Parnassus Lane), while Dr. Timothy Leary created an LSD utopia in William Hitchcock's mansion in the Dutchess County town of Millbrook. Not only did both Bob Dylan and Joni Mitchell once dwell in the Hudson Valley, but in Big Indian there existed a whole countercultural society.

Marybeth Mills, who co-owns Peekamoose Restaurant & Tap Room with her husband, chef Devin Mills, explains the history of the centuries-old building that they ultimately bought. "It was part of an ashram community. Our building was Rudi's Big Indian Country Kitchen, and Rudi was a swami who had a following in the 1960s and '70s." Rudi, born in Brooklyn as Albert Rudolph (1928–1973), was a follower of Tibetan Buddhism who declared himself a spiritual leader in the late 1950s.

"The people at the ashram studied meditation and metaphysics. They worked here at the restaurant and grew their own tomatoes and sprouts for their sandwiches." Mills explains, "They worked here as part of the ashram to cover the expenses of the ashram. And it was very successful for about twenty-five years."

Mills continues, "We've always wanted to own our own restaurant. We were both working in Manhattan under very talented chefs; we had the good fortune to work with some of the best in the industry. My husband cooked under Tom Colicchio at Gramercy Tavern and Eric Ripert of Le Bernardin. I worked with Terrence Brennan at Picholine and with Waldy Malouf at the Hudson River Club." She laughs, "I always worked front-of-the-house, though I did study in Switzerland to be a chef. Believe me, you are much better off having Devin cook for you than me."

He saved his money and went into a lot of debt to go to The Culinary Institute in Hyde Park. And whenever we would come up from the city to visit his mother, we'd see this old building for sale." Mills continues, "And we'd always wanted to come back to this area."

The Millses opened Peekamoose with a commitment to celebrating Hudson Valley produce. "We came from kitchens that had the same respect—especially Gramercy Tavern. They were really—twenty years ago—developing relationships with local, New York farmers and highlighting the ingredients and their quality. That kitchen was about seeing that there is just as much beauty in a carrot as there is some over-processed Kobe beef or something. What we do here is a farmhouse type of cuisine—we absolutely avoid all types of agribusiness. We want to celebrate what grows around here."

HOUSEMADE GOAT SAUSAGE WITH BIODYNAMIC BEETS, FENNEL PUREE & GOAT CHEESE ESPUMA, BEET GREENS CHOUCROUTE

(SERVES 8)

For the goat sausage:

5 pounds fresh Snowdance Farm goat meat (leg/belly)

¾ pound pork fat

3 cloves garlic

½ bulb fennel

5 tablespoons kosher salt

Freshly ground white pepper

1 cup white wine (Lamoureaux Landing Semi-Dry Riesling, New York State)

1 teaspoon coriander seeds

1 teaspoon fennel seeds

½ teaspoon mustard seeds

3 sprigs fresh thyme

½ sprig fresh rosemary

For the biodynamic beets:

2 large beets, peeled and thinly sliced

2 cloves garlic, sliced

1 sprig fresh rosemary

3 sprigs fresh thyme

½ tablespoon coriander seeds

2 cups extra-virgin olive oil

Kosher salt

Freshly ground white pepper

For the goat cheese espuma:

2 cups fresh goat's milk

Salt and pepper to taste

1 tablespoon olive oil

For the fennel puree:

1½ bulbs fennel

Salt and pepper to taste

3 tablespoons extra-virgin olive oil

For the beet greens choucroute:

Beet greens from 2–4 large beets, julienned

1 tablespoon extra-virgin olive oil

½ tablespoon caraway seeds (optional)

1 medium-size Spanish onion, julienned

Kosher salt

Freshly ground white pepper

1 cup white wine (Lamoureaux Landing Semi-Dry
    Riesling, New York State)

1 cup Champagne vinegar

1 tablespoon unsalted butter (optional)

To make the sausage: Using a meat grinder affixed to a stand mixer, grind the goat meat, pork fat, garlic, and fennel. Season with salt and pepper. Chill. In a pot simmer the white wine with spices and herbs. Strain and cool the liquid. Once cool, incorporate the herb-infused wine with the ground goat meat. Allow the proteins to bind. The mixture should have a texture similar to that of meatballs. Adjust the seasoning, then roll into 6-inch-long logs. Vacuum seal the logs in a Cryovac bag and cook in an immersion circulator set to 146°F. Alternatively, you can seal the logs very carefully in plastic zip bags and then poach them in 146°F water (monitor the temperature carefully with a digital probe thermometer). While sausages are cooking, set up an ice bath. Remove the logs and plunge them in the ice bath to halt their cooking. Cut them into ½-inch slices.

To prepare the puree: Roughly chop the fennel. In a medium saucepan combine the fennel and enough water to cover. Add a few pinches of salt. Bring to a boil and cook until the fennel is tender, about 15–20 minutes. Drain and reserve the fennel water. Place the cooked fennel into a blender and puree on high speed while slowly drizzling the olive oil into the blender. For a smoother texture, a little of the reserved fennel water may be added to the puree. Adjust seasoning. Reserve.

To prepare the beets: While wearing rubber gloves, peel the beets and slice them ⅛-inch thick on a mandoline. Reserve the beet greens for the choucroute, below. In a medium saucepan add the garlic, rosemary, thyme, coriander, and olive oil. Over medium heat, bring to a simmer. Add the beets and simmer for 15–20 minutes. Allow the beets to cool in the oil and season with salt and pepper. When ready to serve, remove the beet slices.

To make the choucroute: Wash the beet greens carefully and remove the stems. In a medium saucepan add the olive oil, caraway seeds (if used), and julienned onion. Sweat until the onion is translucent. Season with salt and pepper, then add the beet greens. Cover with wine and vinegar and bring to a boil. Reduce the heat to simmer and continue to cook over medium heat until most of the liquid has evaporated, about 20 minutes. Adjust seasoning and finish with butter, if desired.

To make the espuma: Into a CO_2-charged iSi canister, place the seasoned goat's milk and the olive oil. Shake for 30 seconds.

To serve: Heat a grill or grill pan. Lightly grill the sausage slices for color and flavor, about 2 minutes on each side. On a small plate place a tablespoon of the fennel puree and spread it across the center of the plate. Add a tablespoon of beet greens. Arrange small circles of beets and grilled goat sausage. Garnish with a small mound of goat cheese espuma squirted from the iSi canister. Drizzle with olive oil and serve.

THE TAVERN AT DIAMOND MILLS

25 SOUTH PARTITION STREET
SAUGERTIES, NY 12477
(845) 247-0700
DIAMONDMILLSHOTEL.COM
OWNER: THOMAS STRUZZIERI; EXECUTIVE CHEF: GIUSEPPE NAPOLI

While the Ulster town of Saugerties has deep roots in counter-cultural bohemianism, it also has a tradition of aristocratic horsiness. Every year, the town hosts a summer-long event, Horse Shows in the Sun (HITS), an extensive competition that draws equestrians from all over the country. Happily, the luxurious rooms and baths of the Diamond Mills Hotel offer a cushioned break from the sweat, mud, and rigors of the ring. Each of this boutique hotel's rooms affords a view of pretty Esopus Falls, which, at night, are dramatically spot-lit.

In The Tavern, the hotel restaurant overseen by CIA-trained Chef Giuseppe Napoli, you'll find sophisticated takes on classic American fare. Look for local, Hudson Valley cheeses; rustic charcuterie; and innovative dishes like this open-faced lobster ravioli with black trumpets, fava beans, pancetta, smoked paprika, and tarragon, included below.

THE TAVERN AT DIAMOND MILLS © KELLY MERCHANT PHOTOGRAPHY

Open Face Lobster Ravioli
with Black Trumpets, Fava Beans, Pancetta, Smoked Paprika & Tarragon

(SERVES 4)

For the lobster:

4 (1¼-pound) Maine lobsters

For the lobster stock:

Lobster shells from 4 lobsters (see above)
6 ounces unsalted butter, room temperature
2 coarsely chopped tomatoes
12 dried black peppercorns
½ gallon cold water
1 bay leaf
3 thyme sprigs
3 parsley sprigs
3 ounces carrot, peeled and coarsely chopped
3 ounces leek, rinsed and coarsely chopped
2 lemons (juiced)
3 ounces celery, rinsed and chopped

For the pasta:

2 cups of all-purpose flour, plus more for dusting
1 teaspoon salt
3 large eggs, plus 1 for egg wash
2 tablespoons extra virgin olive oil
Corn meal, for dusting
3 large eggs, plus 1 for egg wash
2 tablespoons extra virgin olive oil

For finishing the dish:

Lobster stock
3 ounces diced pancetta
4 ounces cleaned black trumpet mushrooms
6 ounces fresh shelled fava beans
1 teaspoon smoked paprika

2 ounces heavy cream
10 large leaves tarragon roughly chopped
2 pinches kosher salt
2 pinches ground white pepper

To cook the lobsters: Remove bands and any barnacles. In a large pot big enough to stack all four lobsters, place a steamer. Set out a large bowl of ice water. Steam for 4 minutes and shock in ice water. When lobsters are cooled, remove from ice water and shuck. Save the shells and try to keep meat as whole as possible. Be sure to remove the sand tract and cartilage. Rinse the body and meat until free of greenish tomalley. Set aside.

To make the stock: In a heavy bottomed saucepan placed over medium-high heat, melt 1 ounce of butter. When butter starts to brown, add the tomatoes, lobster shells, and peppercorns. Stir frequently as the sediments will tend to coat the bottom of the pan. When sediments start to brown and shells are very aromatic, deglaze the pan with ½ gallon of cold water. Scrape bottom of pan with a spoon to lift up sediments. Add bay leaf, thyme, parsley, carrot, leek, lemon juice and celery; bring to a low simmer and cook until liquid is reduced to about 4 cups. Strain and press through a fine mesh china cap. Set the liquid aside and discard solids.

To make the pasta: Combine the flour and salt on a flat work surface; shape into a mound and make a well in the center. To the well, add 3 eggs and 1 tablespoon of the olive oil and lightly beat with a fork. Gradually add the flour from the inside wall into the mixture using one hand to hold the

fork and the other to maintain the outer wall. Continue to incorporate the flour until the mixture forms a ball. Knead until smooth and elastic.

Cut the ball of dough in two, and wrap each ball in plastic. Dust the counter and dough with a little flour. Press the dough into a rectangle and roll it through a pasta machine 2 or 3 times, at widest setting. Pull and stretch the sheet of dough with the palm of your hand as it emerges from the rollers. Reduce the setting and crank the dough through the rollers again, 2 or 3 more times. Continue tightening the rollers until the machine is at the narrowest setting; the dough should be paper-thin, about ⅛" thick. You should be able to see your hand through it. Dust the sheets of dough with flour, as needed.

Beat 1 egg with 1 tablespoon of water to make an egg wash. Dust the counter and sheet of dough with flour and lay out the long sheet of pasta; with a 4.5-inch round cutter, cut pasta. Dust the pasta rounds and a sheet pan with cornmeal to prevent the pasta from sticking. Lay each sheet out to dry slightly while assembling the rest.

When the ravioli are all finished, cook the pasta in plenty of boiling salted water for 4 minutes; the sheets will float to the top when ready, so be careful not to overcrowd the pot. Lift the pasta from water with a large strainer or slotted spoon. Follow plating directions below.

To finish the dish: Bring the lobster stock to a simmer in separate pot. Heat heavy bottomed

sauté pan, add remaining butter and pancetta, and cook until the pancetta is crisp. When crisp, add mushrooms and sauté slightly, then add fava beans and smoked paprika. Sauté for one minute and then add the hot lobster stock. Bring to a simmer and reduce the sauce to the desired consistency, then add heavy cream. Simmer until warmed through. Add tarragon and season with a pinch of salt and pepper. Remove from heat.

To plate: For each serving, place pasta sheet flat in the bottom of a wide, warm pasta bowl. Arrange lobster in the center of pasta (lobster tail, 2 claws and 2 knuckles per plate). Ladle sauce over lobster and allow to pool in the bottom of bowl. Add another sheet of pasta and slightly fold back and serve.

THE TAVERN AT DIAMOND MILLS © MICHAEL NELSON PHOTOGRAPHY

THE VILLAGE TEAROOM

10 PLATTEKILL AVENUE
NEW PALTZ, NY 12561
(845) 255-3434
THEVILLAGETEAROOM.COM
OWNER/EXECUTIVE CHEF: AGNES DEVEREAUX

Speaking with a soft Irish lilt, Chef Agnes Devereaux attributes the choice of New Paltz for her restaurant, The Village Tearoom, to the site's location near the Mountain Laurel Waldorf School. Coming from a career in restaurants in France and, later, in New York City (where she bartended at *echt*-locavore Union Square Cafe), Devereaux chose the Waldorf method of teaching for her own children because, "They learn a stone's throw from a garden. The children prepare food on stoves in the classroom and they learn to bake bread. They live in tune with the seasons."

The rhythms of time and nature are central to The Village Tearoom, which is housed in a two-century-old clapboard building in which the rigid geometries of angles have been eased by time. Many of the ingredients used in Devereaux's kitchen would be completely familiar to the building's original occupants: butter, creamline milk, fresh eggs, and locally pasture-raised meats. "We believe in using humble ingredients that we try to prepare carefully. We think the humblest of ingredients can be made into beautiful things." Devereaux's suppliers are as hyper-local and traditional as possible; Devereaux is an active member in Slow Food Hudson Valley.

It wasn't always easy for Devereaux to execute the locavorian mission she envisioned. "When we first opened [in 2004], it was a real challenge to find locally raised meats that were USDA inspected. The local farmers might have been able to sell their meat legally to customers, but as a restaurant I wasn't able to re-sell it. Now, in the Hudson Valley, we're spoiled for local choices." Other things have changed since the birth of The Village Tearoom. For instance, when it opened, the Tearoom's entire menu was composed of a single, three-course prix fixe. Devereaux laughs, "We had to change that one pretty quickly!"

Potato-Toussaint Tart

(SERVES 8)

For the pâté brisée:

¼ pound unsalted butter, chilled

6 ounces unbleached, unbromated all-purpose flour

¼ teaspoon kosher salt

⅛ teaspoon baking powder

2 tablespoons plus 2½ teaspoons filtered water, cold

For the filling:

2 pounds Yukon Gold potatoes, peeled and sliced

10 ounces whole milk (Devereaux recommends that
   you use non-homogenized milk that has been
   pasteurized, rather than ultra-pasteurized.)

8 ounces heavy cream (not ultra-pasteurized)

2 sprigs thyme

2 cloves garlic, peeled and lightly crushed

Salt

Freshly ground pepper

½ ounce unsalted butter

1 medium onion, cut into ½-inch dice

1 organic egg

¼ teaspoon nutmeg

8 ounces Toussaint cheese, rind removed and cut into
   ⅛-inch-thick slices

To make the pâté brisée: Cut the butter into 6–8 pieces. In the bowl of a stand mixer fitted with the paddle attachment, place the flour, salt, and baking powder. Add the chilled butter and, with the mixer set at its lowest speed, cut the butter into the dry ingredients until the pieces of butter are no bigger than ¼-inch. Stir the water into this mixture until it barely holds together in a dough (don't overmix). Scrape the dough out of the bowl, then shape into a flat disc. Wrap in plastic and chill until the dough is firm.

When the dough is firm, roll it out into a disc and fit this into a 9-inch springform pan (see Note) with a removable bottom. Freeze while you assemble the rest of the tart.

Note: Makes enough to line one 8" x 1½-inch springform pan.

To make the tart: Preheat oven to 350°F. When the oven is hot, line the frozen tart shell with a sheet of foil and weight this down with ceramic pie weights or dried beans. Blind bake (prebake) the shell with weights for 20 minutes, then remove the weights and continue to bake the shell for 10 additional minutes. Remove when the shell is crisp and lightly browned.

In a medium pot combine the potatoes with 8 ounces of the milk, the cream, one sprig thyme, and one garlic clove. Season the mixture with salt and pepper and bring to a boil. Lower the heat and simmer for 25–30 minutes, or until the potatoes are tender. Discard the thyme and garlic and allow the potatoes to cool in the liquid.

In a medium-size pan over medium-low heat, melt the butter. Add the onion and remaining thyme and garlic and season with salt and pepper to taste. Sweat this mixture until the onions are translucent, about 18–20 minutes. (Add a little water if pan gets too dry.) When the onions are soft and translucent, remove the pan from heat and discard the thyme and garlic. Set aside to cool.

When cool, drain the potatoes, straining off the milk and cream and reserving it in a liquid measuring cup. You will need 10 ounces of this liquid; if necessary, add more of the remaining milk to equal 10 ounces. In a medium-size bowl

whisk the egg with the nutmeg, then add the milk and cream mixture. Season with salt and pepper and whisk to combine.

Scatter half the onions, half the potatoes, and half the Toussaint cheese in the blind-baked tart shell. Add the rest of the onions and potatoes, then top with remaining cheese. Pour the milk/ cream mixture over the filling and cover with foil. Make sure the foil is tented and not touching the surface of the tart.

Bake the tart for about 45 minutes. Remove the foil and bake an additional 15 minutes, or until the tart is puffy and lightly browned. Let cool for 2 hours before slicing into wedges and serving.

FROM THE GARDEN
GARDEN GREENS:
TUSCAN KALE · RED RUSSIAN KALE ·
MIZUNA · SWISS CHARD · ARUGULA ·
SPRING RABE · ESCAROLE · PAC CHOY ·
RED MUSTARD ·
HERBS:
· DILL · CILANTRO · CHERVIL · PARSLEY ·
HAKUREI TURNIP · FRENCH BREAKFAST · RADISH

WESTCHESTER COUNTY

{ NORTH }

BARTACO

1 Willett Avenue
Port Chester, NY 10573
(914) 937-TACO
bartaco.com
Co-Owners: Sasa Mahr-Batuz and Andy Pforzheimer;
Executive Chef: Adam Halberg;
Beverage Director: Gretchen Thomas

The Byram River is not the Pacific Ocean, nor is Port Chester Baja California. But on any given Saturday night, these facts might elude some of the throng in bartaco. They've come to groove in its glamorized surfer vibe while downing tequila cocktails and tucking into the *echt* surfer food, fish tacos. All to the serious beat of a $35,000 sound system.

This corner of Port Chester wasn't always so.

The site, once a live bait shop-cum-seafood restaurant called Ebb Tide, had been a fried clam bar whose dankness was only somewhat relieved by a Byram-side deck. The Byram—a semi-industrialized waterway that wends through downtown Port Chester (and separates it from Greenwich, Connecticut)—runs, mostly uncelebrated, behind the back ends of businesses to the Long Island Sound. It takes vision to see it as an asset.

But vision is not a problem for Sasa Mahr-Batuz and Andy Pforzheimer. They're the team that got diners in Connecticut and Georgia to swap white bread for *pan tomaca* at the Barcelona Wine Bar chain. Upon taking the space from Ebb Tide, Mahr-Batuz blew out its Byram-side wall. He replaced the formerly blank frontage with a glass wall that rises like a three-car garage door. He paneled the interior with reclaimed barn boards—nailed horizontally and painted white near the ceiling, nautical blue near the floor—and installed a wall of graphic Mexican tiles so stylish that they'd be right at home in a David Hicks interior.

Says Mahr-Batuz, "I want to capture the feeling of walking out of the water and eating the best fish taco that you've ever

had. Clean flavors, bright herbs—but style conscious. Always style conscious." After a pause, he sums it up, "I'm not selling tacos; I'm selling a lifestyle."

It's working. After the wild success of the first bartaco in Port Chester, Mahr-Batuz and Pforzheimer opened three more in Connecticut. Their staggering receipts on a single summer Saturday night are the stuff of local legend.

BAJA FISH TACOS

(SERVES 8)

For the Baja slaw:

10 cups thinly sliced green cabbage
½ cup diced Spanish onion
1 cup chopped cilantro leaves
1½ cups mayonnaise
½ cup lime juice
1 tablespoon minced chipotle in adobo sauce
3 teaspoons honey
1 tablespoon kosher salt
¼ teaspoon cayenne

For the Baja fish:

Canola oil for frying
1½ pounds cod, cut into 3½–4-inch strips
2 cups rice flour
½ cup cornstarch
3 tablespoons kosher salt
1 tablespoon cayenne
1½ teaspoons baking powder
2¼ cups club soda

For the Baja fish tacos:

24 corn tortillas
Chopped onion, for garnish (optional)
Chopped cilantro, for garnish (optional)

To make the slaw: In a large mixing bowl, combine the cabbage, onion, and cilantro. In a separate bowl stir together the mayonnaise, lime juice, chipotle, honey, salt, and cayenne. Pour the dressing over the cabbage and mix well to combine. Set aside.

To fry the fish: Fill a deep, heavy-bottomed pot with 4 inches of canola oil and heat the oil to 350°F. Make a tempura batter by combining the flour, cornstarch, salt, cayenne, and baking powder in a mixing bowl. Add the club soda and whisk vigorously until there are no lumps. Working in batches, dip strips of cod into the batter, then carefully drop the fish into the hot oil. Fry until fish is golden brown on the outside and cooked through on the inside, about 2 minutes. Remove the fish from the oil and drain on paper towels as you finish the dish.

To finish the dish: Warm the corn tortillas on a hot griddle. Place a small scoop of Baja slaw in the middle of each tortilla, then lay a piece of fried fish on top of the slaw. Garnish with onion and cilantro, if desired, and serve.

THE PORT CHESTER REVIVER

(MAKES 1 COCKTAIL)

2 bar spoons chopped cucumber
8–10 mint leaves
½ ounce simple syrup
1½ ounces Millers gin
1½ ounces mango nectar
Juice of 1 lime (about 1 ounce)
Ice

Cucumber spear and mint sprig, for garnish

In a bar glass muddle the cucumber and mint. Add simple syrup, gin, mango nectar, lime juice, and ice. Shake contents until the liquid is cold and aerated. Strain the Port Chester Reviver over ice and garnish with cucumber and mint. Serve.

Birdsall House

970 Main Street
Peekskill, NY 10566
(914) 930-1880
BIRDSALLHOUSE.NET
OWNERS: JOHN SHARP AND TIM REINKE;
EXECUTIVE CHEF: MARCH WALKER

In a lot of ways, Peekskill is hipster heaven. Rents are low, downtown is full of pristine nineteenth-century architecture, and it holds an excellent tattoo parlor. But unlike Brooklyn, Peekskill is virtually untouched by the mobs of wealthy lawyers and bankers who, in their eagerness to co-opt that borough's international cool, priced out the artists who built its fame. Located a solid hour from Manhattan, Peekskill will always be rough trade. It's artist friendly and an outlaw—and that's why we love it.

At the heart of Peekskill's undeniable cool lies the team of John Sharp and Tim Reinke, who teamed up after Reinke's success with Manhattan's beer mecca, Blind Tiger Saloon. Birdsall House debuted in 2010 with a game-changing twenty taps devoted to supremely geeky, mostly locally brewed craft beers. But behind the beer, Birdsall House had a secret weapon; its kitchen (then manned by Chef Matt Hutchins, later of The Hop in Beacon) was slinging on trend, pork-centric cuisine with ingredients sourced from local farms.

Today, Chef March Walker carries on the Birdsall House tradition with a menu that celebrates local beer, local farms, and Peekskill's unique local flavor. In summer linger in Peekskill's hop-lined beer garden or check out its steady roster of live music and events.

Pork & Barleywine Sausage

(SERVES 6)

For the Spezie Birdsall:

2 tablespoons ground ginger

2 tablespoons plus 1 teaspoon mace

4 teaspoons ground cloves

2 tablespoons plus 2 teaspoons ground nutmeg

3 tablespoons ground allspice

4 tablespoons ground coriander

5 tablespoons ground cumin

5 tablespoons fennel seeds

2 tablespoons plus 1 teaspoon mild dried chili powder

For the pork and barleywine sausage:

3 cloves garlic, minced

1 tablespoon minced fresh ginger

¼ cup barleywine or other strong beer (Walker recommends Victory Brewing Company's Old Horizontal or Brooklyn Brewery's Brooklyn Monster)

4 pounds good-quality pork with a ratio of about 30 percent fat/70 percent lean (shoulder is perfect), cubed

5¾ teaspoons kosher salt

1 tablespoon freshly ground black pepper

1 tablespoon plus 1 teaspoon Spezie Birdsall

For cooking the sausages:

1 tablespoon vegetable oil

To make the Spezie Birdsall: Combine ingredients and keep in an airtight jar. Walker recommends using his Spezie Birdsall in many dishes, especially pork chops.

To make the sausage: Place the minced garlic and ginger in a blender with enough barleywine to cover and puree the mixture until smooth. In

a bowl combine this mixture with the pork, salt, pepper, and Spezie Birdsall. Cover and place in the refrigerator to marinate for 1 hour.

In a stand mixer fitted with a meat grinder and a medium die, grind the mixture through once. Toss the pork mixture thoroughly with your hands, then sauté a small piece of the mixture to check the seasoning. If it's bland, add more salt or spice and mix to taste. If it's dry, work in a little cold water or beer. If the sausage is too coarsely ground, grind it once more, but make sure your grinder has been well chilled in the refrigerator first. Once you're content with the flavor, knead the forcemeat very aggressively with your hands until it acquires some opacity and a slight stickiness. This step is very important for the texture of the final sausage; it will help it to stick together and hold moisture.

Stuff the mixture into hog casings according to your sausage maker's directions, or form into patties. If using casings, make sure not to overstuff, and cook gently to avoid bursting. If making patties, be extra careful not to overcook, as these will dry out more easily. Makes about twelve 5-ounce sausages or sausage patties.

To cook the sausage: Preheat oven to 400°F. Heat vegetable oil in a medium-size, ovenproof pan over medium heat. Place sausages in pan and sear very gently until golden, then move pan to the oven to finish cooking, about 5 minutes.

Serving suggestions: Accompany the sausages with pickles, coarse, grainy mustard, and crusty bread. Says Walker, "It's wonderful with malty beers, especially a Belgian tripel or any of the barleywine used in the recipe."

Blue Hill at Stone Barns

630 Bedford Road
Pocantico Hills, NY 10591
(914) 366-9600
BLUEHILLFARM.COM
Owners: Laureen, David, and Dan Barber;
Executive Chef: Dan Barber

When you go to Blue Hill at Stone Barns, you should prepare yourself for unexpected juxtapositions, like the sight of piglets squirming in the mud to be followed immediately by a meal of ravishing elegance. The contrasts are intentional and are all part of Blue Hill's mission to fight for more sustainable foodways using the weapon of sheer, irreducible beauty.

The restaurant is sited in an aristocratic fieldstone barn complex that John D. Rockefeller Jr. commissioned from architect Grovernor Atterbury in the early 1930s. Although it was built in a castle-evoking Norman style, the barn's purpose was purely

rustic. It housed the cows whose teats provided fresh milk to the large Rockefeller family, including David and Nelson, who lived nearby. Now, during the long and luxurious feasts that Blue Hill at Stone Barns serves under the same roof, you'll still feel the seductive tension between basic, rustic reality and the pinnacle of high style.

There are other strange dynamics at work. For instance, it's odd for an enterprise dedicated to the production of meat to dodge the joyful meat-mania that has gripped other restaurants in the Hudson Valley. Says Chef Dan Barber, "While you can raise meat very well in the Hudson Valley—and dairy, for sure—you should also look at eating meat in portions that are more in line with what this environment can provide." The carrot cutlet recipe following is the perfect example of what he means. Says Barber, "If we as Americans are going to cut back on meat consumption—which it seems we really should be doing—we're going to have to figure out ways to make truly satisfying meals that satiate our appetite for protein. And carrots do really well in our soil here, so what if we looked at a carrot—which, when grown in the right variety and picked at the right time in

the right soil—is like meat? It very much *is* like meat. And so, if you braise it with care, and then you roast it to caramelize the sugars as you would caramelize a steak, what you get is a semblance of a steak. And I don't mean that in a kinky way, I mean that in a real way. Cooked this way, the carrot has the umami of a steak. And then you use the meat as a sauce."

Barber continues, "This is a little bit tongue in cheek in that you're flipping the proportions: The seven-ounce steak becomes the one-ounce sauce and the one-ounce carrot garnish becomes the lead actor. But it flips everything on its head, not as a political statement, but as a statement of deliciousness."

And just when you think you have your flexitarian/locavorian feet standing firmly under you, Barber will make you question the no-brainers like ramps. Ramps—an indigenous species with a small ecological footprint—are gathered rather than raised; they are a food that the earth volunteers. What's not to love? "Except," Barber suggests, "the popularity of ramps has driven them to be a little bit in trouble. Chefs now have adopted ramps in huge numbers. This is a frightening thing for the foragers who are finding fewer and fewer ramps. But that's why cuisine is so important: Cuisine is a natural balancer." Cuisine is not a collection of disparate dishes like this cookbook in your hands; it is a cultural system that synchronizes the food needs of a population with the land upon which they live. The classic cuisines of the world have been developed over millennia. In contrast, what we call American cuisine is a hodgepodge of out-of-context dishes borrowed, adapted, or barely remembered from somewhere else.

"In order to provide the seven-ounce steak, you need an agricultural system that's out of kilter. And it's the same thing with ramps, unfortunately, or any vegetable or cut of meat that becomes suddenly popular. We lack a cultural cuisine that allows us to spread the wealth a bit over time and over an agriculture. Instead, you have ingredients like ramps that have become instantly popular with chefs. And with the Internet and farm-to-table social movement, we can—in dizzying speed—suddenly popularize an ingredient and simultaneously signal the end of its life. We see that in the ocean all the time. So we need to be careful. And that's why farm-to-table doesn't work." He continues, "Ramps are the perfect example: Ramps have a small ecological footprint, they're an indigenous species to America, and what a beautiful sign of spring! There's *nothing* wrong with ramps. And yet something is wrong because we tend to support them in a way that ensures their decline."

Point taken. But, just to keep you on your toes, Barber also notes of ramps, "They make a truly delicious pickle that you can enjoy straight through to the next picking."

CARROT CUTLET

(SERVES 6)

For the lamb sauce:

2 (1½-pound) lamb shanks
Salt and freshly ground pepper
2 tablespoons vegetable oil
2 large onions, coarsely chopped
5 cloves garlic, smashed
1 large carrot, peeled and coarsely chopped
1 rib celery, coarsely chopped
1 cup dry red wine
½ cup ruby port
1 sprig rosemary

For the herb salad:

1 cup tarragon leaves
1 cup parsley leaves
½ cup dill leaves
½ cup mint leaves
½ cup chervil leaves

For the apricot puree:

2 cups orange juice
1 cup dried apricots
3 tablespoons Champagne vinegar

For the carrot cutlets:

6 medium carrots, about 8 inches long and
    ¾ inch wide
2 tablespoons olive oil
1 teaspoon granulated sugar
1 teaspoon salt
A generous grind of black pepper

For the breading:

¼ cup finely ground panko bread crumbs
¼ cup finely ground bread crumbs made from
    dried whole wheat bread
2 tablespoons rice flour
1 teaspoon finely ground cumin
2 cups all-purpose flour
1 egg, beaten
Oil for frying

To make the lamb sauce: Preheat oven to 325°F. Season the lamb with salt and pepper. In a large skillet heat 1 tablespoon of the oil. Add the lamb and cook over moderately high heat until browned on all sides, about 8 minutes. Transfer the lamb to a plate and pour off the oil. Add the remaining 1 tablespoon oil to the skillet and add the onions, garlic, carrot, and celery. Cook over moderate heat until browned, about 12 minutes. Add the wine and port and boil the liquid until it's reduced to ⅓ cup, about 4 minutes. Transfer to a roasting pan and add the rosemary. Arrange the lamb shanks in the pan, add ¾ cup water, and cover with foil. Bake for 2 hours, turning the lamb once, until the lamb is very tender.

Transfer the lamb to a bowl and keep warm. Strain the pan juices into a saucepan. Boil over high heat until reduced to ¾ cup, about 7 minutes. Shred the shank meat and add it to the pan juices; season with salt and pepper. Reserve.

To make the puree: In a small pot reduce the orange juice by half. Add the apricots and the vinegar and simmer for 5 minutes. Remove from heat and allow to stand for 10 minutes. Transfer to a blender and puree until smooth. Keep warm.

To make the salad: In a small bowl mix together all the herbs.

To prepare the carrots: Preheat oven to 400°F. Peel the carrots. Lay three sheets of aluminum foil on the counter and place the carrots on top of the foil. Drizzle the carrots with the oil and season with the sugar, salt, and pepper. Wrap carrots tightly in the three layers of foil and place the package on a baking tray. Put the tray in the oven and roast the carrots for 1 hour. After 1 hour flip the package of carrots and continue to cook for another hour, until the carrots are very soft. Remove from the oven and set aside.

When the package is cool enough to handle, unwrap the carrots. Line a baking tray with parchment paper and lay the carrots on the tray, leaving some space between each carrot. Top with another piece of parchment paper and another baking tray. Place a heavy weight, such as several cans of food, on top of the tray to press down the carrots. Press for 10 minutes. If the carrots are cooked properly, they will not break but will instead press into little cutlets.

To bread and fry the carrots: In a small bowl combine the panko, bread crumbs, rice flour, and cumin. In another bowl place the all-purpose flour. In a third bowl place the beaten egg. Working in sequence, dip each carrot first into the all-purpose flour, shaking off any excess. Then dip each carrot into the egg wash. Finally, dredge each carrot in the bread crumb mixture. Meanwhile, in a sauté pan over a medium flame, heat about ½ cup oil. When hot, carefully place the carrot cutlets in the oil and fry them for 4 minutes per side, or until they are golden brown. Transfer the fried cutlets to a plate lined with paper towel to drain, then season well with salt and pepper. Spoon the lamb sauce around the cutlet; serve with a dollop of apricot puree and garnish with herb salad.

PICKLED RAMPS

½ pound ramps

2 cups white wine vinegar

1 cup granulated sugar

2 teaspoons mustard seed

1 bay leaf

Wash the ramps thoroughly and trim off the root ends and green parts. Set aside about ½ pound of ramps. In a pot bring the wine vinegar, sugar, mustard seed, and bay leaf to a boil. Place the ramps in an airtight container fitted with a hasp and seal. While the liquid is still warm, pour the brine over the ramps and seal the airtight container. The pickled ramps will keep for several months in the refrigerator.

A Conversation with Chef Dan Barber

My brother, David [Barber], and my relationship to farming started with our grandmother, who began Blue Hill Farm in the Berkshires in the late 1960s. My brother and I were farming that land as kids. And my grandmother wasn't a political activist or anything. She just loved the open space and she wanted it preserved. She knew that in order to preserve the beauty, she had to farm it. It was very smart. So we were farming to preserve the beauty but ended up being inculcated with the issues of agriculture. That sounds kind of light, but it's important. And the place, Blue Hill Farm, is quite stunning. It has views that are really iconic for New England agriculture. It's a place that still informs my cooking.

My brother and I were approached by Mr. Rockefeller to offer an idea for what the Stone Barns Center could be with a fine dining restaurant attached. That's really what happened. And Mr. Rockefeller liked us; he liked my brother and his financial plan. He liked my sister-in-law [Laureen Barber] and her sensibilities. And, he liked my food.

It happened, for lack of a better word, organically. Our idea was to create a restaurant that looked at and celebrated the Hudson Valley. But with its own farm that supplied the food—also, the food would come from other farmers that were interested in becoming our customers. The idea of co-creating a menu with farmers still appeals to me. Carlo Petrini, who is the founder of Slow Food, said that we need to stop thinking of ourselves as either consumers or producers. Instead, we all need to think of ourselves as co-producers—and eaters are co-producing, too. I thought that was a really great way to put it, and so that was the underlying philosophy of Blue Hill at Stone Barns and of the Stone Barns Center for Food and Agriculture.

Jack Algiers is the vegetable farmer and Craig Hainey is the livestock guy and they've been on this project since the beginning. How do I talk about them? They're intimately involved in the planning of the menu because they're rotating their crops or planting particular crops and adopting different breeds according to where the menu is going. And they are simultaneously reacting to and dictating the menu, which is all part of the co-producer thing.

And I have to give credit to my sister-in-law for the design of the place. I mean, she really believed in the ideas that permeate our food and our farming. The idea behind the design is that you're combining old and new to reach a broad audience. Given our food and our farming, we didn't want it to feel like a Shaker museum from the late 1800s. She really brought a modern sensibility to the design. My food is really quite modern. And these ideas of local, sustainable, and supporting a community are all rooted in age-old and inherited wisdom—but at Blue Hill at Stone Barns, they're interpreted in a modern context. Laureen expresses that beautifully in the design. You know you're in these old, historic barns, but you feel like you're part of something very modern and up-to-date. That's not a contradiction; that's an important aspect to our identity.

We made more mistakes than I can count, and we're still making them pretty heartily. And I'm like anybody else: I wake up the morning and think, I wish I could start over. And that's pretty much what we try to do. In just this past year, we got rid of the menu completely; you sit down without any menu at all. It's almost like every couple of years, we start all over again because we're so linked to what's going on around the world. There's a really exciting global social movement happening in fine dining. The food's changing and we're keeping pace with that. But, also, we're telling a story. Is our restaurant a political statement? I don't know . . . I guess so. It's not the direct intent, but eating is politicized, and it has to be in some way. It's more like we go to restaurants as places to escape, right? I mean, that's the beauty of going to restaurants—you let someone else serve you and you escape from your daily ritual. And if we do our job right, it seems to me that we can still offer that, but also, we can have a restaurant that's a place of connection. That's our idea: How can we connect diners to the natural world? To a lost but reemerging system of farming? To the history, the open space, and the beauty of the Hudson Valley?

Sure, you could do all this by writing a book, and you could do it by lecturing. You could do it through a lot of ways, but I would argue that one of the more provocative and, increasingly, powerful ways is through food. Through food and through the totality of a menu. It's a great way to pierce the things that we can't see or spend the time trying to understand. Ecology, ecological diversity, and ecological vitality are all very hard things to talk about. But it's not very hard when you serve a delicious meal, because the menu connects all the dots. And luckily, I'm on a stage where I am, with Mr. Rockefeller's help, allowed to speak about issues in a way that broadcasts pretty profoundly. I wouldn't be able to do this if I were just a chef in a space that wasn't situated on a beautiful farm with these historic early twentieth-century stone barns. I have this bully pulpit, in a way.

It always angers me because some things—like a new breeder developing a new variety that has worked well in the system and some story that's attached to it—just get lost in a plate of food. We really re-jiggered the restaurant to address this—I mean, talk about mistakes. I was doing that for five years. We were dealing with all this beautiful produce and the stories attached to it, and it all had great potential for the diner to understand the issues that we just talked about. And I was just blowing it left and right because, unless you have a connection to the ingredient, you're not going to get very far with that. So, yeah, that was a big one.

Not everyone agrees with [Blue Hill's didactic mission], and so I have to be very careful. There's definitely a sector of the dining public that doesn't want to hear about it during a meal. So, in those cases we're either doing it wrong—in other words, we're approaching them incorrectly—or we should be leaving those people alone and then, hopefully, trying to win them over with great food.

We're called farm-to-table, but the trick for the future (if we have this conversation in ten years) is to tie the pieces further together. It's not just about supporting a local farm. It's more about thinking about a menu that connects with a whole system of agriculture. That's what any good cuisine does: peasant French, peasant Italian, Chinese, Indian. These are cuisines that produced different local interpretations, famous dishes and cooking techniques, but that mostly arose from supporting a system of agriculture. They're rooted in peasantry. And, in many ways, I'm trying to get back to that.

In the past, good land stewardship was trying to eke out of the land whatever could be produced. But being evolved now supports the same idea—to get good nutrition and eke out what you can from the land. And that sustains—that's why we call them cuisines. They sustain for thousands of years. As farming changed and environments changed and cultures developed, for sure, they became more complex. But at the root of it, we are talking about building a package that can support a healthy landscape. And that's not just about buying local; if it's about buying local, that's just too easy. Anyone can buy zucchini, tomatoes, and eggplant from Hudson Valley farmers and call themselves "farm-to-table." I think the future needs a new paradigm. And that's what the Stone Barns Center is inching its way toward.

CRABTREE'S KITTLE HOUSE

11 KITTLE ROAD
CHAPPAQUA, NY 10514
(914) 666-8044
KITTLEHOUSE.COM
PARTNERS: JOHN CRABTREE AND GLENN VOGT;
EXECUTIVE CHEF: JAY LIPPIN

While it's no secret that a restaurant has operated at 11 Kittle Road since the 1920s, in fact much of the Kittle House story lies underground, both figuratively and literally. Not only was the eighteenth-century structure operated as a roadhouse during Prohibition, but, since the 1980s—when the Crabtree family purchased it—the building's cellar has housed a world-class wine collection.

Crabtree's Kittle House is one of only about seventy restaurants in the world to hold *Wine Spectator Magazine*'s Grand Award. You might have heard of some of the others in its cohort—the French Laundry in Yountville, California; Taillevent in Paris; and Daniel and Eleven Madison Park in New York City. You get the point: A Grand Award is a pretty big deal.

But even though the Kittle House's wine program has made it an oenophile icon, only a small segment of diners drop in for that $25,000 Domaine de la Romanee Conti. Most

of the Kittle House's regulars are blissfully unaware of the 65,000 bottles below. Instead, they come for what has made the Kittle House beloved for more than thirty years: its warm heart.

Says Kittle House partner, Glenn Vogt, "There are several key reasons why we have been able to survive in this challenging business for as long as we have. The most important reason is hospitality. We've always focused on making our guests feel comfortable and well cared for, first and foremost. The second reason is the inherent quality in our food and beverage programs. Though chefs have come and gone from the Kittle House, the quality of the product and preparation has never wavered. We've used the same approach with wine and spirits. We're presenting a world-class wine list with over five thousand selections for those who enjoy an elevated wine drinking experience—but we're also offering a selection of wonderful and affordable options on a much shorter and easier-to-navigate wine list."

Then, of course, there's the fact that the Kittle House is an excellent neighbor. Over the years, the Kittle House has supported many charities—in summer look for their weekly "Sparkle for a Cause" garden parties that raise money for local charities.

Hudson Valley Foie Gras Sauté with Black Mission Fig & Caramelized Honey Sauce

(SERVES 3 AS AN APPETIZER)

6 tablespoons honey
4 tablespoons fig vinegar (available at specialty shops and Amazon.com)
4 ounces brown chicken or duck stock
½ teaspoon chopped fresh lemon thyme
2 Black Mission figs, quartered
3 (4-ounce) foie gras medallions (cleaned and separated into lobes)
Coarse salt and freshly ground pepper to taste
1 sprig lemon thyme, for garnish

To prepare the foie gras: In a medium-size saucepan over high heat, pour the honey and allow it to deepen in color, lightly caramelizing. When the honey starts to bubble, add the vinegar and the brown stock and stir the mixture with a wooden spoon to combine. Add the chopped lemon thyme and the quartered figs and stir very gently. When the figs are warm, approximately 3 minutes, remove them from the sauce and set aside. Let the sauce simmer on low heat.

Season the foie gras medallions with coarse salt and fresh pepper. Place a medium-size sauté pan over high heat. When very hot, carefully add foie gras. Sear for approximately 1 minute on each side (depending on the thickness of the medallion).

To plate: Arrange the figs on the plate and place the foie gras on top of the figs. Drizzle the caramelized honey sauce across the foie gras medallions and over the plate. Place the thyme sprig on top of the foie gras and serve.

WARM VALRHONA CHOCOLATE GIFT

(SERVES 9)

For the chocolate sponge cake:

4 ounces granulated sugar

16 eggs

9 ounces cake flour

3 ounces Valrhona cocoa powder

For the ganache filling:

3 quarts heavy cream

10 pounds dark Valrhona chocolate

For the pastry cream:

3 cups granulated sugar

21 large egg yolks

3 quarts milk

6 ounces cornstarch

2 vanilla beans, scraped

1 pound unsalted butter, cut into small cubes

For the gift:

1 box frozen phyllo pastry

To make the chocolate sponge cake: Preheat oven to 350°F. Spray a half-sheet pan (18 x 13-inch) with nonstick spray and line the bottom with a sheet of parchment paper. In a stand mixer fitted with the whisk attachment, combine sugar and eggs and whip at medium speed. Sift together the flour and the cocoa powder. Add the flour and cocoa to the sugar and egg mixture and blend thoroughly. Pour the batter into the prepared sheet pan. Bake for about 15 minutes, or until the cake is cooked through. To test, insert a bamboo skewer. If nothing clings to the skewer when you pull it out, the cake is done. Invert onto a rack and peel off parchment.

To make the ganache filling: In a double boiler set over simmering water, heat the cream. When hot, fold in the chocolate. Reserve.

To make the pastry cream: In a stand mixer fitted with the whisk attachment, blend the sugar and egg yolks together on medium speed. In a saucepan over medium heat, place milk, cornstarch, and scraped vanilla beans. Scald the mixture, stirring, but do not boil. Carefully pour the hot milk mixture into the sugar and egg mixture while mixing on medium speed. When combined, return the entire mixture to the saucepan and cook, stirring constantly, until thick. Stir in butter, then pour mixture into a bowl. Combine with ganache and set aside.

To assemble the gifts: Cut the chocolate sponge cake in half to form two layers. Place one layer on a parchment-lined tray whose sides are at least 2 inches high. Spread layer with the ganache mixture and then top the ganache with the other half of the chocolate sponge cake. Refrigerate.

Once the cake has completely cooled, cut it into equal sections of approximately 2 by 3 inches. Place two stacked leaves of phyllo dough on a board and place one piece of the layered cake onto the center of the dough. Wrap the phyllo around the top and sides to completely cover the cake. Wrap all the cakes the same way.

Preheat oven to 350°F. Place a wrapped gift with the seam side down onto a parchment-lined sheet pan and bake until golden brown. Serve with vanilla ice cream, whipped cream, or crème anglais.

FORTINA

17 Maple Avenue
Armonk, NY 10504
(914) 273-0900
FORTINAPIZZA.COM
OWNERS: CHRISTIAN PETRONI, JOHN NEALON, AND ROB KRAUSS;
EXECUTIVE CHEF: CHRISTIAN PETRONI

There's something innately superstar about Chef Christian Petroni. Even when he cooked on the line in Chef Anthony Goncalves's White Plains tapas bar, Peniche, it was apparent that Petroni would be going places. It could have been his self-effacing humor, wide smiles, and camera-friendly banter—but, somehow, it was obvious: This guy wouldn't be on the line too long. Petroni's stint at the helm of the Greenwich, Connecticut, branch of Barcelona Wine Bar landed him repeated appearances on the Food Network's *Chopped,* where a combination of good humor and serious skills made him one of the few chefs to escape reality television without shame. In 2012 Petroni debuted Cooked and Co., a small cafe-cum-prepared food shop that he owns with three other Westchester kitchen veterans, Melissa Iscaro, Denise Ruggiero, and Herb Lindstrom. Friday tasting dinners at Cooked and Co. often featured Petroni theatrically

pouring vats of polenta directly onto dining tables.

But at Fortina, the vast Armonk restaurant that Petroni launched in 2013 with partners John Nealon and Rob Krauss, Petroni finally has a canvas as big as his spirit. With soaring ceilings and 130 seats—and that's just inside, there are almost as many outside—Fortina runs dual wood-fired ovens, one for pizza, one for everything else. The restaurant's name is taken from a property (the "Little Fort") that Petroni's family owns on Ponza, an island off Naples. Its menu manages the delicate balance between blatantly lustful and charmingly sophisticated. Here you'll find the occasional nugget of Petroni's humor (for instance, on the menu the dry-cured meat *capicola* becomes "gabagool"), giant #10 cans of imported tomatoes are used as pizza stands, and one pie (the Tenderoni) is named for a Chromeo song.

Jokes aside, Petroni and his partners are deadly serious when it comes to Fortina. You can expect Petroni's carefully crafted, wood-fired dishes to be joined by an on trend beverage program that offers eighty-plus labels of wine, classic cocktails, and a long and stunning craft beer list.

Burrata Fettunta with English Peas & Brown Butter

(SERVES 4–6 AS A STARTER)

For the fettunta:

8 slices of crusty Italian bread (Petroni prefers filone)
½ cup of extra virgin olive oil
3-4 cloves of garlic
Maldon sea salt, to taste

For the finished dish:

1 pound very fresh burrata cheese
1 cup of arugula
1 tablespoon olive oil
1 teaspoon lemon juice
¾ cup raw English peas
3 tablespoons vin cotto (you may substitute saba or
   a 12–18 year old aged balsamic vinegar here)
2 tablespoons butter
¼ teaspoon sel gris, or to taste

To make the *fettunta*: Cut bread into ½-inch slices. Grill (or broil) until the bread is brown and slightly charred. Scrape surface with garlic cloves. Saturate the slices with olive oil and finish with Maldon salt to taste.

To serve: Place the slices of *fettunta* onto plates. Divide the burrata onto the slices of *fettunta*. In a bowl, toss the arugula leaves with olive oil and lemon, to taste. Set aside. In a small pan set over medium heat, melt and cook the butter until it becomes lightly brown and begins to smell slightly nutty. Remove from heat. Place the arugula leaves over the burrata and garnish with peas. Drizzle plates and *fettunta* with *vin cotto* and brown butter. Scatter with *sel gris* and serve.

GLEASON'S

911 SOUTH STREET
PEEKSKILL, NY 10566
(914) 402-1950
GLEASONSPEEKSKILL.COM
OWNERS: TIM REINKE AND JOHN SHARP;
EXECUTIVE CHEF: MARCH WALKER; BARMAN: JASON SCHULER

Sure, the southern tip of the Hudson Valley lies squarely in The Great Pizza Continuum that extends from the iconic "apizza" joints in New Haven into the foundational pizzerias of New York City. But, though southern Westchester holds pizzerias that date back to the 1930s and 1940s, the farther north you travel in the valley, the harder it gets to snag a great pie.

This fact had not gone unnoticed by the shrewd team behind Peekskill's Birdsall House, who, in the fall of 2012, debuted Gleason's in Peekskill. The heart of this stylish pizzeria is Chef March Walker's novel pizza dough that blends artisanal commercial yeast with a yeast that Walker cultured himself from Belgian ale. The dough is allowed a slow two- to three-day proof in the refrigerator, a span that allows it time to develop an intriguing tang. The result is a distinctly flavorful round topped with whatever is in season.

As at Birdsall House, the team's other venue, Walker sources many of his ingredients from local farms.

But Gleason's secret weapon is the painstakingly crafted cocktails of Jason Schuler. Schuler, who owns and operates Drink More Good in Beacon—a "head shop" for bartenders that vends boutique and house-made bitters, "roll your own" tea bags, and artisanal, house-made sodas—took on Gleason's bar and made it a destination in its own right. Look for craft distilled spirits, artisanal mixers, and drink names that echo the spirit of the vintage B-movie posters on Gleason's walls—like *The Black Dahlia,* purported to leave drinkers "grinning from ear to ear."

LAMB & MORTADELLA LASAGNA WITH PARSNIP BÉCHAMEL

(SERVES 12–14)

For the ragu:

2 big bunches fresh rosemary
1 big bunch thyme
1 (750ml) bottle red wine
1 large white or yellow onion, coarsely chopped
2 ribs celery, coarsely chopped
1 large carrot, coarsely chopped
6 cloves garlic, peeled and sliced
Olive oil, as needed
Salt and pepper to taste
2 pounds ground lamb
1 cup tomato paste

For the parsnip béchamel:

2 large parsnips, peeled and sliced into thin rounds
2 cups whole milk
2 cups water
Salt and pepper to taste
1 cup heavy cream
½ cup unsalted butter
½ cup all-purpose flour
Nutmeg to taste

For the pasta:

1½ cups all-purpose flour
2 large eggs
Scant pinch of kosher salt
A little water

For the lasagna:

2 cups finely grated Parmigiano Reggiano or Grana Padano
12 thin slices mortadella

To make the ragu: One day before you plan to assemble the lasagna, in a small saucepan over low heat, combine the rosemary and thyme with the red wine. Let the herbs and wine steep for an hour or so on very low heat, turning it lower if it starts to bubble. Meanwhile, put the onion, celery, carrot, and garlic in a food processor and chop fine (don't overprocess the vegetables—you could also do this by hand). Heat a 5-quart Dutch oven and coat the bottom with olive oil. Sauté the vegetables in the olive oil over moderate heat, stirring often, until they are evenly caramelized. Season to taste with salt

and pepper. Add the lamb to the vegetables and continue cooking, browning the meat well (this should take another 15–20 minutes), scraping up any crispy brown bits. Add the tomato paste and cook, stirring, for a few more minutes. Strain the herb-flavored wine into the Dutch oven to deglaze, scraping up all the crispy bits, and stir well to incorporate. Turn the heat to low and allow the ragu to simmer for 3 hours or so, adding water as needed to prevent it from sticking or scorching. This recipe will make more than you need, so save some for later. It freezes very well.

To make the parsnip béchamel: In a medium saucepan place the parsnips, milk, and water. Season with salt and pepper and simmer until the parsnips are very tender. Add the cream and transfer the mixture to a blender. Puree the mixture until it is very smooth. In a medium saucepan melt the butter. Add the flour and stir well to make a smooth roux. Cook the roux on low heat until it is blonde in color. Gradually whisk in the parsnip puree and bring the béchamel to a simmer. Season to taste with nutmeg, salt, and pepper. Strain through a fine mesh and reserve.

To make the pasta: In a food processor place the flour, eggs, and salt and pulse until they come together. Alternatively, you could simply combine these ingredients by hand. With either method you will need to add a little water at the end, a few drops at a time, until the dough comes together. Ultimately it should be a firm, and not sticky, dough. When the dough is firm and consistent, flour it lightly and then cover with plastic wrap. Allow the dough to rest at room temperature for an hour. Meanwhile, take out your pasta machine.

After the pasta dough rests for an hour, cut the ball of dough in half and form it into a roughly rectangular shape narrower than the width of your pasta rollers. Roll the dough a few times through the machine with the rollers set at the widest setting, dusting the dough with flour if it

becomes sticky. Continue to pass the dough through the machine at this setting until the dough is silky. Narrow the rollers, one setting at a time, passing the dough through until you have a thin sheet. For most machines you will stop one short of the narrowest setting. Cut the sheets about the same length as your lasagna pan and dust them lightly with flour. Set aside.

Bring a large pot of salted water to a boil. Have a large container of ice water handy, as well as a skimmer and an oiled cookie sheet or platter. Blanch the pasta sheets for about 1 minute in the water, cooking them just until firm. Remove pasta from the water with the skimmer and shock in ice water to prevent further cooking. When they are cold, place the sheets of pasta on the oiled cookie sheet. Reserve.

To assemble the lasagna: Preheat oven to 400°F. Butter a 9-inch or 12-inch baking pan, then spread a thin layer of béchamel on the bottom. Lay one layer of pasta on the bottom of the pan, piecing pasta sheets together as needed to make a full layer. Spread about 1 cup lamb ragu in a thin layer over the pasta, then spread about ½ cup béchamel over the ragu. Sprinkle ⅓ cup Parmigiano Reggiano over the top and add three slices of mortadella. Repeat this process three more times, ending with a layer of pasta on top. You will wind up with five layers of pasta and four layers of lamb ragu, mortadella, and béchamel filling. Spread a little of the remaining béchamel over the top sheet of pasta, sprinkle this with the remainder of the Parmigiano Reggiano, and then cover the pan loosely with foil.

Bake the lasagna for about 15 minutes, or until everything is hot and the cheese has melted, then remove the foil and bake for 30 more minutes, or until the lasagna is well browned and crusty on top. Allow the lasagna to rest for 10 minutes before serving. Serve with a simple mixed salad.

Jason Schuler has built a better, cleaner, and more natural mousetrap with his Beacon bartender's shop and soda factory, Drink More Good. The factory handcrafts dizzyingly adult soda syrups that are flavored with natural ingredients including raw organic ginger, sarsaparilla, cassia, kola nuts, organic sugar, and whole vanilla pods. Unlike national sodas—which are bottled in vast factories, then trucked across the country to distributors—these concentrates are locally made and leave a minimized ecological footprint. Plus, when diluted according to directions with carbonated water (one ounce syrup per eight ounces water), the pop bears between 30 percent and 50 percent less sugar than most supermarket brands and contains no high fructose corn syrup.

Not surprisingly, Drink More Good sodas have been adopted by Hudson Valley trendsetters, most notably Blue Hill at Stone Barns and Captain Lawrence Brewing Company. You can find DMG behind the bars at both of those landmarks, plus at several farmers' markets in Westchester, Dutchess, and Brooklyn. DMG products are also available at the Brewster DeCicco's Market and at DMG's retail store/factory on Beacon's Main Street.

© DRINK MORE GOOD

Schuler's interest in sodas was an organic evolution from his work as a high-end barman (one hates the word mixologist) working in LA under the iconic Steve Livigni. When Livigni developed the beverage program at Blue Cow Kitchen, Schuler learned cocktail precepts from the best. "I learned the fundamentals from him, which was eye opening, considering that I had been in restaurants and bars for almost fifteen years before that." Schuler continues, "It's a humbling experience to suddenly realize how little you know about the actual craft and art of a thing—but the experience opened my world to so many more opportunities to learn and become a better barman."

Schuler swapped coasts and took a job in Peekskill, where he designed the stunning cocktails at Gleason's. In the effort to find superior ingredients for his drinks, Schuler began to make his own sodas for Gleason's. One day a Gleason's customer offered Schuler money for his sodas, which he intended to drink at home. Inspired, Schuler soon began selling his syrups in farmers' markets from a homemade bar bearing taps and carbonated water that he kegs himself. Eventually Schuler was able to open his first tiny store at 259 Main Street in Beacon, which he jammed wall-to-wall with fetishized bar stools, Luxardo cherries, and hard-to-find bitters; Schuler joked that DMG's first home was a "barman's headshop." In 2014 DMG moved to larger space down the block at 383 Main Street, with a glassed-in factory floor and more retail room.

383 Main Street, Beacon, NY 12508; (845) 797-1838; drinkmoregood.com

THE KNEADED BREAD

181 NORTH MAIN STREET
PORT CHESTER, NY 10573
(914) 937-9489
KNEADEDBREAD.COM
OWNERS: JENNIFER AND JEFFREY KOHN; BAKERS: JEFFREY KOHN
AND MAMADY CISSE

People don't just to *go* to The Kneaded Bread; they *are devoted to* The Kneaded Bread, as though this cozy Port Chester bakery were some sort of compelling, carb-driven religion. And, in a way, the Kneaded Bread bakery feels like a church with an overflowing marble altar piled high with artisanal breads, French pastries, and tall American layer cakes. For its faithful, a visit to The Kneaded Bread is a more regularly observed ritual than Sunday service; weekend mornings would not be the same without Kneaded Bread's scones, croissants, muffins, buns, and doughnuts.

But The Kneaded Bread wasn't always the sure bet that it looks now. Back in 1998 when Jennifer and Jeffrey Kohn debuted The Kneaded Bread in gritty Port Chester, there was no Tarry Lodge, Tarry Market, or Tarry Wines just across the street. This was before bartaco and Arrosto, and before the Capitol Theater. Port Chester was just a tough inner-ring suburb with serious inner-city problems. It took the Kohns' foresight to see the value in Port Chester's pristine nineteenth-century urban architecture, which had been left untouched thanks to the preservation power of poverty. It took their intelligence to observe that, though rents are low in Port Chester, the town is virtually surrounded by some of the richest diners in the suburbs—and we're talking that serious Greenwich, Connecticut, and Rye, New York, kind of rich. Finally, it took a gamble to think that these customers would venture to Port Chester to buy artisanal bread—which is a luxury and not a necessity (plus you might find a reasonable facsimile closer to home).

Amazingly it all paid off—and in spades. Once locals got hooked on The Kneaded Bread's quality, they could never look at a supermarket loaf again. Even better, The Kneaded Bread was a Port Chester pioneer that paved the way for other food and entertainment businesses. This little temple to artisanal baked goods showed that Port Chester could become a dining mecca.

MULTI-GRAIN BREAD

(YIELDS 2 PULLMAN LOAVES, 2 POUNDS EACH)

For the levain:

2 ounces flour

2 ounces water

For the bread:

3 ounces flax seed

3 ounces sesame seed

3 ounces millet

1 pound unbleached, unbromated patent flour

8 ounces coarse, stone-ground whole wheat flour

2 ounces levain (starter)

8 ounces clover honey

10 ounces filtered water

2 ounces salt

To make the levain: Two days before you intend to bake the bread, combine the flour and the water in a mixing bowl. Cover the mixture with plastic wrap and allow the levain to ferment at room temperature for 2 days.

To make the dough: In the bowl of a stand mixer fitted with a dough hook, combine the flax, sesame, and millet. Add the flours, levain, honey, and water. Mix on low speed for 2 minutes, scraping down the sides of the bowl to help incorporate the flour. Add the salt. Increase the mixer speed to medium and knead for about

8 minutes. Remove the dough and place it in an oiled bowl or plastic container and cover. Let the dough rise at room temperature for 1–1½ hours, or until it is double in volume.

To bake the bread: Oil two standard 2-pound Pullman loaf pans (15¾ x 3¾-inch). Turn the dough onto a floured work surface and cut it into two equal portions. Slap dough to deflate and cover with a cloth. Let dough rest for 15 minutes.

Uncover the dough and, using as little flour as possible, shape the two sections of dough into two roughly rectangular portions. Place the shaped sections into the oiled Pullman pans, cover loosely with towels, and allow dough to rise until the loaves have grown again by half their original volume, about 1 hour.

Preheat oven to 450°F. Fill a spray bottle with water. Place the loaves in the preheated oven and immediately spray the loaves and oven with water for 5 seconds. Close the oven door and bake the bread. After 20 minutes check the loaves and rotate them (if necessary) to ensure that they are evenly baked. Continue baking the loaves for about 25 more minutes to make a total of about 45 minutes baking time. Remove the loaves from the oven and place them on a cooling rack. When cool, serve.

La Tulipe Desserts

455 Lexington Avenue
Mount Kisco, NY 10549
(914) 242-4555
latulipedesserts.com
Co-Owners: Maarten and Frances Steenman;
Baker: Maarten Steenman

In some ways, La Tulipe Desserts in Mount Kisco is a super-local enterprise. Its owners, Maarten and Frances Steenman, met more than twenty years ago when they were both working in a bakery in town. Holland-born Maarten Steenman is a second-generation pastry chef who had apprenticed at some of the finest patisseries in Europe—to be honest, sleepy Mount Kisco was lucky to have him. Once united, the Steenmans opened La Tulipe Desserts and set about creating their signature, incredibly painstaking desserts for locals. Thing is, one of those locals turned out to be Chelsea Clinton, who famously asked La Tulipe to create her vegan, gluten-free wedding cake.

But most locals do not need the high-profile recommendation of the Clintons (who happen to live nearby in Chappaqua) to appreciate La Tulipe. The bakery's fans have known for ages that La Tulipe will deliver the goods with consummate style, whether that means whipping up a vegan, gluten-free wedding cake for an American princess or slinging the bakery's signature treat, its gemlike chocolate-raspberry macarons.

CHOCOLATE-RASPBERRY MACARONS

(MAKES 38 MACARONS)

For the raspberry ganache filling:

½ cup raspberry puree

⅓ cup water

2¾ teaspoons lemon juice

9 ounces chocolate (64 percent cacao), chopped

14 tablespoons unsalted butter, cut into pieces
  and softened

5⅓ teaspoons raspberry liqueur

For the macarons:

2 extra-large egg whites

¾ teaspoon lemon juice

Pinch of salt

½ cup plus 2½ tablespoons 10x powdered sugar

1–2 drops red food coloring

¼ pound almond flour

3 tablespoons Valrhona cocoa powder

To make the ganache: Bring the raspberry puree, water, and lemon juice to a boil. In a medium bowl place the chopped chocolate. Working in small batches, use a silicone spatula to stir the hot raspberry mixture into the chocolate. Do not use a whisk and do not overmix, as the mixture will separate. Gently stir the mixture after every addition, stirring until chocolate is completely melted. Add small pieces of the soft butter and raspberry liqueur. The acidity from the puree will cause this base to separate a little, but the ganache will come together when the butter and the liqueur are added. Stir to emulsify the ganache, then pour it onto a tray to cool (it will cool faster with greater surface area—plus, it will allow for greater moisture loss) at room temperature.

To make the macarons: Three days before you intend to bake the macarons, separate the egg whites and store them in the refrigerator. This extra step breaks down the elasticity of the egg whites and improves the texture of the resulting macarons. On the day that you plan to bake the macarons, fit a stand mixer with the whisk attachment. Place the rested egg whites in the mixer bowl and whip them with the lemon juice and salt until the mixture holds stiff peaks. Add the 2½ tablespoons of powdered sugar and the food coloring and whip until combined.

Into a separate bowl sift the almond flour, cocoa powder, and remaining powdered sugar. Sift the ingredients one additional time. Using a silicone spatula, fold the almond flour/sugar mixture into the whipped egg mixture until it is shiny and forms smooth ribbons. Fold the mixture very gently, as you do not want the meringue to collapse. Preheat the oven to 310°F. Line two baking sheets with parchment paper. Spoon the mixture into a pastry bag and then pipe the batter into seventy-six circles, each about 1½ inches in diameter. Allow the macarons to dry at room temperature for about 20–30 minutes before you place them in the oven. After they have dried, bake the macarons in the preheated oven for 10 minutes. Allow them to cool before filling.

Working one at a time, spread about 1 teaspoon ganache onto the flat side of a macaron, then top that with another macaron, flat side placed directly on the ganache, rounded side up. Repeat this process to make thirty-eight sandwiched macarons. Serve.

LITTLE SPICE BAZAAR

27 EAST MAIN STREET
MOUNT KISCO, NY 10549
(914) 218-3333
FACEBOOK.COM/LITTLESPICEBAZAAR
CHEF/OWNERS: BONNIE SARAN AND KAREN GERA

Modest. Affable. And, dare I say it—cute? Whatever you want to call her, Little Spice Bazaar's Chef Bonnie Saran is a great big liar.

For all her cuddliness, Bonnie Saran is a restaurant animal—and as shrewd as any scarred, thirty-year veteran. Before debuting Little Kebab Station (the first of her three side-by-side Mount Kisco restaurants), Saran used the business degree that she earned in India to work as a consultant to Indian restaurants in New York and New Jersey. Called upon during financial crises, Saran knew the paths to restaurant failure like the back of her own hand. Having seen the catastrophes wrought by overreaching, Saran's first venture, Little Kebab Station, was a parable of achievable goals.

With no liquor license and ten seats (well, twelve if you count the two chairs at the complimentary tea station), LKS was barely an actual restaurant. Yet its message—telegraphed by spice-colored walls, a painted frieze of Indian food trucks, and Bollywood stars pasted over ugly fluorescents—was clear. Little Kebab was fun, DIY, and miles from the stuffy sitar-and-samosa Indian restaurants of the past. Rather than serving ponderous curries, Saran introduced Westchester to Bombay frankie rolls: *kathi* wraps of highly spiced kebab meat, fluffy fried egg, lemon, and fiery onion and mint chutnies. At Little Kebab, Saran offered lighter, modern takes on Indian standards (but never spared the flavor). Often she used locally sourced ingredients.

Almost as soon as Little Kebab Station debuted, Saran snagged popular and critical favor, and claimed the loyalty of many local celebrities, most notably, Martha Stewart herself. Stewart remains a vocal supporter.

Saran's second venture, Little Spice Bazaar, debuted in 2012 and is even more casual than LKS, if that's possible. It's a loud, buzzy *lassi* shop that also offers sit-down salads. Little Spice Bazaar's Ayuvedic, probiotic *lassis*—made with tangy house-made yogurt, fresh fruit, and medicinal spices and herbs—is an instant addiction for everyone who tries it, even those who have never done yoga or attempted a cleanse. Besides *lassis, papri chats,* and the stunning *bhel puri* (recipe follows), Little Spice Bazaar offers teas and an array of Indian culinary and medicinal spices. Also look for a small, carefully curated selection of Indian groceries that includes incense and health and beauty aids.

BHEL PURI

(SERVES 4)

2 cups puffed rice (available at many Indian grocery stores)

10 crushed papadi (these Indian wheat crisps are available at many Indian grocery stores)

¼ cup plus 2 tablespoons sev (crunchy chickpea flour noodles, available at many Indian grocery stores)

¼ cup diced boiled potatoes

¼ cup chopped onion

3 teaspoons roasted cumin seed powder, plus more for garnish

2 teaspoons chaat masala (you can find this spice blend online or at many Indian specialty stores. Alternatively, you can blend it yourself—recipes, which vary slightly, can be found online.)

¼ cup plus 1 tablespoon chopped cilantro

½ cup tamarind chutney (recipe follows)

½ cup mint chutney (recipe follows)

1 tablespoon pomegranate seeds

¼ teaspoon chili powder (or to taste)

In a medium-size bowl, toss together the puffed rice and eight of the ten *papadi* (crush these by hand). Add ¼ cup of the *sev,* the potatoes, onion, roasted cumin seed powder, chaat masala, and ¼ cup of the cilantro. Add the tamarind and mint chutneys. Toss everything together until the ingredients are well combined. Garnish with the two remaining *papadi* (crushed by hand), pomegranate seeds, the remaining tablespoon of chopped cilantro, the remaining 2 tablespoons of *sev,* and a sprinkling of cumin seed powder and chili powder. Serve immediately.

MINT CHUTNEY

(MAKES 1 PINT)

2 cups coarsely chopped mint leaves

1½ cups coarsely chopped cilantro

½ cup coarsely chopped red onion

2 tablespoons fresh lemon juice

2 tablespoons granulated sugar

2 green chiles, finely chopped (optional)

2 cloves garlic, chopped

½ teaspoon salt

In a blender puree all the ingredients together using a small amount of water (use as little as possible). Puree until very smooth.

TAMARIND CHUTNEY

(MAKES 1 PINT)

1 slab dried tamarind (about 200 grams, available at many Indian groceries)

100 grams jaggery (available at many Indian groceries) or 1½ cups granulated sugar

2 teaspoons cumin seeds, toasted

1 teaspoon coriander seeds

1 tablespoon black salt (available at many Indian groceries or online; kosher salt may be substituted)

¼ teaspoon chili powder

1 teaspoon powdered ginger

Pull the block of tamarind into 1-inch pieces and place these in a small saucepan. Cover with 2½ cups water and bring this mixture to a boil. When boiling, reduce heat and simmer the mixture, stirring, until the tamarind is mostly dissolved. Place a strainer over a small bowl and pass the tamarind mixture through the strainer. Discard the seeds and return the tamarind to the pot. Add the remaining ingredients and return the mixture to a boil. Taste to correct for sugar and salt, then stir in a tablespoon (or so) of water—the chutney will thicken when it cools. Remove the mixture from heat. Cool completely and refrigerate. This tamarind chutney can be kept refrigerated for up to 1 month.

Ocean House

49 North Riverside Avenue
Croton-on-Hudson, NY 10520
(914) 271-0702
OCEANHOUSEOYSTERBAR.COM
Owners: Brian and Paula Galvin; Chef: Brian Galvin

Ocean House was never supposed to be the great restaurant that it has become. In 2004 Brian and Paula Galvin took on a vintage diner—one that had stood squarely on North Riverside Avenue in Croton-on-Hudson since the Great Depression—with nothing but the most modest of culinary intentions. Says Chef Galvin, "Our plan was to do a basic seafood restaurant, get the freshest fish, and prepare it as simply as we could. We never in our wildest imagination thought that we'd get a 28 [out of a possible 30] in *Zagat*. The *New York Times* review came two months after we opened, and it just took off."

To be honest, Ocean House is a hard sell on paper. While its interior has been transformed into a spare, sea-and-sky-colored dining room, from the exterior Ocean House still looks exactly like a vintage diner. Long and narrow, the pre-fab structure once rode the rails to Croton-on-Hudson from the Bixler Manufacturing Company in Norwalk, Ohio. When this diner was created (sometime between 1931 and 1937), the Bixler design was touted for its airy, houselike elegance. Unlike the streamlined, bulletlike shape of other Depression-era diners, the Bixlers bore tall, double-hung windows and ornate, gable-end facades—these were the chateaux of the pre-fab diner set. Ocean House still has its windows and an arched facade, and still seats only nineteen diners. Plus it's a BYOB; the original diner's single bathroom prevents Ocean House from being licensed to sell liquor.

No matter. Ocean House's legion fans are happy to queue on the street, bottles in hand—though, most likely, they've left their cell phone numbers at the door and are cooling their heels in a nearby tavern.

Basically folks are delighted to do whatever it takes to get a crack at Ocean House's carefully curated array of brimming East and West Coast oysters, sparklingly fresh seafood, and warming soups that include Galvin's seductively smoky New England clam chowder and his Portuguese fish stew, included below.

Chef Galvin, with genuine modesty, deflects the credit that is always attributed to his stunning cooking at Ocean House. "The space dictated what we were going to do," he says. "Our business plan was to be a very mom-and-pop kind of place, but it just kind of kept rolling and turned into what we have now."

PORTUGUESE FISH STEW

(SERVES 4)

2 tablespoons extra-virgin olive oil
1 clove garlic, finely minced
1 bulb fennel, cored, cut in half, and sliced very thin
1 cup peeled, seeded, and chopped plum tomatoes
2 links chorizo sausage, chopped
1 cup dry vermouth
4 cups fish stock
16 washed mussels
12 washed littleneck clams
2 cups cooked white beans
Pinch of saffron
1 sprig fresh thyme
Salt and pepper to taste

In a large saucepan heat the olive oil. Add the garlic, fennel, tomato, and chorizo and sauté for 2–3 minutes. Add the vermouth and stock and cook over medium heat until the liquid simmers. Add the mussels, clams, and white beans and cook until the shellfish opens. When the clams and mussels are open, stir in the saffron and thyme. Season with salt and pepper to taste and serve immediately.

PEEKSKILL BREWERY

47-53 SOUTH WATER STREET
PEEKSKILL, NY 10566
(914) 734-2337
PEEKSKILLBREWERY.WORDPRESS.COM
OWNERS: KARA, MORGAN, AND KEITH BERARDI;
BREWMASTER: JEFF O'NEIL; EXECUTIVE CHEF: SEAN CORCORAN

First of all, let's all admit that there was a bad moment in the 1990s when every crappy town had an equally crappy bar that made its own beer. Oh, *at first* it was a thrill to eat our burgers while looking at gleaming fermentation tanks, but pretty soon it became obvious that those beers—though made on-site—were mostly second rate. Worse, the effort to make beer sucked attention from brewpub kitchens, which often resorted to serving basic pub grub, and by that we mean generic, freezer-to-Frialator food. Sadly, after the 1990s it became apparent that the brewpub genre was favored by the sort of diner who wasn't particular about quality in either beer or food.

Cue Kara, Keith, and Morgan Berardi, the wife-husband-sister team behind Peekskill Brewery. This young power trio had the audacity to hire Ithaca Brewing Company's star brewer, Jeff O'Neil, while they were still running a gritty brewpub in a tiny, L-shaped space at 55 Hudson Street. When they did this, jaws dropped. But what the Berardis knew (that the rest of us didn't) was that Peekskill Brewery was set to explode.

In a short few months after PB snagged O'Neil's talents, the Berardis re-launched their brewpub in the roomy four stories of an elegant former furniture factory built in 1928. Not only did the move triple the former brewery's beer production, but it also afforded a public gallery, a private event space, and a rooftop biergarden with sunset Hudson views. The new brewery holds one of the only *kuhlschips* in the United States; the shallow pool collects ambient yeast for beermaking—it literally rests below a window open to Hudson River breezes. This means that some of Peekskill Brewery's beers are literally brought to life with Hudson Valley air.

On Peekskill Brewery's ground and second floors, Chef Sean Corcoran holds sway with locally sourced cuisine that often incorporates O'Neil's craft-brewed beers. Look for hearty charcuterie, locally sourced cheeses, and house-made soft pretzels—and, always, the perfect match for pint after pint of beer.

Seared Chicken Liver with Caramelized Onions & Balsamic Vinegar

(SERVES 6)

For the polenta:

5 cups roast chicken stock

1 cup polenta

2 tablespoons unsalted butter

½ cup grated Parmigiano Reggiano

Salt to taste

For the chicken livers:

1 teaspoon neutral oil (canola or grapeseed)

1 pound free-range chicken livers, cleaned

Salt

Flour for dredging

1⅓ cup julienned onion

¼ cup balsamic vinegar

To make the polenta: In a medium saucepan bring the chicken stock to a boil. Slowly add the polenta, whisking constantly, until it's fully incorporated. Lower the heat under the saucepan and keep the mixture at a simmer, whisking constantly. Cook the polenta for 7–8 minutes, or until it is thickened. When finished, remove the pan from the heat, whisk in the butter and cheese, and season to taste with salt. Set aside.

To cook the chicken livers: In a large sauté pan, heat the teaspoon of oil. Season the livers with salt, then dredge them in the flour, shaking off the excess flour. When the pan is almost smoking, add the livers and cook for about 45 seconds on each side. Remove the livers from the pan and set them aside as you prepare the remainder of the dish. Add the julienned onions to the hot pan and sauté in the liver fat until the onions are dark brown and richly caramelized. Return the livers to the pan and then deglaze the pan with balsamic vinegar. Cook the balsamic vinegar with the livers until the liquid is reduced by half. Remove the pan from the heat.

To plate: Divide the polenta among six dinner plates. Place two or three livers in the center of the polenta and garnish with the onions. Drizzle with the balsamic glaze and serve.

PURDY'S FARMER & THE FISH

100 TITICUS ROAD
NORTH SALEM, NY 10560
(914) 617-8380
FARMERANDTHEFISH.COM
OWNERS: MICHAEL KAPHAN AND EDWARD TAYLOR;
CHEF: MICHAEL KAPHAN

For more than two centuries, the old farmhouse at 100 Titicus Road sat backed by a sloping meadow that was used to produce food. But when Farmer & the Fish stepped into the site in March 2012, the building had been home to a series of restaurants that treated the Revolutionary War–era building with reverence but left its fertile surrounding land fallow.

That all changed when Edward Taylor and Michael Kaphan took over the farmhouse and plowed up the field's pretty green grass. Under the direction of Kaphan, the "farmer" of Farmer & the Fish (and an Ag school graduate from SUNY Cobleskill), the duo planted the field with the potatoes, heirloom tomatoes, herbs, peas, beans, eggplants, kale, chard, and lettuces that they intended to use in their new restaurant. Taylor, the

partnership's "fish," owns Down East Seafood, a large wholesale seafood company based in New York City.

But what's more shocking than plowing up the field, Taylor and Kaphan stripped off the farmhouse's quaint, but rickety, twentieth-century porch enclosure, effectively opening the restaurant's arms to the world. The pair also removed some of the farmhouse's Revolutionary War–era walls, uniting what had previously been several small, dark, and formal rooms into one open and exciting space.

Daring—even contentious—but ultimately rewarding. In summer Farmer & the Fish's porch spills customers out onto the lawn. They're drinking, laughing, and as happy as—well, clams—to wait for Kaphan and Taylor's uniquely Hudson Valley take on New England seafood. In winter those historic hearths are lit to make the perfect focus for mellow evenings in a centuries-old house. Farmer & the Fish seems poised to go for two more centuries. Says Kaphan, "We see ourselves as custodians of the land. We just want to be good custodians."

The Farmer & the Fish Lobster Boil

(SERVES 4)

For the gremolata:

1 clove garlic, minced
½ bunch parsley, finely chopped
1 sprig rosemary
5 sprigs thyme
Zest of 1 lemon
Zest of 1 orange

For the boil liquid:

10 sprigs thyme
5 sprigs rosemary
½ bunch Italian (flat leaf) parsley
3 cloves garlic
1 teaspoon black peppercorns
4 lemons, cut in half

For the lobster boil:

4 (1½-pound) lobsters
16 clams (littlenecks, topnecks, or steamers)
2 ears sweet corn, cut in half
1 pound red creamer potatoes
1 cup clarified butter
2 tablespoons gremolata
Salt and pepper to taste
2 lemons, cut in half

Special equipment:

4 clam bags (see Note)

To make the gremolata: In a bowl combine the garlic, herbs, and lemon and orange zest thoroughly. Refrigerate until needed.

To prepare the boil: Fill a 20-quart stockpot two-thirds of the way with water. Add the herbs, garlic, peppercorns, and lemons and bring to a boil, then simmer for 20 minutes. Meanwhile, prepare the rest of the dish.

To prepare the clam bags: Place one lobster, four clams, one-half ear of corn and ¼ pound of potatoes in each clam bag. Tie the top of the bag in a knot. Once the boil liquid has simmered for 20 minutes, drop the bags into the pot and set your timer for 10 minutes. When the timer goes off, carefully remove the bags. Place the corn, potatoes, and clams in a mixing bowl; add ¼ cup of the clarified butter (reserving the rest), 2 tablespoons gremolata, salt, and pepper. Mix well and set aside. Split the lobsters in half lengthwise and place one on each plate. Distribute the potatoes, corn, and clams evenly over the top of each lobster. Garnish with one-half lemon on each plate. Place reserved drawn butter in small bowls for dipping and serve.

Note: Clam bags are frequently used in the Northeast for clam/lobster boils. A good kitchen store should have them, or you can find them online at Butcher & Packer, butcher-packer.com.

Restaurant North

386 Main Street
Armonk, NY 10504
(914) 273-8686
RESTAURANTNORTH.COM
PARTNERS: CHEF ERIC GABRYNOWICZ AND STEPHEN PAUL MANCINI

Stephen Paul Mancini and Chef Eric Gabrynowicz are the restaurant Dream Team, it's that simple.

It begins with Chef Eric Gabrynowicz—ice-blue eyes, energy radiating off him like lines off a Keith Haring figure. His résumé reads like a straight flush. After graduating with honors from The Culinary Institute of America, Gabrynowicz shone so brightly that he turned an externship at Danny Meyer's Union Square Cafe into a rare and coveted full-time post. From there Meyer groomed Gabrynowicz with turns in Tabla and Blue Smoke (both Meyer landmarks), before returning him to Union Square as its sous-chef under Chef Michael Romano.

Now, other chefs of Gabrynowicz's caliber would have cashed in at that point—and perhaps hired a GM in a solo venture that snagged all the cash and kudos for himself. But Danny Meyer, the legendary front-of-house guru, had taught Gabrynowicz better than that. In 2010 Gabrynowicz teamed up with another Danny Meyer protégé, Stephen Paul Mancini, to form an unbeatable front-and-back-of-house team.

Mancini—irrepressibly enthusiastic, if not a wild-eyed zealot—started his restaurant career in a post-college stint as a busboy at Gramercy Tavern. By twenty-seven this Scarsdale-raised *enfant terrible* was beverage director of Union Square Cafe, the youngest ever in a restaurant that rated #1 in the *Zagat Survey*. Though busy, he still had time to push the boundaries by home curing prosciutto and making wine in his Harlem apartment. In 2008 the *New York Sun* called Mancini "The Mad Scientist of 16th Street" for his nuclear yellow experiments in the Italian liqueur limoncello (conducted in the basement of USC). When Danny Meyer opened Maialino in the Gramercy Park Hotel, he appointed Mancini its opening beverage director. Despite his youth, Mancini is the total front-of-house package with first-class wine, cocktail, and service chops.

Together, Gabrynowicz and Mancini created Restaurant North, a sunny and sophisticated restaurant that simultaneously expresses the duo's aristocratic restaurant background and their youthful joy. Restaurant North supports local farms, winemakers, distillers, and brewers, but never at the price of fun. North's excellence has not gone unnoticed—not only is North a critical darling, but in 2012 Chef Gabrynowicz snagged *Food & Wine* magazine's People's Best New Chef (Northeast).

Meiller's Farm Short Ribs with Sweet Potato Puree

(SERVES 4)

For the short ribs:

4–6 bone-in beef short ribs, preferably from
    Josef Meiller's Farm and Slaughterhouse
    (Pine Plains, New York)
Salt and pepper
1 carrot
1 onion
2 stalks celery
1 bottle good quality red wine
2 fresh bay leaves
2 tablespoons black peppercorns
Chicken stock to cover

For the sweet potato puree:

1 pound sweet potatoes, peeled and coarsely chopped
4 tablespoons unsalted butter
¼ cup cream
Salt and pepper

For the sweet potato chips:

Blended oil for frying (Gabrynowicz uses a 90/10 blend
    of canola/olive oil)
1 sweet potato, peeled and sliced thin
Salt

For the roasted Brussels sprouts:

1 pound Brussels sprouts, trimmed and cut in half
2–3 tablespoons extra-virgin olive oil
Salt and black pepper to taste

To prepare the ribs: Preheat oven to 300°F. On the bone side of each short rib, trim the excess fat and score the ribs diagonally across the bone. Season the ribs all over with salt and pepper. In a large Dutch oven, sear the ribs meat side down until crusted. Remove the ribs and set aside; in remaining fat, sauté carrot, onion, and celery. When the vegetables are soft and slightly caramelized, deglaze the pan with the red wine. At this point add the bay leaves and peppercorns and return the meat, bone side up, to the Dutch oven. Add chicken stock until the ribs are covered, place lid on the Dutch oven, and place in the preheated oven. Braise the ribs for 4–5 hours, or until the meat is fork tender.

When ribs are fork tender, remove the Dutch oven and set it aside. Allow the ribs to cool in the Dutch oven for 1 hour. Gently lift the meat from the pan (reserving the liquid) and place it on a cookie sheet. Remove the bones from the short ribs. Place another cookie sheet on top of the meat and weight it down to press. Refrigerate. Strain the reserved braising liquid through a chinois or fine mesh strainer and return the strained liquid to the pan. Cook over medium heat until the liquid is reduced to a syrup consistency. Set aside.

After the ribs are completely cooled (8–10 hours), trim the excess fat and sinew from the meat. Discard. When ready to plate, reheat the cleaned meat in a Dutch oven with the reduced liquid. Baste frequently.

To make the sweet potato puree: In a medium-size pot, cover the potatoes with cold water and season the water with salt. Bring to a boil, then reduce heat to simmer and cook until potatoes

are fork tender. Drain. In a separate saucepan melt the butter and then add the cream. Add the milk/butter mixture to the potatoes and incorporate using a hand blender. For extra fluffiness, finish in a drink blender with an additional tablespoon of both cream and butter. Season with salt and pepper.

To fry the chips: Fill a wide pot halfway with the 90/10 blended oil. Heat to 320°F. Add the chips one by one and fry, about ten at a time, until golden brown. Remove with a slotted spoon or spider onto paper towels. Immediately season with salt.

To roast the Brussels sprouts: Preheat oven to 350°F. Toss Brussels sprouts, olive oil, and salt and pepper in a bowl until coated. Place cut side down on a cookie sheet. Roast in the oven for approximately 20–23 minutes, or until tender.

To assemble the dish: Place a dollop of the sweet potato puree down as a base, then add a few roasted Brussels sprouts and top with the glazed short ribs. Finish with the fried chips.

ROASTED OYSTERS
WITH PICKLED GARLIC SCAPE COMPOUND BUTTER

(SERVES 4–6 AS A FIRST COURSE)

For the pickled garlic scapes:

1 dried chile
1 cup cider vinegar
1 star anise pod
4 teaspoons kosher salt
4 teaspoons granulated sugar
15 garlic scapes

For the garlic scape compound butter:

1 pound unsalted butter, softened
6 pickled garlic scapes, sliced thin on a bias
3 Meyer lemons, zested and juiced
½ cup finely (but gently) chopped herbs (Gabrynowicz suggests chive, chervil, and tarragon)

For the oysters:

Kosher salt
24 oysters

To pickle the scapes: In a small saucepan combine the chile, vinegar, anise, salt, and sugar. Bring to a boil and pour over the garlic scapes. Press down with a weight (Gabrynowicz uses plates) so that the scapes stay submerged in the brine.

To make the compound butter: In a medium-size bowl, blend the butter, scapes, lemons, and herbs gently. Try not to bruise the herbs. Reserve at room temperature.

To roast the oysters: Preheat oven to 425°F. Spread a ½-inch layer of kosher salt on a baking sheet and set aside. (The salt acts as a stabilizing bed for the roasting oysters so that their precious liquids won't spill.) Clean the oysters by scrubbing them under cold water with a brush. When clean, pat the oysters dry on a towel and place the unopened oysters flat side up on a high-heat grill (preferably charcoal) for approximately 2 minutes, or until they open. Carefully remove the oysters from the grill with tongs and place them flat on the bed of kosher salt. Remove their top shells.

To assemble the dish: Spoon about 1 tablespoon of the compound butter over each cooked oyster. Roast in the oven for about 2 additional minutes. Serve and slurp.

Hudson Valley Terroir

About 12,000 years ago, when glaciers receded from the Hudson Valley, what they left in their wake was a uniquely composed soil so dense in nitrogen, sulfur, and other nutrients that, in global satellite images, discrete regions of Orange County show up as a jet-black streak. Stephen Paul Mancini of Restaurant North explains the value of the Hudson Valley black dirt: "In Burgundy, they call it 'terroir.' No one cares how old your vines are, what they really care about is the dirt. And that dirt can change, as far as its composition, in the space of ten feet. So, the appellation could be Grand Cru or Premiere Cru within a ten-foot walk up a hill. Literally. And so taking from that old model—especially in the Hudson Valley, especially on Long Island—we're not really looking at geography as much as we are digging in and checking the soil. In the Hudson Valley, that's especially true in the Black Dirt Region. Guy Jones at Blooming Hill Farms has about one hundred acres of black dirt where he's producing amazing onions, garlic, and potatoes." He adds, "People like Guy Jones are very prideful about their black dirt."

Black Dirt Spirits, used in Mancini's North of Manhattan cocktail (below), are made by the distilling offshoot of Warwick Valley Winery, located in Pine Island, squarely in the Black Dirt Region. Says Mancini, "All of the products used to make Black Dirt Spirits—whether apple jack or bourbon—are grown in the Hudson Valley on black dirt. So the Black Dirt Bourbon uses 100 percent black dirt corn, malted barley, and rye; and the apples in Black Dirt Apple Jack are all grown on black dirt, too."

NORTH OF MANHATTAN

(SERVES 1)

2 ounces Black Dirt Bourbon or Black Dirt
   Apple Jack
1½ ounces New York State apple cider
½ ounces of ginger cordial or Q Ginger Ale
1 slice of Jonagold apple, for garnish

Stir the first three ingredients over ice. Strain into a martini glass and garnish with a slice of Jonagold apple.

Tarry Lodge

18 Mill Street
Port Chester, NY 10573
(914) 939-3111
TARRYLODGE.COM
Owning Partners: Mario Batali, Joseph Bastianich,
Nancy Selzer, and Andy Nusser;
Executive Chef: Andy Nusser; Chef de Cuisine: Sam Epps;
Lead Sommelier: Laura Miller

One of the most amazing things about the team behind Tarry Lodge is that—though it is composed of elite (as in TV-famous, nationally recognized, and multiple James Beard Award winning) Manhattan restaurateurs—there isn't a hint of anti-suburban snobbery in the venture.

The partnership of Joseph Bastianich and Mario Batali has yielded some of New York's most iconic restaurants: Babbo, Esca, Lupa, and Del Posto, just to name a few (there are more than twenty worldwide). Then, along with the restaurants there is the formidable television influence of Mario Batali. He's joined in his celebrity by Lidia Bastianich, Joseph Bastianich's mother (and, frequently, his business partner). Her series of motherly cooking shows and books have edified and entertained PBS viewers since 1998. Of course, there is also Joseph Bastianich's serious work in winemaking and wine education to consider, not to mention his campy, Vaderesque turns on the Fox Network show, *MasterChef*.

It is not an exaggeration to assert that, since the 1990s, the trio of Batali/Bastianich/Bastianich has led the American discourse in Italian food and wine. Which just begs the question: Why would they bother to debut a restaurant in a burnt-out site once held by a notoriously decrepit Italian-American red sauce joint in an economically depressed suburb (hidden twenty-six miles north of Manhattan) *and still keep the original restaurant's name?*

The answer has something to do with the bankability of memory. The Batali-Bastianich team wanted to tap the deep well of emotion held by locals for an Italian-American landmark. Says Joseph Bastianich, "After we bought the

Tarry Lodge, we realized what a great amount of nostalgia there was for the name and the restaurant and the location. Everyone knew Tarry Lodge. Everyone celebrated their high school graduation there or their birthday there in 1950 or 1940 or whatever. So we thought, 'This place has a lot of nostalgia associated with it. We should re-conceptualize it and bring it back to what might have been its former glory.'"

Yeah, but the old Tarry Lodge was never like this. The team installed Chef Andy Nusser, who made his bones during a five-year stint at the helm of Babbo that earned the restaurant three stars from Ruth Reichl in the *New York Times* and simultaneously introduced a new, lavishly carnal style of Italian eating (which has been endlessly emulated ever since). After Babbo, the trio of Nusser, Batali, and Bastianich struck gold with Casa Mono and Bar Jamon, a restaurant-bar that celebrates the food of Nusser's youth on Spain's Costa Brava. Nusser had always been a figure in the Batali/Bastianich empire. At the very beginning, Nusser cooked side-by-side with Batali in the minuscule kitchen of Pò, which was the very first Batali and Bastianich enterprise. At Pò, Batali/Bastianich and Nusser also snagged the talents of Nancy Selzer, who shot northward in their ranks and was a partner at Casa Mono/Bar Jamon. She also was an opening partner in both Tarry Lodges (in Port Chester and Westport, Connecticut).

What this team created at Tarry Lodge (in reverence to the original) is a reimagined ideal of an old-time Italian restaurant in America. There are the oceans of Carrera marble, the penny and hex floor tiles, and the sepia lighting of a *Godfather* movie. There is *zuppa di pesce,* rigatoni with meatball and sausage, and—you guessed it—eggplant parm. But, also, there is a top-class Italian wine list, carefully sourced salumi (some from Batali's father, Armandino), farro, and tender wood-fired pizzas. Tarry Lodge emerges as a kindly gesture toward Italian Americana done with a seasoned restaurant group's eye.

EGGPLANT PARMIGIANA

(SERVES 4)

For the tomato sauce:

¼ cup extra-virgin olive oil

1 Spanish onion, cut into ¼-inch dice

4 cloves garlic, peeled and thinly sliced

3 tablespoons chopped fresh thyme leaves, or
    1 tablespoon dried

½ medium carrot, finely grated

2 (28-ounce) cans peeled whole tomatoes,
    crushed by hand and juices reserved

Salt

For the eggplant:

2 large eggplants

Salt, as needed

Olive oil for greasing pans

2 cups flour

4 eggs, lightly whisked

2 cups seasoned dry bread crumbs

For the finished dish:

1 quart tomato sauce (above)

2 cups loosely packed fresh basil leaves

2 cups sun-dried tomatoes

1 pound fresh mozzarella, diced

2 cups grated Parmigiano Reggiano

1 pint toasted panko bread crumbs

To make the tomato sauce: In a 3-quart saucepan heat the olive oil over medium heat. Add the onion and garlic and cook until soft and light golden brown, about 8–10 minutes. Add the thyme and carrot and cook for 5 more minutes, or until the carrot is quite soft. Add the tomatoes and juice and bring to a boil, stirring often. Lower the heat and simmer for 30 minutes, or until the sauce is as thick as hot cereal. Season with salt and reserve.

To cook the eggplant: On the night before you plan to make the dish, cut the eggplant into ½-inch slices and lightly salt each slice. Line a colander with the slices and allow them to drain overnight. On the following day preheat oven to 450°F and pat the eggplant dry on paper towels. Lightly oil two baking sheets. Into each of three wide-mouthed bowls, place the flour, eggs, and bread crumbs. Dredge each eggplant slice first in flour, then egg, then bread crumbs. Arrange each slice on the oiled pans—do not overcrowd. Repeat this process until all the eggplant slices are coated and placed on the pans. Bake the slices for about 10 minutes on each side, or until golden brown.

To assemble the dish: In the bottom of an ovenproof baking dish, spread an even layer of the tomato sauce. Arrange the baked eggplant slices over the sauce. Ladle about 2 ounces of tomato sauce on top of each piece of eggplant. Place one basil leaf on top of each slice of eggplant, then place one sun-dried tomato on top of the basil leaf. Top each leaf with three cubes of mozzarella. Liberally sprinkle grated Parmigiano Reggiano over the eggplant. Repeat the process of layering the eggplant, tomato sauce, basil, sun-dried tomato, mozzarella, and Parmigiano Reggiano for two to five times until all the eggplant slices are used. Top each stack with toasted panko and bake for 20 minutes until the surface is bubbling and golden brown. Serve.

Wild Atlantic Halibut
with Truffle Brodo, Mussels & Ceci

(SERVES 4)

For the ceci beans:

1 bag dried ceci beans (chickpeas)

2 tablespoons extra-virgin olive oil

1 carrot, diced

1 small onion, diced

1 stalk celery, diced

Salt to taste

For the halibut:

4 (5-ounce) pieces wild halibut, skin removed
(striped bass, tilefish, fluke, or monkfish are
all good substitutes)

2 tablespoons extra-virgin olive oil

3 tablespoons unsalted butter

1 cup dry white wine

2 cups vegetable stock

2 cups cooked ceci beans (recipe follows)

1 tablespoon chopped black truffles (fresh truffles
are preferable, but preserved truffles in oil make
a reasonable substitute)

Juice of 1 lemon

1 bunch escarole, cleaned, trimmed, and sliced
into thin ribbons.

1 dozen mussels, cleaned and scrubbed

To cook the beans: On the night before you
plan to serve the dish, place the ceci beans in
a large bowl. Add water to cover with a couple
of inches to spare. Allow the beans to soak
overnight at room temperature. Into a medium-
size saucepan, pour the olive oil and add the
carrot, onion, and celery. Sauté the vegetables
until they are translucent. Add the drained ceci
to the vegetables and add water until beans are

covered. Cook the beans until tender, season to
taste with salt, and reserve.

To make the dish: Choose a sauté pan that is
big enough to fit all four pieces of fish without
overcrowding. Place the pan over high heat and,
when it is hot, add 2 tablespoons olive oil. When
the olive oil is almost smoking, add the pieces of
fish skin side up [where the skin had been, with
presentation side down]. Sauté the fish for about
2 minutes, or until you see the edges begin to
turn golden. Add 1 tablespoon butter, then check
the bottom of the fish. When each piece is golden
brown and not sticking to the pan, flip it over and
cook the fish for an additional 30 seconds. When
they are done, remove the fish pieces from the
pan (leaving the pan on the stovetop). Set the fish
aside while you assemble the rest of the dish.

To the pan in which you've cooked the fish,
add the white wine, vegetable stock, cooked
chickpeas, chopped truffles, and lemon juice
and bring this mixture to a boil. Add the escarole
to the pan and cook it until wilted. Add the
mussels and then return the fish to pan. Cover
the pan and cook the mussels and fish until all
the mussels have opened. If some mussels don't
open, discard them. Don't overcook.

To plate: Remove the mussels from the pan
and arrange them around the outside edge of
a platter. Using a slotted spoon, scoop out the
chickpeas and escarole and place them in the
center of the plate. Place the fish on top. Add the
remaining butter to the pan containing the fish
and vegetable liquid and bring this mixture to a
boil. Pour this sauce over the fish and serve.

TRUCK

391 OLD POST ROAD
BEDFORD, NY 10506
(914) 234-8900
TRUCKRESTAURANT.COM
CHEF/OWNER: NANCY ROPER

Named for the farm trucks that rumble down the edge of the Hudson Valley on New York State's Route 22, Nancy Roper's TRUCK manages to pay two different geographic homages in a single stroke. On one hand this stylish, idealized vision of rustic Americana is an ode to the local purveyors that provide TRUCK's raw ingredients. Much of the food that TRUCK serves is cultivated nearby—and this includes everything from de rigueur locally raised lettuces to the more daringly sourced Long Island Sound oysters of Jeff Northrup's New York Oyster Company in Westport, Connecticut.

But TRUCK also takes nourishment from the New Mexico of Chef Nancy Roper's youth. Its menu gives small-town America a Southwestern spin with accessible, family-friendly tacos, burritos, and quesadillas. TRUCK proves that multiple generations can enjoy meals of healthful, locally raised food together—and this includes fussy kids (who may have been—God help them—raised on prepackaged lunches). For parents, TRUCK offers excellent margaritas, craft-distilled spirits, and beer. For everyone, TRUCK slings dreamy, nostalgic desserts that include perfect, Lilliputian cones of frozen custard and the adorably miniature Snowball Cake, included here.

TRUCK SNOWBALL CAKE

(MAKES ONE 6-INCH CAKE, SERVES 4)

For the cake:

5 ounces organic unsalted butter, softened, plus
    more to butter cake pan
1 cup organic granulated sugar
¼ teaspoon sea salt (Roper prefers Maldon)
2 teaspoons baking powder
1½ cups organic cake flour
¼ cup cream of coconut (not coconut milk)
¼ cup water, room temperature
1 tablespoon rum
2 eggs

For the coconut cream cheese frosting:

8 ounces organic cream cheese, softened
2 ounces organic unsalted butter, softened
1 teaspoon pure vanilla extract
½ cup powdered sugar
1 cup sweetened coconut

To make the cake: Carefully cut a circle of parchment paper the exact size of the bottom of a 6-inch cake pan. (These can be purchased at professional bakeware stores.) Butter the cake pan with melted butter and line the bottom of the pan with the parchment round. Preheat oven to 350°F.

In the bowl of a stand mixer fitted with the paddle attachment, cream the butter and sugar on medium speed until the mixture is light and creamy. Meanwhile, in a large mixing bowl, stir together the salt, baking powder, and flour. In another bowl stir together the coconut cream, water, and rum and set aside. Once the butter and sugar are light and fluffy, add the eggs one at a time, beating until combined after each addition. When the eggs are fully incorporated, shut off the mixer and

scrape down the sides and bottom of the bowl to ensure that all ingredients are combined.

With the mixer set to its lowest speed, add one-third of the flour mixture to the mixing bowl. Pour in half of the coconut mixture. Continue alternating the dry and wet mixtures until all the ingredients are incorporated. Turn the mixer to medium speed and beat the batter for 3 minutes. Once the mixture is uniform, pour the batter into the prepared cake pan. Bake for 27–30 minutes, or until a cake tester comes out clean. Remove the cake from the oven and allow it to cool in the pan for 10 minutes. Invert the cake onto a baking rack and set aside.

To make the frosting: In the bowl of a stand mixer fitted with the paddle attachment, mix cream cheese, butter, and vanilla extract until the mixture is uniform and no clumps remain. Add in powdered sugar and ½ cup coconut, mixing until everything is well combined.

To assemble the cake: Once the cake is cool, slice it into two even layers with a serrated knife. Spread about 1 tablespoon frosting on a cardboard round or cake stand so that the cake adheres to a firm base. Place the bottom layer of the cake cut side up onto the cardboard or stand. Spread about ½ cup frosting onto this layer. Cover with plastic wrap and chill in the fridge for about 10 minutes. When the frosting is firm, top the first layer of the cake with the second layer, making sure that the rounded top of the cake remains on top of the assembled layer cake. Spread the remaining frosting over the top and sides of the assembled cake, making sure that all parts are covered. Finally, cover the sides and top of the cake with the remaining shredded coconut to create a furry snowball shape.

WESTCHESTER
COUNTY
{ SOUTH }

42 THE RESTAURANT

1 RENAISSANCE SQUARE
WHITE PLAINS, NY 10601
(914) 761-4242
42THERESTAURANT.COM
CHEF/OWNER: ANTHONY GONCALVES

It's a tough word to use with a straight face, but we're going to go ahead and call Chef Anthony Goncalves a maverick. He stepped into his first professional kitchen at Trotters Tavern in White Plains in 2001 when it was (for the previous four years) what Goncalves calls a "rock and roll place" with live music, chicken wings, and burgers. Up until 2001 Goncalves had been strictly front-of-house personnel, but he was forced into the kitchen after four chefs left Trotters Tavern in quick succession. "After working with these guys

and being in the kitchen—you know, trying to make it happen—I came to a place where I really knew what I wanted Trotters to be about." Goncalves had neither culinary school nor professional cooking experience, but he did have innate talent and an idiosyncratic understanding of food. It helped that Goncalves had grown up with a rich culinary tradition given to him by his close Portuguese-American family. Trotters dropped the word Tavern, and with Goncalves at the helm it became a Westchester sensation known for its virtually unclassifiable cooking that blended elite ingredients, Portuguese flavors, and American classics.

Chef Goncalves could have had an excellent career at Trotters. After all, the restaurant was conveniently located near the county seat, plus it was firmly entrenched as the watering hole for Westchester's movers and shakers. But in 2008 Goncalves teamed up with real estate developer Louis Cappelli to debut 42 the Restaurant on the 42nd floor of the new Ritz-Carlton Westchester towers. This stunning, glass-wrapped penthouse offers staggering views from the Hudson River to Long Island Sound. On clear days, diners can look through floor-to-ceiling windows and see both the twinkling lights of Manhattan and the dense, verdant canopy of northern Westchester.

At 42 (and its attached tapas bar, Bellota), Chef Goncalves dazzles with a unique brand of cooking that manages, like its setting, to keep an eye on multiple worlds. Having begun in American comfort food at Trotters Tavern, Goncalves spent several years at 42 working in the high-flying molecular gastronomy then popular at Spain's Arzak, El Bulli, and Berasetegui. Currently Goncalves has dialed back from the chemicals and potions of molecular gastronomy, but he's not regretful of where he's been. "Look, I needed to go through all that to get to where I am now. It takes a lot of work to get to a point of confidence. Now, if I'm making something and I start to smile, that's when I know this dish is going on the menu. It takes a long time to get to that point."

Razor Clam Crudo with "Shaving Cream"

(SERVES 6 AS AN APPETIZER)

For the clams:

2 pounds razor clams
Juice of half a lemon
6 ounces lemon olive oil, divided

For the sea lettuce vinaigrette:

4 ounces Moscato vinegar
8 ounces sea lettuce

For the shaving cream:

1½ cups clam juice
1½ cups white wine
2 sheets gelatin

Special equipment:

Whipped cream maker (see Note)

To clean and marinate the clams: Set up an ice bath and rest the razor clams in the bath placed in the refrigerator for 1 hour. Repeat three more times, changing the ice each time, in order to purge the clams of impurities. Shuck and trim the razor clams, retaining broth and shells. Vacuum seal the clean razor clams in a bag with a squeeze of lemon and 2 ounces of lemon olive oil. If you don't have a vacuum sealer, place the oil and clams in a zip bag and press out all the air. Immediately refrigerate the clams.

To make the vinaigrette: In a blender add the Moscato vinegar, sea lettuce, and remaining 4 ounces of lemon olive oil. Blend until emulsified, pour into a bowl, and refrigerate until needed.

To make the "shaving cream": In a saucepan over medium heat, simmer the clam juice and white wine until it is reduced by half. Meanwhile, bloom the gelatin sheets in 2 cups cold water. When clam juice/wine mixture is reduced, remove from the heat and strain it through a fine sieve. Return the strained mixture to a clean saucepan, add the softened gelatin sheets (discarding the water), and bring the mixture to a simmer. When the mixture is beginning to boil, remove the pan from the heat and place directly in an ice bath to cool the mixture quickly. Pour the chilled clam juice/wine mixture into the whipped cream maker and charge the canister according to the manufacturer's directions. Refrigerate the filled and charged canister until you're ready to plate.

To plate: Remove the razor clams from the bag and cut into a tartare-size dice. Place clams in a mixing bowl, add sea lettuce vinaigrette, and toss to combine. Plate the clams and use the ISI charger to gently add "shaving cream" to the razor clams.

Note: For this recipe you will need a CO_2-powered whipped cream maker. Chef Goncalves recommends those manufactured by iSi, available at Amazon.com.

ALVIN & FRIENDS

14 MEMORIAL HIGHWAY
NEW ROCHELLE, NY 10801
(914) 654-6549
ALVINANDFRIENDSRESTAURANT.COM
OWNER: ALVIN CLAYTON;
EXECUTIVE CHEF: MAURICE MAJOR

Alvin Clayton spent much of his childhood in Trinidad with a grandmother whose hospitality was so deeply ingrained that even delivery men bringing packages to her home were offered something to drink. Today her benevolent face overlooks the bar at chic Alvin & Friends, a contemporary southern and Caribbean restaurant that also functions as New Rochelle's de facto living room. When you're there, expect to rub elbows with everyone in town including, frequently, the mayor.

Clayton, an accomplished painter whose work hangs in the collections of Robert De Niro and Denzel Washington, might be familiar to anyone who has ever flipped through

the pages of *Elle, Vogue,* or *Esquire.* Clayton's stunning looks gained him an early career in modeling—even today Clayton is recognized as the cover model from countless L.L. Bean catalogs. But, happily, Clayton never relied on his face. In between his stints in front of the cameras, Clayton also worked in restaurants and eventually partnered with Denzel Washington and Debbie Allen in the Los Angeles contemporary southern restaurant, Georgia's.

Cue Alvin & Friends, the result of Clayton's relocation to the East Coast. It debuted in 2010 with a cuisine that effortlessly blends southern American and Caribbean culinary traditions. Its menu manages to embody *every* American's idea of soul food. When you visit, don't miss Clayton's gently lethal rum punch or the sophisticated fried chicken whose secret weapon is the poultry's par-cooking in Louisiana hot sauce. Also, it's wise not to skip Alvin's jerk duck breast, included here—like the restaurateur who invented it, it's sophisticated but with a warm heart.

JERK DUCK BREAST

(SERVES 6)

6 duck breasts

Salt and pepper to taste

1½ cups extra-virgin olive oil, plus a splash to season
    the duck

1 bunch cilantro, leaves removed from stems

1 bunch parsley, leaves removed from stems

1 bunch scallions (5–8), including some of the green part

10 sprigs thyme, leaves removed from stems

6 cloves garlic

¼ cup soy sauce

½ cup brown sugar

3 Scotch bonnet chiles

¾ cup ground allspice

One day before you intend to serve this dish, trim edges of duck breasts until each one is roughly oval in shape. Lightly score the fat of each slice with six slashes—each slash should be deep enough to reach all the way through the fat and slightly into the flesh. Season the duck with salt and pepper and add a splash of olive oil. Toss to combine in a bowl. Set duck aside.

In a food processor pulse the cilantro, parsley, scallions, thyme, garlic, soy sauce, brown sugar, scotch bonnets, allspice, and oil until it forms a coarse and wet mixture. If it seems dry, add more oil until the marinade is a coarse puree—but don't overprocess the herbs. Pour the marinade over the duck slices and, as Chef Major says, "Work in well with a lot of love." Cover with plastic and refrigerate for 24 hours.

To a medium-size sauté pan set over a medium-high heat, add the duck skin side down. Immediately reduce the heat to medium and cook the breasts, rendering their fat. Drain the pan of excess fat as you cook the duck breasts,

discarding the fat. Continue this process for about 5 minutes. At this point the skin of the breasts should be almost fully rendered of its thick, white fat, and their surfaces should be mahogany brown and crisp. Turn the duck breasts over and reduce heat to medium low. Continue to cook for 2–3 more minutes for medium rare, or longer for desired doneness. Let rest for 3 minutes before slicing. Serve.

CHIBOUST

14 MAIN STREET
TARRYTOWN, NY 10591
(914) 703-6550
CHIBOUST.COM
CHEF/OWNER: JILL ROSE

Here's the sort of thing that people don't realize about the glamorous world of restaurateurs: Often, their work is pretty grim. In 2004, when Chef Jill Rose was pulling together what would become one of Tarrytown's chicest spots, Chiboust, she found herself kneeling on the sidewalk in a strong, off-river January wind, bolting together a pastry case that she had bought on eBay. Says Rose, "I told my mother, 'Listen, I just signed this lease and I want you to come see it.' My mother walked in and she cried," laughs Rose. "And then when I was finished renovating, she walked in and she cried *again*. I was mortified. In her mind, you know, like a brick wall—she's of a different generation—that rustic, organic feel was not desired. If you have a brick wall, it should be painted. It should be perfect. I'm saying, 'It's finished!' She's saying, "No, it's *not* finished. You're not going to make it.'"

Rose's long, 12-foot-wide space had previously been a Laundromat. Its dirt basement had not been fully excavated—or, not sufficiently excavated for Rose's needs—and its soaring ceilings were decapitated by a dropped ceiling. Though a serious pastry chef coming out of Manhattan's Lespinasse and La Caravelle, Rose performed as much of the renovation labor herself as she could.

"It's funny because I was actually looking at some spaces in the city but I was living in Tarrytown, and there was just nothing here—nowhere to eat. There were a lot of Italian restaurants like Lago de Como, which I liked—it had some good years and then it fell by the wayside or went downhill. I was living here and it was, like, on my day off, 'Where do I go? There's nowhere here to eat.' One day I saw a for rent sign and I thought, 'Huh. This town could use a restaurant.'" The idea that the space had previously been the town's dreariest business, its Laundromat, was a positive for Rose. "I thought it would have good plumbing and electric and could probably handle a bakery oven and whatever I would need for a restaurant.

"I wanted a dessert-centric restaurant to take advantage of what I brought to the table in pastry, and I thought my reputation from the city would help in launching a restaurant. That's where I saw myself being most beneficial. Knowing that a small restaurant can't afford to have pastry chefs, I wanted that focus to be here at Chiboust. It wasn't something that had really been done in the suburbs.

"When I first started cooking, I was doing cooking—I wasn't doing pastry—and I have an affinity for the savory side. I always wanted to get back to that. I wanted the food to be simple and not complicated, clean, and, basically, a neighborhood bistro. You know—with good desserts." With characteristic independence, Rose adds, "I didn't aspire to do more than I thought that *I* could produce."

DOLCE DI COGNAC

(SERVES 6–8)

For the nut base:

1 cup sliced almonds, toasted and crushed
½ cup light brown sugar
⅓ cup melted unsalted butter

For the chocolate cognac cream:

1 cup Belgian chocolate "Extra Bitter"
    (72 percent cacao)
6 egg yolks, room temperature
3 tablespoons brewed espresso
1 tablespoon cognac
1¼ cups heavy cream

To make the nut base: In a stand mixer blend the almonds, brown sugar, and butter until the mixture is fully combined. Press into the bottom of an 8-inch round cake ring to form the base of the cake.

To make the chocolate cognac cream: In a double boiler (or very carefully in the microwave, being sure not to burn), melt the chocolate. In a medium-size bowl whip the egg yolks. Incorporate the chocolate, espresso, and cognac with the yolks and blend well. Separately whip the heavy cream until it holds soft peaks. Using a rubber spatula, fold the cream into the chocolate mixture. Do not overmix. Spread onto the nut base and chill for 1–2 hours. Unmold the cake ring and garnish with shaved chocolate.

Chutney Masala Bistro

4 West Main Street
Irvington, NY 10533
(914) 591-5500
CHUTNEYMASALA.COM
CHEF/OWNER: NAVJOT AURORA

If you go down the hill, around the corner, and then over the tracks, you'll find a pretty brick building, a vestige from Irvington's nineteenth-century industrial past. But, chances are you'll smell this building before you even see it—and your mouth will be watering by the time it comes into view. This is where Chutney Masala's Chef Navjot Aurora spins his spicy web, snaring hapless commuters as they step from the train.

Aurora's cooking manages to show perfect fidelity to his native India while simultaneously offering a didactic hand up to diners for whom the cuisine is unfamiliar. Chutney Masala's menu is as much a lesson as a bill of fare, and on it you *won't* find the Anglo-Indian standby—chicken tikka masala (a dish that's reputed to have been invented in Glasgow). There'll be no judgment if you ask for the Scottish innovation; Chutney Masala's servers will simply guide you to a better and more delicious dish.

Though faithful to Mother India, Chutney Masala is not closed-minded. Its two floors are decorated by the stunning work of the nineteenth-century photographer, Raja Deen Dayal, who unflinchingly depicted the Raj, India's troubled era as a British colony. On Aurora's beverage list, along with the expected Kingfisher and Taj Mahal beer, you'll find thoughtful gin and cucumber cocktails that selectively reference Britain, taking the good (and thoughtfully leaving the bad).

HARA BHARA KEBAB

(SERVES 8 AS AN APPETIZER)

For the tamarind chutney:

1 (4-ounce) piece tamarind from a pliable block (available at Indian specialty stores)

¾ cup hot water

¼ cup packed jaggery (available at Indian specialty stores) or dark brown sugar

1 teaspoon coriander seed

1 teaspoon cumin seeds

½ teaspoon garam masala powder

½ teaspoon cayenne

½ teaspoon salt

For the kebabs:

2 pounds potatoes, peeled

3 pounds spinach, chopped

1 pound green peas

1 pound paneer (available at Indian specialty stores)

1 cup roasted chana dal (available at Indian specialty stores)

2 tablespoons vegetable oil plus more for deep frying

¼ cup whole cumin seeds

⅓ cup peeled and chopped ginger

⅛ cup kasuri methi (dried fenugreek powder, available at Indian specialty stores)

½ cup garam masala (available at Indian specialty stores)

1 bunch cilantro, chopped

¼ cup chopped green chile

½ cup lemon juice

Salt to taste

2 tablespoons red chili powder

To make the chutney: In a small bowl gently mash tamarind with water until its pulp is softened. Strain the tamarind into a 2-quart saucepan, pressing firmly, then discard seeds and thick fibers. Add jaggery and cook the mixture over low heat, stirring, just until the jaggery is dissolved. Place the mixture in a bowl and reserve.

In a small skillet over moderate heat, toast the coriander and cumin seeds, stirring, until fragrant and a shade darker, about 2 minutes. Cool completely, then grind into a powder in a spice grinder. Stir ground spices, garam masala, cayenne, and salt into tamarind mixture. Reserve.

To make the kebabs: In a medium pot of boiling water, cook the peeled potatoes until soft but not mushy. When cooked, drain the potatoes and refrigerate them.

Meanwhile, in a large pot of boiling water set over high heat, blanch the spinach until wilted. While it is cooking, in a medium bowl set up an ice bath. When the spinach is wilted, remove it to the ice bath (leaving the pot of water boiling). When spinach is cool, drain it, squeezing the excess water from the spinach. Set aside.

Boil the peas until soft, remove to the ice bath, drain, and place peas in a bowl. Mash with a fork and set aside.

Grate the cooled potatoes along with the paneer in a food processor fitted with a grating disc (you can also do this on a box grater). Place the grated potatoes and paneer in a large bowl. Chop the roasted *chana dal* in a food processor and add to the potatoes and paneer.

In a medium pan heat 2 tablespoons oil and sauté the cumin seeds, chopped ginger, and *kasuri methi* until the ginger is soft. Place in a bowl with the cooked potatoes, spinach, and peas. Add garam masala, paneer, cilantro, chile, lemon juice, salt, and chili powder. Form the

mixture into patties ¾ inch thick by 2 inches in diameter. Panfry the patties in vegetable oil until crisp and golden.

To serve: Plate with tamarind chutney and serve while still hot.

THE COOKERY

39 CHESTNUT STREET
DOBBS FERRY, NY 10522
(914) 305-2336
THECOOKERYRESTAURANT.COM
EXECUTIVE CHEF/OWNER: DAVID DIBARI;
CHEF DE CUISINE: SAMMY JIMENEZ;
GENERAL MANAGER/BEVERAGE DIRECTOR: RALPH RUBINO

Almost everything about The Cookery pushes someone's buttons. Not only is its dining room small and loud, but you can't reserve a table for fewer than six diners. The restaurant is located on a virtually unparkable block, and Chef David DiBari's menu is lavish with transgressive foods like crispy duck tongues, jiggly bone marrow, and the roasted, split heads of lambs. At The Cookery you'll find no veal chop, and there is no $200 bottle of Barolo. Some conservative diners will find themselves at sea.

And yet it works. In spades. On any given night The Cookery is jammed with rabid fans, only some of whom have come for DiBari's outré foodstuffs. Mostly, The Cookery's customers return for heartbreaking pastas, unspeakably carnal charcuterie, and supernaturally fluffy meatballs. They're there for DiBari's hand-stretched mozzarella that's so tender, it's only barely coherent. While whole pigs and duck tongues might snag the camera-phone snaps, it's the finesse of The Cookery's kitchen that keeps diners coming back.

DiBari, who was not yet thirty years old when he opened The Cookery in 2009, had nevertheless been working in professional kitchens for more than half his life. Having grown up in Verplanck, New York, DiBari started working at the Paradise Restaurant, located a few doors from his home, at the tender age of fourteen. After attending The Culinary Institute of America, DiBari's trajectory took him through some of the highest profile kitchens in Manhattan: Windows on the World, David Bouley's Danube, Patroon. Most notably, DiBari worked for three years in the notorious kitchen of Mario Batali's Babbo; it was an experience that prepared him for restaurant ownership at an age when most young men can't cover their car payments.

"It's been an evolution, but The Cookery will always be my baby. There might be other restaurants, other concepts, but this will always be my launching pad. It's just full of soul and good energy, and everyone here collaborates." At the time of writing, DiBari was already in the midst of launching his third venture, The Parlor, a wood-fired pizza restaurant. It joins DoughNation, DiBari's mobile wood-fired pizza truck.

THE COOKERY'S
ROAST SUCKLING PIG

(SERVES 8–12)

For the brine:

2 gallons water
1½ pounds salt
2 tablespoons fennel seeds
1 tablespoon ground star anise
1 tablespoon red pepper flakes
2 bay leaves
1½ pounds granulated sugar
1 (20-25 pound) suckling pig, skinned and gutted

For the quince honey glaze:

2 tablespoons quince or apple vinegar
4 tablespoons honey

For the roasted suckling pig:

¼ cup whole cloves garlic
3 large carrots, cut into 2-inch lengths
½ head of celery (about 6 stalks), cut into 2-inch lengths
3 white onions, quartered
10 Yukon Gold potatoes, cut in half

To brine the pig: On the day before you intend to cook the pig, bring the water, salt, spices, and sugar to a boil in a large stockpot. Stir to dissolve the sugar, then remove the brine from the heat. Chill the brine until it is very cold. Select a container large enough to fit the pig with room to spare, then place the pig in it and pour the cooled brine over the top. Make sure that the entire pig is fully submerged; weight the pig down with a heavy bowl or plate, if necessary, to keep it covered in brine. Brine the pig, refrigerated, for 24 hours.

To make the glaze: Combine the vinegar and honey and reserve.

To toast the pig: Preheat oven to 300°F. In a roasting pan large enough to hold the whole pig, place the garlic cloves, carrots, celery, onions, and potatoes. Use the vegetables as a bed on which to lay the pig. Arrange the pig on the vegetables so that the back legs stretch forward. Roast the pig in the preheated oven for 7 minutes per pound, or at least 3 hours. About 5 minutes before the end of the roasting time, raise the oven temperature to 500°F. Roast the pig at high heat for 5 minutes to crisp the skin. After 5 minutes remove the pig from the oven and place it on a board or platter. Brush the pig with the quince glaze until it shines. Using a silicone spatula, stir the vegetables remaining in the roasting pan to coat them with the pork juices, being sure to scrape up any of the tasty brown bits stuck to the bottom of the pan. Arrange the vegetables around the pig and serve.

Kale Salad

(SERVES 4)

For the soft-poached eggs:

4 large eggs

For the salad:

1 pound fresh black or red kale, de-stemmed, cut into bite-size pieces, and washed thoroughly
½ small red onion, sliced thin
4 tablespoons coarsely chopped toasted almonds
¾ teaspoon quince vinegar
½ teaspoon extra-virgin olive oil
4 soft poached eggs (recipe follows)
Salt and black pepper to taste

To soft-poach the eggs: In a medium pot of boiling water, carefully submerge the eggs. Cook the eggs in gently boiling water for exactly 5 minutes. While the eggs are cooking, prepare an ice bath. When the eggs have cooked for 5 minutes, shock them in ice water to halt further cooking. Allow the eggs to sit in the ice for at least 15 minutes before you proceed. Take this time to prepare the rest of the salad.

To make the salad: Toss the kale, onion and almonds together. Lightly whisk vinegar and oil together and use to dress the salad, to taste. Season with salt and pepper. Place on a platter. Peel the eggs very carefully by cracking and peeling their shells under cold running water. Allow the water to slip underneath the membrane that lies between the shell and the egg white. This will allow you to peel the eggs more easily without breaking them. Cut the boiled eggs in half, lengthwise, exposing their runny yolks. Arrange the eggs over the salad and serve.

Cauliflower Ravioli

(SERVES 6)

For the cauliflower filling:

2 tablespoons olive oil

1 head cauliflower, coarsely chopped

2 tablespoons peeled, chopped garlic

¼ pound (1 stick) unsalted butter

Pinch of chopped fresh thyme

1 cup milk

6 ounces brioche bread, coarsely chopped

1 ounce Grana Padano cheese

Pinch of red pepper flakes

Salt and pepper to taste

For the pasta dough:

1 teaspoon salt

3 whole eggs

8 egg yolks

¾ teaspoon extra-virgin olive oil

3¾ pounds flour

2 eggs, beaten, for an egg wash

For the pasta sauce:

12 tablespoons unsalted butter

36 slivers garlic

2 pinches of red pepper flakes

A few 6-ounce ladles of the water in which you have
    cooked the ravioli

3 teaspoons grated Parmigiano Reggiano

Few pinches of bread crumbs

Drizzle of lemon olive oil

To prepare the filling: In a large stockpot heat the oil and add the cauliflower. Sauté the cauliflower until it is well caramelized. Add the garlic, butter, and thyme and cook the mixture for another 5 minutes. Pour in the milk, then add the bread and the Grana Padano. Allow the bread to absorb the liquid, thickening the mixture. Cool the filling. When the mixture is cool, puree in a food processor until smooth. Reserve.

To make the pasta: In a stand mixer fitted with the dough hook attachment, combine the salt, eggs, and olive oil. Slowly add the flour until the mixture forms a ball. Add more flour, sparingly, if the dough seems too wet. The pasta dough should form a ball, but it will be sticky to the touch. Form the dough into two balls and allow them to rest on a floured surface for about half an hour.

After the dough has rested, roll it out: Using a rolling pin on a floured surface, roll it into two long rectangles. The dough should be about ½ inch thick. Set up a pasta maker fitted with rollers and dial to the machine's widest setting. Flour one pasta sheet on both sides, then begin rolling the sheet between the rollers. Progressively dial down the width of the rollers, making the dough thinner with each pass. Stop at the second to narrowest setting; repeat the rolling process with the second sheet. After both sheets have passed through the machine at the second to narrowest setting, lay them out onto a floured surface.

To form the ravioli: You will need a square or round ravioli mold (available online or at many cookware stores). Lightly flour the bottom half of the mold and lay one sheet of pasta dough over the mold. Use the other part of the mold to make depressions in the pasta sheet; these will be the pockets that you fill with cauliflower stuffing. Lightly brush the dough with egg wash.

Fit a pastry bag with a ½-inch round tip and fill the bag with the cool cauliflower stuffing. Use the pastry bag to fill each dimple in the pasta dough

with the ravioli stuffing. You will use approximately 1 ounce per ravioli. Lay the other sheet of pasta dough on top of the filling and lightly press it onto the bottom sheet with your hands. Carefully replace the top of the mold and, with a rolling pin, roll over the entire mold to press. Flip the ravioli mold over and the entire sheet of ravioli will pop off. On a pan lined with parchment paper and then floured, place the ravioli and freeze until you are ready to use. Freezing the ravioli makes them easier to separate without breakage. Repeat the molding process until you have used all the dough.

To finish the ravioli: Drop the frozen ravioli in salted boiling water and cook for at least 3–4 minutes. If the ravioli have not been frozen, they will cook in 1½–2 minutes. Place a sauté pan large enough to accommodate all the ravioli over medium heat, and into that place the butter, garlic, and red pepper flakes. When the butter is brown, turn off the heat and add a few 6-ounce ladlesful of pasta water. Add the cooked ravioli to the pan and cook them in the sauce, swirling, until the sauce thickens, reduces, and becomes a silky coating on the ravioli. Remove the pan from the heat, then add the Parmigiano Reggiano and swirl until it is incorporated. Plate the ravioli and garnish with bread crumbs and a drizzle of lemon olive oil.

HALF MOON

1 HIGH STREET
DOBBS FERRY, NY 10522
(914) 693-4130
HALFMOONHUDSON.COM
OWNERS: BRUCE BERNACCHIA AND ANGELO LIBERATORE;
EXECUTIVE CHEF: VINCENT BARCELONA;
CHEF DE CUISINE: ENRIQUE ESTRADA

Named for the ship on which Henry Hudson first sailed up his (eventually) eponymous river, the idea for this sister restaurant to Harvest-on-Hudson was triggered by a stroke of someone's bad luck. When Landry's, the parent company of the tourist-driven Chart House chain of restaurants, fell into dire financial straits (it also owns Bubba Gump's Shrimp, by the way), some of its prized waterfront real estate fell onto the market. As foodies know, the chain—which once hogged some of the most spectacular water views in the country—used its gorgeous siting to sell overpriced chain store cuisine. Its Dobbs Ferry jetty (a promontory that was built in the nineteenth century as a lumber depot) was no different from the other Chart Houses. The spot yielded stunning views of the Hudson and the imposing Palisades beyond. However, when the team behind Harvest-on-Hudson, Fort Pond Bay, took over the Chart House keys, Chef Vincent Barcelona discovered an alarming number of microwaves in the kitchen. And there was a lot of cleaning to do. A *lot* of cleaning. More diplomatically, Barcelona observes, "They had let it go; it had fallen into disrepair."

The new restaurant's theme was to be simple: Exploit the sources that the Fort Pond Bay Company had already developed with its two Montauk properties (East by

Northeast and the Stone Lion Inn) to offer sparklingly fresh Long Island seafood on the banks of the Hudson. Instead of Muzac and plastic nautical maps, Half Moon offers, according to Chef Barcelona, "Beach cuisine: clambakes and microbrews. Fish cooked on the *plancha*. Duck tacos. Bottles of beer served in buckets of ice." Its wraparound decks offer staggering views to the glittering lights of Manhattan. To the north you'll see the twinkling arc of the Tappan Zee.

Whatever Barcelona is doing, it seems to be working. What was once a moribund, semi-forgotten chain restaurant (at whose heart lay banks of freezers and microwaves) is now a thronged restaurant serving as many as 600 diners per night!

PLANCHA-SEARED SEA BASS WITH GREEN MANGO, CHERRY TOMATO & CHINESE LONG BEAN SALAD WITH FRAGRANT TAMARIND COCONUT & MINT EMULSIONS

(SERVES 4)

For the tamarind vinaigrette:

¼ cup lime juice

2 tablespoons finely ground palm sugar

½ teaspoon Thai fish sauce

1 teaspoon tamarind paste

½ teaspoon kosher salt

1 (½-inch) piece fresh ginger, peeled and sliced

1 Thai chile, finely chopped

1 tablespoon extra-virgin olive oil

For the fragrant coconut emulsion:

1 cup unsweetened coconut juice

3 tablespoons unsweetened coconut milk

3 tablespoons fresh lime juice

1 small jalapeño

1 stalk lemongrass

1 (2-inch) piece fresh ginger, peeled and sliced thinly

2 tablespoons granulated sugar

12 Kaffir lime leaves, finely chopped

For the mint emulsion:

¾ teaspoon cornstarch

½ teaspoon salt

1½ cups fresh mint leaves

½ cup corn oil or other neutral oil

For the green mango, cherry tomato, and Chinese long bean salad:

4 Chinese long beans, trimmed and cut into 2-inch pieces

1 small green mango, peeled and julienned

1 small ripe mango, peeled and julienned

1 cup bean sprouts

24 cherry tomatoes

½ cup fresh cilantro leaves

Tamarind vinaigrette

Salt and pepper

For the black sea bass and final plating:

4 fillets of black sea bass, skin on, pin bones removed

Salt and pepper

¼ cup grapeseed oil

To make the vinaigrette: Place all the ingredients except the olive oil in a blender. Add 3 tablespoons water and blend the mixture until smooth. With the machine running, add the olive oil and blend until the mixture is emulsified. Set aside.

To make the coconut emulsion: Put all the ingredients except the Kaffir lime leaves into a medium saucepan and bring the mixture to a simmer. Add the Kaffir lime leaves and simmer for a few more minutes. Set aside to cool to room temperature.

To make the mint emulsion: Fill a medium bowl with ice and water. Put the cornstarch and ½ teaspoon salt into a small saucepan with 3 teaspoons water. Over medium heat bring the mixture to a boil, whisking until it is thick and clear. Transfer this to a small bowl and set the bowl over (not into) the ice water bath.

Fill a large bowl with water and ice and set aside. Bring a small pot of water to a boil and add the mint leaves. As soon as the water returns to a boil, drain the leaves into a colander. Immediately transfer the mint leaves to the ice water to stop further cooking. Squeeze the mint leaves to drain as much water as possible, and then transfer to a blender. Add the corn oil and blend this mixture until smooth. Add the cornstarch mixture and blend the mint and cornstarch mixtures until they are emulsified. Strain through a fine mesh sieve, pressing on the solids to extract as much of the emulsion as possible. Set aside.

To make the salad: In a large bowl toss all the salad ingredients with tamarind vinaigrette to taste. Season with salt and pepper and set aside.

To finish the dish: Dust the fillets with salt and pepper. In a large, flat sauté pan, heat the grapeseed oil over medium heat. Place the sea bass skin side down in the pan and sauté for 1 minute on medium heat. Reduce heat to low and sauté for 3 more minutes. Flip the fillets over and

continue to cook them on low heat for 2 more minutes. Remove the fillets from the sauté pan and set aside. In a small pan return the fragrant coconut emulsion to a simmer.

On four large dinner plates, divide the salad and place it off center on the plates. Pour ¼ cup of the fragrant coconut milk emulsion into the center of each plate. Place one fillet on each plate, leaning onto the salad, and then drizzle 1 teaspoon of mint emulsion on the side of each fillet, allowing it to spill into the coconut milk. Serve.

Harper's

92 Main Street
Dobbs Ferry, NY 10522
(914) 693-2306
HARPERSONMAIN.COM
Owner/Executive Chef: Chris Vergara;
Owner/General Manager: Justin Montgomery;
Beverage Director: Clark Moore

One of the things that happens in any tightly knit restaurant community is that, inevitably, chefs start to take cues from each other. In the hotbed dining scene of Westchester's River Towns—Hastings-on-Hudson, Dobbs Ferry, Irvington, and Tarrytown—it's no different. Says Chef Chris Vergara about his inspiration for Harper's in Dobbs Ferry, "A lot of Harper's had to do with conversations that I was having with Chef David DiBari of The Cookery." The penny dropped for Vergara, who'd been cooking at Meritage (a Scarsdale restaurant that he has co-owned with Jamie Steinthal since 2004), when he saw what was happening in the kitchen of The Cookery. "David was, and still is, doing beautiful food that was exciting and different. The fact that he had such a success with this at The Cookery told us that there was a clientele in the River Towns that was ready for what we wanted to do."

The difference between glitzy, moneyed Scarsdale and the bohemian River Towns couldn't be more profound. According to Vergara, Dobbs Ferry "is one of the more artistic communities in Westchester. They're just more adventurous." In the Dobbs Ferry kitchen of Harper's, Vergara was finally able to practice nose-to-tail cooking. "We buy whole animals and, when you do that, there are always cuts that are difficult to sell. But, in the River Towns it seems like it's more difficult to sell the loin than it is to sell the neck. When it comes to total product utilization, it's a lot easier to sell an off-cut here."

Though it demands much more from a kitchen to break down whole carcasses, Vergara is adamant about buying whole animals. "It's both a quality thing and a control thing at the same time. I mean, I know where the lamb was raised, I know what it ate. I know who raised it, and I know when it was slaughtered. Plus, I have complete control over custom cuts. I can cut my steaks however I want; I can cut my loins and racks however I want. I could bone out the neck or leave it whole. That, and we have the option of hanging it, which you don't get when you buy precut Cryovac-ed meat products."

It wasn't always easy for Vergara, who relates the story of trying to break down his first whole pig. "I lucked out because, when I bought the business at Meritage [when he

was twenty-five], it came with a band saw. But when I bought my first pig, I had no idea what I was doing. I'd never taken apart a whole animal. So I'm standing in the basement kitchen and I'm basically hacking this thing to pieces, and the guy who was mopping the floor at the time, his family owned a *carniceria* in Mexico. He was my dishwasher. After fifteen minutes of watching me fumble around with this pig, he took the knife away from me and showed me how to do it. And he got a raise after that: He put down the mop and picked up a boning knife."

But the challenges of storage, labor, and time all argue against buying whole animals, which is why, as we speak, those Cryovac-ed blister packs are being popped in kitchens all over the world. Vergara will never go that route. "Because the difference in quality is that drastic, I'll take the Pepsi Challenge with the lamb that we're using against any lamb in the country from any farmer. It's amazing. It eats like veal, and that gamy flavor that you usually associate with lamb is more subtle and nuanced in our lamb. It's like nothing else. It's the same thing with our pork; it tastes like pork, you know what I mean? Instead of chicken or whatever the hell you get from those god-awful factory farms."

In the recipe following, Vergara features one of the lesser known (and appreciated) cuts. "I love that you're taking the breast, which is impossible to buy anywhere, and turning it into this delicious thing. That has a lot of appeal on a lot of levels. The lamb breast—or the shoulder for that matter—isn't something that you just throw into a pan, flip, and it's done. It takes a little bit of time, and there's a transformation that happens when the connective tissue breaks down. It yields this thing that is, in my opinion, better than any loin that you can get."

SLOW ROASTED LAMB BREAST
WITH WARM VEGETABLE SALAD, YOGURT & MINT

(SERVES 6)

For the lamb marinade:

1 cup parsley, stems removed
¼ cup thyme leaves
1 tablespoon rosemary leaves
2 cloves garlic
4 salted anchovy fillets, rinsed
Zest and juice of 1 lemon
¼ cup extra-virgin olive oil
1 teaspoon red pepper flakes
1 tablespoon salt
1 tablespoon freshly cracked black pepper

For the lamb:

5 pounds bone-in lamb breast, membrane removed
Salt
1–2 cups dry white wine

For the lemon vinaigrette:

1 tablespoon Dijon mustard
Zest and juice of 1 lemon (about 3 tablespoons)
1 teaspoon minced garlic
½ cup extra-virgin olive oil
Salt and pepper

For the warm vegetable salad:

3 medium-size fennel bulbs, cut in sixths with
    the core intact

2 medium-size red onions, peeled and sliced in
    ½-inch rounds

2 tablespoons extra-virgin olive oil

Salt and pepper to taste

1 pound fingerling potatoes, cooked until just
    tender and halved lengthwise

2 tablespoons dill

2 tablespoons mint

2 tablespoons parsley

Lemon vinaigrette

For the minted yogurt:

12 ounces Old Chatham Sheepherding Co.
    plain sheep's milk yogurt

2 tablespoons honey

2 tablespoons white wine vinegar

1 tablespoon extra-virgin olive oil

1 tablespoon ground toasted cumin seed

Zest and juice of 1 lemon

1 tablespoon mint, cut into a chiffonade

Salt and black pepper to taste

To prepare the marinade: In the bowl of a food processor (or in a mortar and pestle), place all ingredients and process until well combined but still chunky.

To cook the lamb: Preheat oven to 275°F. Lightly season the lamb breast with salt. Thoroughly rub the marinade into the meat on all sides. Select a roasting pan that fits the entire lamb snugly and place the lamb in, meat side up. Pour white wine into the pan and cover the pan with aluminum foil. Roast until tender, 3–5 hours, checking every hour or so to make sure that the pan isn't dry. (If it is, add water.) When it's fully cooked, the rib bones should pull easily away from the meat.

When done, allow the lamb to cool to room temperature. Place a roasting pan of equal size directly on top of the lamb and load with 2–3 pounds of weight. Move the lamb to the refrigerator and press for 4–6 hours, but preferably overnight. This will squeeze out the extra fat and give the lamb uniform thickness. When cool, slice into equal-size portions. Set aside.

To make the lemon vinaigrette: In a small bowl whisk together the mustard, lemon, and garlic. While continuing to whisk, add the olive oil in a thin, steady stream and whisk until the vinaigrette is emulsified. Season to taste with salt and pepper.

To prepare the salad: In a small mixing bowl, combine the fennel and red onions. Toss with olive oil and salt and pepper to taste. Grill over medium-high heat, turning occasionally, until the vegetables are tender but not mushy. In the same bowl repeat with the fingerlings and grill until they are well marked. Toss potatoes with the fennel and red onions (reserving the dill, mint, parsley, and lemon vinaigrette for plating). Set aside.

To make the minted yogurt: Whisk all ingredients together, then taste and adjust seasoning. Reserve.

To assemble the plates: In a medium pan over medium heat, warm the fennel, onion, and potato mixture over low heat. Toss in reserved dill, mint, and parsley and dress to taste with lemon vinaigrette. Over medium heat in a charcoal or wood-burning grill, grill the lamb portions until they are nicely charred and lamb is warmed through. Arrange the vegetable salad on a platter and top with lamb. Serve the yogurt on the side.

Barman, Myth

I'd heard rumblings about the mythic Clark for more than a year before I met him. At the River Roadhouse, Thalia Rayow, perennial bartender to off-shift restaurant workers, claimed that Clark was the best bartender working in Westchester. Chef David DiBari of The Cookery and The Parlor admitted to me once, over many whiskeys (looking somewhat pained), that this mythic Clark was absolutely the Real Deal; sadly, he wasn't under his employ.

Like Billy the Kid, Clark Moore was a hard man to track down. At that point, Moore was pulling the occasional shift over at the "Roadie" when he wasn't slinging drinks at the Tapp in Tarrytown or grading papers. A naturally occurring River Towns eccentric, the thin and bearded Moore teaches writing at Westchester Community College, where he manages to sneak his beloved Beat writers into his Beginning English Composition curriculum; he corrects his class's papers while sitting at the bar. Happily, Moore finally found a permanent home as Harper's beverage director, where you can find him slinging artfully composed drinks whose names bear the occasional William Burroughs allusion.

Says Harper's chef/owner, Chris Vergara, "The idea behind the cocktail program at Harper's was—in a cheeky way—to under-promise and over-deliver. So you walk into a place that doesn't have tablecloths and there's no pretense of a fancy restaurant, but then you sit down at the bar and meet Clark, and he's making amazingly well-thought-out, farmers' market cocktails. All of a sudden you're sitting on those crappy stools at the concrete bar thinking, 'Where the hell am I? This is really good!'"

MINT & PEAS COCKTAIL

(SERVES 1)

6–8 mint leaves
2 bar spoons blanched spring peas
1 very light pinch of salt
1 light pinch of black pepper
¾ ounce mint syrup
¾ ounce fresh lime juice
2 ounces Square One organic cucumber vodka
¼ ounce yellow Chartreuse
1 light splash of club soda

Place the mint, peas, salt, pepper, syrup, and juice in a mixing glass and muddle. Add vodka and Chartreuse and lightly shake with ice. Strain into a round Old Fashioned glass filled with crushed ice. Splash with soda and garnish with mint leaves and flowers.

Harvest-on-Hudson

1 River Street
Hastings, NY 10706
(914) 478-2800
harvesthudson.com
Owners: Bruce Bernacchia and Angelo Liberatore;
Executive Chef: Vincent Barcelona

Here's why every diner in the Hudson River Valley owes a debt to Bruce Bernacchia and Angelo Liberatore: When others saw a degraded parcel of land that was being used as a Robison Oil truck depot (because of its proximity to shipping via the Hudson), Bernacchia and Liberatore had the insane vision to see the land as a sort of neo-Tuscan plantation, Harvest-on-Hudson.

In the late 1990s—and that's way before the other Hudson-side restaurant pioneers: X2O, Red Hat on the River, and RiverMarket Bar & Kitchen—Bernacchia and Liberatore took the flight of Westchester's Hudson-side industry as an opportunity to uncover the land's inherent beauty. The pair purchased the trash- and rubble-strewn lot and began a long process of remediation that uncovered panoramic views of the Hudson River and the regal, red swoop of the Palisades beyond. Bernacchia and Liberatore surrounded

their new restaurant with raised planting beds that they filled with growing vegetables and herbs. In summer these morph into outdoor rooms whose living walls are literally made of homegrown food. It's not just decoration, either—Chef Vincent Barcelona, a Le Bernardin alum, takes much of what grows in Harvest's gardens for his kitchen. Expect a menu that celebrates the shared Italian heritage of Barcelona, Liberatore, and Bernacchia.

Since its debut in 2000, Harvest has become known for its stunning river views, but we prefer the view closer in—say, at our feet, where the Hudson's bankside soil was reclaimed from its industrial past.

Whole Roasted Montauk Skate Wing with Preserved Harvest Garden Tomatoes, Vinegar Peppers & White Anchovy Tomato Vinaigrette

(SERVES 4 AS A MAIN DISH)

For the vinegar garden peppers:

Enough freshly picked Anaheim or cherry peppers to fit snugly into 2 (quart-size) Ball or Mason jars
1¼ cups white vinegar
1½ cups water
⅛ cup sea salt

For the tomato and white anchovy vinaigrette:

4 Sicilian white anchovy fillets, chopped
5 whole canned San Marzano tomatoes, seeds removed, and chopped into large dice
Juice of 2 lemons
¼ cup extra-virgin olive oil
Salt and pepper to taste

For the skate:

2 large skate wings on the bone, each cut in half to make 4 equal servings
3 tablespoons canola oil
Salt and pepper

1 tablespoon unsalted butter
4 home-canned Roma (plum) tomatoes, peeled (an equal number of canned San Marzano tomatoes may be substituted)
12 Sicilian white anchovy fillets (optional)
4 garden cherry peppers preserved in vinegar, cut into quarters
4 garden Anaheim peppers preserved in vinegar, cut lengthwise into strips
Tomato anchovy vinaigrette

To pickle the peppers: Wash the peppers well and place them in two clean, 1-quart Mason or Ball jars. In a medium-size saucepan boil the vinegar, water, and sea salt. Pour this mixture over the peppers and immediately screw on the lids until barely snug (don't fully tighten; once the mixture cools, you'll need to tighten the lids fully for storage). Allow the peppers to pickle in the refrigerator for 1 or 2 days before use.

Note: Harvest's vinegar peppers may be kept in the refrigerator or a cool cellar or pantry for up to 1 year unopened.

To make the vinaigrette: In a medium bowl place the anchovies and tomatoes. Whisk in the lemon juice and, while whisking, add the olive oil. Season to taste with salt and pepper and reserve.

To prepare the skate: Preheat oven to 400°F. Clean the skate by running it under cold water to remove its natural slime. Use a cleaver or heavy knife to trim each wing's bony edges back to where the meat begins. Heat two ovenproof sauté pans, each large enough to fit two pieces of skate wing. Split the oil between the pans and heat until it begins to smoke. Lay two pieces of wing in each pan and agitate the pans to prevent the fish from sticking. Lower the heat under the pans to medium and continue cooking the skate for about 2 minutes.

Flip the wings and sauté for 2 more minutes, then place the pans in the oven for 8 minutes. Remove the skate from the pans onto a platter and, using a spatula or a fork, remove the skin from both sides of each piece. (It will pull away from the flesh easily.) Season the skate with salt and pepper. Divide the butter between the pans and, when the butter is hot, return the fish to the pans. Reduce the heat under the pans to low and sear the fish, basting continuously with butter, until the bottoms of the wings are golden and lightly crusted.

To plate the dish: Place the skate in the center of a large serving platter and arrange the tomatoes, anchovy fillets (if used), and the two types of vinegar peppers around it. Drizzle the fish and vegetables with vinaigrette. Serve.

JUNIPER

575 WARBURTON AVENUE
HASTINGS-ON-HUDSON, NY 10706
(914) 478-2542
JUNIPERHASTINGS.COM
EXECUTIVE CHEF/OWNER: ALEX SZE

For such a soft-spoken man, Chef Alex Sze has a lot of nerve. With no cooking experience whatsoever, Sze somehow managed to scam his way into the kitchen of Washington, DC's Citronelle under the Gallic icon, Chef Michel Richard. Richard, having hired Sze as a pastry chef, was soon confronted with Sze's total lack of experience. Still, he spotted something in the recent UConn biology graduate and took Sze under his wing. Over a period of three years at Citronelle, Richard led Sze through every aspect of working in a professional French kitchen, eventually allowing the young chef (for so he had become) to man Citronelle's grill and sauté stations.

Sze took what he learned at Citronelle to move into other elite restaurants in and around D.C. before returning to the Northeast (Sze was raised in Hamden, Connecticut).

In 2009, when Sze was only twenty-seven, he debuted Juniper, a tiny BYOB in sleepy Hastings-on-Hudson. Instantly, Juniper drew the loyalty of devoted regulars and raves from the critics. Even other chefs were vocal fans; Hastings-on-Hudson resident, Chef Andy Nusser (of Mario Batali's Tarry Lodge), calls Juniper "a gem."

What's not to love? With its open kitchen, light-filled windows, and glass counter holding pastries and desserts, Juniper emanates a breezy, almost offhanded energy that disguises its secret weapon: the finesse in Sze's ever-changing, French-inflected menu. Dishes like red beet and yogurt gazpacho (recipe follows), might come and go overnight, but whatever is on Juniper's menu, we know that it'll be good.

Red Beet & Yogurt Gazpacho
with Poached Shrimp Sausage, Trout Roe, Pickled Golden Beets, Horseradish Mousse, Dill, Rye Croutons

(SERVES 4 AS A STARTER)

For the shrimp sausage:

1 cup (½ pound) chopped shrimp
1 teaspoon grated ginger
3½ tablespoons sliced green onion
½ teaspoon salt
¼ cup cream
Pinch of white pepper

For the rye croutons:

2 slices rye bread
Olive oil

For the horseradish mousse:

½ cup crème fraîche
1 teaspoon horseradish
Salt to taste

For the pickled beets:

1 pound golden beets
¾ cup granulated sugar
⅔ cup white wine vinegar
⅔ cup water
1⅓ tablespoons mustard seeds
½ teaspoon salt

For the red beet gazpacho:

2 sliced shallots
2 sprigs fresh thyme
1 bay leaf
3½ teaspoons salt
¼ cup olive oil

1 pound peeled chopped beets
4 cups vegetable stock
½ cup plain yogurt
2 tablespoons white balsamic vinegar
Pepper to taste
4 sprigs fresh dill, for garnish
2 tablespoons trout roe

To make the shrimp sausage: Beat all the ingredients together in a large mixing bowl. Pour mixture into the center of a piece of plastic wrap and form a 1½-inch-thick sausage log. Twist ends of plastic to seal.

Bring a large pot of water to a boil. Drop in the plastic-wrapped sausage and turn off heat. Poach in hot water for 8–10 minutes until cooked through.

To make the rye croutons: Preheat oven to 325°F. Brush the bread with olive oil and cut into squares. Place on a sheet pan and bake for 10–12 minutes until golden brown.

To make the horseradish mousse: Whip crème fraîche until it holds stiff peaks. Fold in horseradish. Season with salt and reserve.

To pickle the beets: Toss beets with olive oil. Wrap in foil. Roast in a 350°F oven for 35 minutes. Cool and peel off skin. In a large saucepan bring sugar, vinegar, water, mustard seeds, and salt to a boil. Remove from heat, add beets, and pickle in the refrigerator for at least 24 hours.

To make the red beet gazpacho: In a large sized saucepan, sweat shallots, thyme, bay leaf, and salt in olive oil over medium-low heat for 5–10 minutes, or until the shallots are soft and translucent. Add chopped beets and vegetable stock. Bring to a boil over high heat, then turn down to low and simmer for 30 minutes, or until beets are fork tender. Remove bay leaf. Add

yogurt and white balsamic vinegar, then place everything in a blender and blend for 5 minutes until smooth. Chill.

To serve: Pour gazpacho into four bowls and garnish with sausage, rye croutons, horseradish mousse, pickled beets, dill, and trout roe.

LULU CAKE BOUTIQUE

40 GARTH ROAD
SCARSDALE, NY 10583
(914) 722-8300
EVERYTHINGLULU.COM
CO-OWNERS/BAKERS: JAY MUSE AND VICTOR GONZALEZ

Located smack in the center of downtown Scarsdale, Lulu Cake Boutique might be a tiny designer's atelier or an expensive jewelry shop. Instead, it's a bijoux bakery for all the world as precious as the rest of the glittering shops that line the moneyed streets just outside its doors.

It seems a given that the two bakers who ultimately created infinitely detailed specialty cakes for Madonna, Mariah Carey, Whoopi Goldberg, and Jimmy Fallon should choose to set up shop in the swank locale of Scarsdale. But it turns out that nothing could be further from the truth; the ideal siting of Lulu Cake Boutique was just luck, pure and simple.

Says co-owner/baker Jay Muse of Lulu's debut back in 1999, "I had no clue. I just read the real estate section in the *Times* every Sunday, just looking for a bakery that was even halfway decent. Often, they were located way out in the Bronx or they were way too expensive. I had no idea that Scarsdale was as rich as it was. When we started, I didn't even think I'd be doing specialty cakes. I thought we'd do muffins, all kinds of muffins, and that *we'd clean up.*" He laughs. "I didn't realize that you can't make any money selling muffins. And then someone came in and wanted a wedding cake; they offered us five hundred dollars. We thought we'd hit the jackpot!"

That was 1999, a long time ago. Since then, Lulu Cake Boutique has evolved into Westchester's signature cake designer. Lulu's trademark style is, simply put, fabulous. Look for Lulu cakes to regularly adorn the best-selling bridal magazines (but, be warned, their prices may have risen).

HUDSON VALLEY APPLE CAKE

(YIELDS ONE 9 X 13-INCH CAKE)

¾ cup melted unsalted butter, cooled (or you may substitute oil)

¾ cup applesauce

2 eggs

1½ cups granulated sugar

1 teaspoon vanilla

2½ cups all-purpose flour (preferably unbleached and organic)

2 teaspoons ground cinnamon or allspice

½ teaspoon salt

1 teaspoon baking soda

4 cups diced tart apples (such as Northern Spy or Rome Beauty)

1 cup shredded tart apples (such as Northern Spy or Rome Beauty)

1 cup toasted walnuts (optional)

1 cup Muscat or sultana raisins (optional)

Preheat oven to 350°F. Butter a 9 x 13-inch cake pan. In a large bowl using a handheld electric mixer or whisk (or in the bowl of a stand mixer fitted with the paddle attachment), beat the melted butter, applesauce, and eggs together until the mixture is creamy. Slowly add the sugar and vanilla and beat well.

In a separate bowl combine the flour, cinnamon or allspice, salt, and baking soda. Slowly add the flour mixture to the egg mixture and mix until just combined. Do not overmix. The batter will be quite thick. Fold in the apples (and nuts and raisins, if used). Scrape the batter into the prepared pan and set it in the center of the oven. Bake the cake for 45 minutes to an hour, or until the center springs back when lightly touched and a tester inserted into the center comes out clean. At this point the cake should be beginning to pull away from the sides of the pan. Cool and serve.

MP Taverna

1 BRIDGE STREET
IRVINGTON, NY 10533
(914) 231-7854
MICHAELPSILAKIS.COM
EXECUTIVE CHEF/OWNER: MICHAEL PSILAKIS

In some ways Italian food has become as American as apple pie: Pizza is just as vital to the American canon as the fabled wedge of fruit pastry. But having grown up on Long Island in a Greek American family, Chef Michael Psilakis dared to ask this question: What do the foods of Italy have that the foods of Greece don't?

If any chef was poised to change American attitudes toward Greek cuisine, it was Psilakis. His kitchen career is practically the stuff of culinary school legend. In one single year, in 2008, Psilakis won both *Food & Wine* magazine's Best New Chef and *Bon Appetit* magazine's Chef of the Year awards. While he was at it, Psilakis's collaboration with Donatella Arpaia—Anthos—received a Michelin star and was nominated for a James Beard Award for Best New Restaurant. After closing Anthos, Psilakis set off on his own with several high-profile Manhattan restaurants including Kefi and FISHTAG. In all, Psilakis remained loyal to his Greek background but with an urbane, New York point of view.

Psilakis's trio of MP Tavernas (in Irvington; Roslyn, Long Island; and Astoria, Queens) dispatch with the conceptual roadblocks that have hindered Greek food in America. On its menu, meatballs are listed simply as meatballs and not as six unpronounceable syllables with too many Ks. Says Psilakis, "The thing to remember is that MP Taverna is a Greek brasserie. So think about Italian food and how it's evolved in the United States, and especially in New York City. Forty years ago, when you went into an Italian restaurant, you had to see the straw-wrapped fiascos of Chianti. You had to hear Italian music playing. You had to see Italian people eating at the tables. But now when you go into an Italian restaurant, all you see is a pretty restaurant. We're trying to do the same thing for Greek restaurants. MP Taverna does not look like a Greek restaurant at all; it looks like a brasserie. MP Taverna has the comfort of the known."

GRILLED BRANZINO

(SERVES 4)

4 (1–2 pound) branzinos, scaled and gutted

Extra-virgin olive oil

Salt and pepper

3 cloves garlic, sliced thin

10 fingerling potatoes, par-cooked

24 cherry tomatoes, halved

24 kalamata olives, pitted

24 green olives, pitted

2 sweet onions, sliced into rings and grilled

1 tablespoon dried oregano

½ cup feta cheese

Juice of 2 lemons

1 tablespoon chopped parsley

1 tablespoon chopped basil

1 tablespoon chopped dill

Preheat a grill to medium-high. Brush each fish with olive oil and season with salt and pepper. Place the fish on the hot grill and grill them, flipping once, for approximately 8 minutes, or until the fish are cooked through and lightly charred. Set aside.

In a large, heavy-bottomed pan, add 2 tablespoons extra-virgin olive oil and heat until shimmering. Add the garlic and par-cooked potatoes and sauté until lightly brown. Add tomatoes, olives, grilled onion rings, dried oregano, and feta cheese. Toss the mixture briefly in the pan, then transfer to a serving platter. Place the grilled fish on top of the warm salad. Squeeze fresh lemon juice over the fish, then drizzle with more extra-virgin olive oil. Sprinkle with fresh herbs and serve.

THE PARLOR

14 CEDAR STREET
DOBBS FERRY, NY 10522
(914) 478-8200
CHEF/OWNER: DAVID DIBARI

One way to consider Chef David DiBari's second bricks-and-mortar venture, The Parlor, is to think of this pizzeria as David DiBari unchained. While The Cookery, also in Dobbs Ferry, was merely mischievous when it deemphasized the accepted standards in Italian restaurants—say, thick tablecloths and pricey Barolo—The Parlor steps almost joyfully into the role of provocateur. On The Parlor's corrugated, graffiti-tagged walls, you won't find one inch of Carrera marble, and, just look around, here are no subway tiles. Instead, The Parlor's decor is just what you bring to it. Literally. But for an underlayment of graffiti (itself crowd sourced in a contest), The Parlor's decor invites you to scrawl YOUR NAME HERE.

Adhering to a strict DIY ethos, the design—and much of its execution—comes from the minds of The Cookery team. DiBari himself hunted for the worn cafeteria tables and Catholic girls' school chairs that populate The Parlor's dining room in the trenchlike antiques fields of Brimfield, Massachusetts. Aside from some installed corrugated metal, the space's walls and ceiling have simply been stripped to whatever lay beneath. In some cases, that's surreally juvenile wallpaper; in others, it's bare brick and floor joists. An homage to DiBari's girlfriend, Cathy Cercena—an image of her smiling lips—graces The

Parlor's wood-fueled oven. This is a restaurant created by and for its cooks.

Says DiBari, "The Parlor is the first time that I could fully represent a piece of me in a restaurant. I feel like, finally, I've been able to do everything and express everything in a really limited space." On the walls you'll find everything from the logos of local punk bands to publicity shots of the 1980s hair bands that informed DiBari's Hudson-side youth in Verplanck, New York. "The Parlor was basically a canvas for me to show who I am and where I'm from."

At The Parlor the decor's pared-down, three-chord aesthetic backs a menu of exemplary craftsmanship that includes locally sourced produce, house-smoked meats, and hand-stretched mozzarella. If you can imagine it, The Parlor is as close to an artisanal pizza dive as the Hudson Valley comes. "It's about cutting out all the pretense. I always say it's okay to eat serious and have fun. To have fun is all we want to do in life and, for me, cooking is having fun. I feel like, if I'm not having fun, then I shouldn't be doing it."

Pizza with Fresh Lemon, Garlic, Basil & Smoked Scamorza

(MAKES SIX 10-INCH PIES)

For the pizza dough:

2 cups warm water
1 ounce active dry yeast
20 ounces King Arthur flour
½ ounce kosher salt

For the pizza:

36 paper-thin slices fresh lemon
30 thin slices garlic
18 fresh basil leaves
1½ pounds smoked scamorza cheese,
    cut into 36 slices
⅓ cup grated Parmigiano Reggiano
⅓ cup olive oil
Fleur de sel to taste

To make the pizza dough: In the bowl of a stand mixer fitted with the dough hook, place the warm water. Add the yeast and about half of the flour. Add the salt. With the mixer set to low, stir the mixture until it forms a smooth, liquid batter with the consistency of heavy cream. When the batter is smooth, allow it to rise in the mixing bowl for 15 minutes, or until it is foamy, bubbly, and about double in size.

When doubled, switch the mixer to medium speed and carefully add the remaining flour. If it is very humid in your kitchen, you may need to add more flour. Knead the dough in the machine on medium speed for about 5 minutes. When you're done, the dough will be wet and should fall off the hook easily. Place the dough in a floured pan or bowl and allow it to rest for 30 minutes.

After it has rested, portion the dough into six 7-ounce balls. Place the balls in lightly greased quart containers with lids. Allow the dough to rest, sealed in lidded containers, in the refrigerator for at least 1 hour. Alternatively, you can leave the dough in the refrigerator overnight.

To make the pizza: Heat a wood-fueled pizza oven to about 800°F. About 15 minutes before you plan to make the pizzas, remove the containers of dough from the refrigerator to allow the dough to rise in temperature. This relaxes the dough and makes it easier to work. After 15 minutes gently press the dough with your hands, pushing the air to the outer edges of the ball. Keep pressing until you have a round, flat disc. Begin to stretch and pull the dough disc into a thin, 10-inch round. Cover the pie with six slices of lemon, five slices of garlic, three basil leaves, four slices of *scamorza*, 1 tablespoon grated Parmigiano Reggiano, and a drizzling of olive oil. Slide the pizza onto a paddle and bake, spinning the pie twice, in your wood-burning oven. Each pie will take 60–90 seconds to cook.

Scott Vaccaro of Captain Lawrence Brewing Company

444 SAW MILL RIVER ROAD
ELMSFORD, NY 10523
914-741-BEER (2337)
CAPTAINLAWRENCEBREWING.COM

Unlike other young entrepreneurs armed with a business plan and a wad of investment capital, Captain Lawrence's Scott Vaccaro was not concerned with looking "money." In 2006, when Vaccaro was twenty-seven years old and launching his original brewery in Pleasantville, New York, he was living in his parent's house and sleeping in the twin bed of his boyhood. In fact, when a pint of Captain Lawrence beer could be bought in Manhattan's

Gramercy Tavern, Vaccaro still lived at his parent's house and sometimes delivered his beer in person via his Volkswagen Jetta.

"My salesman at the time was my cousin Joe. And while I was building the whole place out, he was knocking on doors and trying to figure out, alright, who is even interested in talking about a local beer? Which restaurants wanted to support the idea before even tasting it? We got some good feedback, and, basically, we went from town to town. How many bars sold draught beer (because we were only going to do draught beer when we opened up)? How many were just saying 'No. We only sell Bud, Miller, and Coors'?

"The day my beer was ready, we knew exactly where to go with it. In May of the first year—we opened in January 2006, so five months into it—Joe Marino of American Beer in Brooklyn called up saying that he wanted to distribute our beer in Brooklyn, New York City, and Manhattan. So I thought, 'I'll give this a shot and give Marino a call.' It was probably the smartest thing I ever did."

Signing Danny Meyer's restaurants—Union Square Cafe, Tabla, Eleven Madison Park, Gramercy Tavern—was another huge breakthrough for Vaccaro. "When we presented in front of their manager's meeting, it was basically all or nothing. You're either approved in all of his restaurants or none. So Blue Smoke has been a big one, Shake Shack another."

In 2012, Vaccaro moved his Captain Lawrence Brewing Company from its original Pleasantville digs to a new space at 444 Saw Mill River Road in Elmsford. The move nearly doubled CLBC's size, plus Vaccaro gained the ability to produce twelve-ounce bottles. Nowadays, you can find classic CLBC brews—Freshchester Pale Ale, Liquid Gold, and Smoked Porter—on supermarket shelves next to Sierra Nevada and Guinness. Rumor has it that those bottles are delivered by actual truck (and not via Volkswagen Jetta).

Plates

121 Myrtle Boulevard
Larchmont, NY 10538
(914) 834-1244
platesonthepark.com
Executive Chef/Owner: Matthew Karp

Bigger is not better. Larchmont's tiny, somewhat creaky boutique restaurant might be small in square footage but it makes up for that in bona fides. Chef Matthew Karp was raised in nearby Scarsdale, which happens to be a nursery of local culinary stars. Adam Kaye (Blue Hill at Stone Barns), Stephen Paul Mancini (Restaurant North), Zak Pelaccio (Fish & Game), and Shea Gallante (Italian Kitchen) also come from its streets. Karp earned his Master's in Culinary Arts from the Cordon Bleu in Paris. From there he staged all over Europe in Michelin 2- and 3-star restaurants, eventually winding up in New York City at Restaurant Daniel and Bouley. Given his trajectory toward ever more elegant restaurants, it's a surprise that Karp landed in sleepy Larchmont at all.

But the space that would eventually become Plates was hard to refuse. The restaurant is housed in a turn-of-the-twentieth-century frame house that was built as a resting place for the railroad workers that toiled on the nearby tracks. The historic wood and stucco structure is rumored to have once been a speakeasy, and there is still something secretive about it—it's nestled beside a romantic pocket park. On some nights, white mist hovers around its foundation.

Unlike the toney restaurants that mark Karp's past, Plates does not strive to be a once-in-a-lifetime splurge. Instead, Karp's approachable American cuisine features seasonal, sophisticated takes on standards—but those can range from reconceived Ring Dings to the beautiful dishes that follow.

Soft-Shell Crab with Summer Fruits & Vegetables

(SERVES 4)

For the fruits and vegetables:

1 watermelon
1 cantaloupe
1 Crenshaw melon
1 tablespoon olive oil
Salt and pepper to taste
5 ears corn
1 tablespoon unsalted butter
1 cup chicken stock
8 ramps
A splash of olive oil

For the crab tempura:

1 cup flour
¼ cup cornstarch
1 cup water
¼ cup beer
2 quarts canola oil
4 soft-shell crabs

To prepare the fruits and vegetables: Using a melon baller, scoop fifteen balls from each of the watermelon, cantaloupe, and Crenshaw melons. Place these in a bowl with olive oil and season to taste with salt and pepper. Using a heavy knife,

cut the corn kernels from the cobs. Reserve 2 cups and set aside. In a medium saucepan over medium heat, melt the butter and sauté the remaining kernels of corn. When tender, transfer them to a blender. Add the chicken stock and puree until smooth. Set aside. Heat a grill or grill pan over high heat. When hot, lightly dress the ramps with olive oil and grill until tender. Season with salt and pepper and set aside.

To make the crab tempura: In a medium-size bowl whisk together the flour, cornstarch, water, and beer. Chill the batter while you heat the oil. In a heavy-bottomed, 4-quart saucepan, heat the canola oil to 375°F. When the oil is hot, dip two crabs into the tempura batter and then into the oil. Fry the crabs for 3 minutes. Drain on paper towels. Repeat for the remaining two crabs.

To plate the dish: Place the melon balls in the center of four plates. Place reserved corn and corn sauce around the melon and then center the crabs on top. Garnish with grilled ramps and serve.

TUNA CRUDO

(SERVES 4)

4 ounces sushi grade tuna
4 ounces hamachi tuna
Salt and pepper to taste
Juice of 1 lemon
2 tablespoons olive oil
2 teaspoons shredded mint
2 teaspoons shredded basil
½ cup chopped celery

Slice both tunas paper thin. Season with salt and pepper and then carefully toss in a bowl with the lemon juice, olive oil, mint, and basil. Arrange artfully on a cold plate and serve. Garnish with celery.

POLPETTINA

102 FISHER AVENUE
EASTCHESTER, NY 10709
(914) 961-0061
POLPETTINA.COM
CO-OWNER/EXECUTIVE CHEF: MIKE ABRUZESE;
CO-OWNER: KYLE INSERRA

It's counterintuitive in a current restaurant world so dominated by PR launches and first-in-the-door bloggers, but sometimes stealth is a great quality for a restaurant to have. In 2011 the plucky (and tiny) Polpettina debuted on a sleepy street corner in Eastchester with a few tables and a seriously sketchy bathroom that sported a mop sink and was accessed through the kitchen. Polpettina's youthful owners—the perennially T-shirt clad Mike Abruzese and Kyle Inserra—cleared their throats and declared that their intention was to serve comfort food standards like meatballs, french fries, and pizzas. Which would have been straightforward (and completely unremarkable) if that's what the pair actually did.

Lured through the door with guilty hopes of greasy, orange pizza slices and disco fries, diners were amazed to find locally sourced cheeses, Hudson Valley produce,

and a fairly ambitious craft beer program. Along with Polpettina's basic pizzas—which are hardly basic and include house-made mozzarella, San Marzano tomatoes, and La Quercia salumi—you'll find luxurious oddities like pasta tossed with sea urchin butter and the lamb and foie gras meatballs.

Postscript: Polpettina's overwhelming success enabled it to expand into the space next door to accommodate twice as many tables (plus a luxurious new bathroom).

LAMB MEATBALLS WITH FOIE GRAS SAUCE, MINT & PECORINO

(SERVES 6–8 AS AN APPETIZER)

For the foie gras sauce:

3 tablespoons extra-virgin olive oil

3 shallots, sliced

3 cloves garlic, chopped

1 pound Hudson Valley foie gras (grade B or C is fine), cut into 1-inch pieces

1 cup cream sherry

3 cups heavy cream

Sea salt to taste

Freshly ground pepper to taste

For the meatballs:

1 pound ground lamb

1 egg

2 slices good white bread, trimmed of crust and torn or chopped

2 tablespoons chopped mint

¼ cup chopped parsley

3 cloves garlic, chopped

1 teaspoon sea salt

½ teaspoon freshly ground pepper

½ teaspoon smoked paprika

½ cup extra-virgin olive oil

¼ cup shaved pecorino cheese

To make the sauce: In a saucepan over low heat, heat the olive oil and then add the shallots and garlic, sautéing them until translucent. Raise the heat to medium-high and toss in the foie gras. Sauté the pieces until they're nicely caramelized (be very careful not to burn the foie gras). When the foie is nicely caramelized, pour in the sherry and cook the mixture, scraping up the brown bits, until the liquid is reduced to a syrup consistency. Add the heavy cream and simmer until the sauce is reduced by half. When reduced, transfer mixture to a blender (ideally, a Vitamix) and blend the sauce until it is very smooth. Pass the sauce through a fine mesh strainer and season with salt and pepper to taste. Set aside.

To make the meatballs: In a medium-size bowl mix the ground lamb with the egg, bread, 1 tablespoon of the mint, parsley, garlic, salt, pepper, and smoked paprika. Shape the mixture into 1-inch-diameter balls. In a very large skillet (preferably cast iron), heat the olive oil. Add the meatballs and fry them over medium-high heat until they're thoroughly browned and cooked, approximately 4 minutes. Blot the meatballs on a paper towel–lined plate. Serve with warm foie gras sauce, the remaining mint, and shaved pecorino.

POLPETTINA ROASTED CHICKEN

(SERVES 4)

3 sprigs fresh oregano
2 cloves garlic, crushed with edge of knife
2 teaspoons kosher salt
2 tablespoons extra-virgin olive oil
Juice of 2 lemons (reserve the lemon halves)
1 (3½-pound) whole chicken, cut into eighths
Freshly ground black pepper to taste

Preheat oven to 450°F. Make a pile of the oregano, garlic, and salt and mash the ingredients into a paste using the flat side and edge of your chef's knife. Transfer the paste to a large bowl and stir in olive oil and half of the lemon juice (reserving the remainder). Add the chicken pieces and toss to coat. Heat a large cast-iron skillet over medium-high heat and place the chicken in it, skin side down. Cook the chicken pieces until the skin is caramelized and brown, about 5–7 minutes. Turn the chicken pieces over in the pan and add the remaining lemon juice and reserved lemon halves. Transfer the skillet to the preheated oven and roast until the chicken skin is crisp, 20–25 minutes. Serve.

RED BARN BAKERY

4 SOUTH ASTOR STREET
IRVINGTON, NY 10533
(914) 231-7779
REDBARN-BAKERY.COM
CHEF/OWNER: RANDELL DODGE

When you think of a bakery, do you think of sin? Maybe the image of a girly cupcake pops into your mind—piled high with gritty frosting and a few pastel candies strewn across the top. *Naughty.*

But, get this—Randell Dodge's Red Barn Bakery does not do sin. She challenges the usual sin rhetoric associated with bakeries by offering sophisticated cakes, pies, and savories that are geared toward consenting adults. At Dodge's sleek Irvington shop, you'll find her working with 100 percent organic ingredients that are tied to the seasons and are often locally sourced. What emerges from her kitchen is absolutely beautiful and, often, good for your body. Look for many gluten-free and vegan options, too.

Red Barn Bakery sells only fair trade, organic coffee, plus Dodge sources at local farms and is a regular vendor at local farmers' markets. But the warmest thing about

Red Barn is that its community mindedness goes both ways. In a recent Kickstarter campaign (KickstartTheCookie), Dodge succeeded in raising $20,000 from Red Barn's loyal customers for new mixers, ovens, and other equipment. Everyone thinks that's really sweet.

SAVORY WILD FIDDLEHEAD TART

(MAKES ONE 8-INCH TART FOR 4–6 SERVINGS)

1 sheet of your favorite savory tart shell recipe

1 organic egg white for wash

5 tablespoons (approximately) organic extra-virgin olive oil

1½ cups sliced organic onions

1½ pounds wild fiddleheads, cleaned and trimmed

1 teaspoon organic fresh thyme leaves

2–3 cloves garlic, finely chopped

Salt and pepper to taste

1 cup sliced organic leeks

2 tablespoons unsalted organic butter

¼ cup aged organic goat cheese

2 large organic eggs

1½ cups organic heavy cream

1 cup flat leaf parsley, minced

Pinch of nutmeg

¼ cup fresh goat cheese

1 tablespoon snipped chives

Toasted pine nuts (optional)

To make the tart: Preheat oven to 350°F. Roll the pastry out on a silicone mat and fit into an 8-inch tart shell. Pierce the dough several times with a fork to allow steam to vent (this is called "docking") and then freeze the unbaked tart shell for at least 20 minutes before baking. After chilling, line the shell with foil and fill it with dried beans. Blind bake (prebake) the tart for 15 minutes. Meanwhile, in a small bowl lightly whisk the egg white. After the shell has baked for 15 minutes, brush the egg wash all over the interior of the shell. Bake for an additional 5 minutes, then remove from oven and set aside.

Coat a roasting pan with olive oil and add the onions and fiddleheads. Drizzle with a bit more olive oil and toss with thyme, garlic, and salt and pepper to taste. Roast the vegetables in the oven for 20 or so minutes, tossing occasionally. After 20 minutes pull out just the fiddleheads and return the rest of the vegetables to the oven. Bake for another 40 minutes, or until fully translucent.

In a separate pan on the stovetop, sauté the leeks in butter until wilted and translucent. Remove from heat. In a food processor combine the aged goat cheese with 1 tablespoon olive oil and process until smooth. In a separate bowl combine the two eggs with heavy cream, parsley, salt, pepper, and nutmeg.

To assemble the tart: Spread the aged goat cheese mixture over the baked tart shell. Arrange the sautéed leeks over the top, followed by the roasted onions and fiddleheads. Pour the egg and cream mixture over the fiddleheads and onions. Dot with the fresh goat cheese and scatter with chives. If desired, you can also sprinkle toasted pine nuts over the top. Bake for 20–25 minutes, or until the pastry is puffy and brown. Serve warm or at room temperature with an herb salad.

Sweet Grass Grill

24 Main Street
Tarrytown, NY 10591
(914) 631-0000
SWEETGRASSGRILL.COM
CHEF/OWNER: DAVID STARKEY; CHEF DE CUISINE: RICK KREBS

Presaging the fetishized Chipotle Grill by several years, David Starkey's modest first venture, Tomatillo in Dobbs Ferry, felt like a revelation. There, in playful, honky-tonk digs, Starkey offered a lighter, locally sourced version of good old American Tex-Mex, dubbing his style "Mexchester cuisine." Tomatillo was welcomed by locals who could treat their families to quick, crowd-pleasing burritos without shame—not to mention without antibiotics, GMOs, or unnecessary food miles, either. Tomatillo's happy hours of discounted craft beer and margaritas only sealed the deal; like evenings spent streaming Netflix rather than watching broadcast TV, Tomatillo suddenly felt like the better choice.

With the 2009 debut of Sweet Grass Grill in Tarrytown, Starkey took on a more grown-up, New American menu while still keeping his sourcing as local as ever. Even the building materials for Sweet Grass come from its immediate neighborhood; Sweet Grass's bar was hewn from an oak tree that had fallen on the nearby Rockefeller Preserve. As at Tomatillo, Starkey sources ingredients from the Stone Barns Center for Food and Agriculture. His is also supremely vegan and vegetarian friendly; there is no lonely veggie option in the bottom-of-menu ghetto here.

Says Starkey, "We try to source everything that we possibly can locally because we know we'll be getting the freshest product while keeping our carbon footprint small. But what I really enjoy about sourcing locally is that it allows you to know your farmers. They become your partners. You can't have a farm-to-table restaurant without knowing your farmers."

CHILLED GARDEN PEA SOUP

(SERVES 4)

1 cup chopped spring onions

2 tablespoons olive oil

4 cups shelled fresh peas (retain the pods for the stock; see Note)

1 cup chopped basil

½ cup chopped mint

Salt to taste

2 tablespoons blanched, peeled edamame

1 tablespoon chives

¼ cup whole Greek yogurt

In a medium sauté pan over medium heat, sauté the spring onions in 1 tablespoon of the olive oil until they are translucent. Meanwhile, fill a small stockpot with 1½–2 quarts of salted water and bring it to a boil. When the spring onions are translucent, remove them from the heat and set aside. When the water is boiling, drop in the pea pods and cook, simmering, until they have lost their vibrant color and become somewhat tender (this should take 10–20 minutes). Skim the pods from the pot and discard, retaining the cooking liquid. Add the sautéed spring onions and return the liquid to a boil. When boiling, add the shelled peas and cook until tender, about 10 minutes.

Remove the pot from the stove and begin finishing the soup. In a medium bowl prepare an ice bath. Using a skimmer, remove about 1 cup of the peas and shock them in the ice bath. As the peas are cooling, set up a blender. Pour 2 cups of the hot peas, onions, and vegetable stock into the blender and blend until the mixture is smooth. Pass this through a fine mesh strainer and reserve; do not discard the solids that remain in the strainer. You will need them later in the recipe. Repeat this process of blending and straining with all but 1–2 cups of the remaining pea/onion/vegetable stock mixture. Allow the reserved portion to cool slightly.

To the blender add the reserved solids, the cold shocked peas, basil, mint, and the reserved vegetable stock. Blend until the mixture is a smooth liquid. Pass this through a strainer into the remaining stock mixture and discard all the solids. Season with salt to taste and chill until ready to serve.

To plate: Pour the soup into four bowls. Garnish each with blanched edamame, chives, 1 tablespoon cold Greek yogurt, and a drizzle of the remaining olive oil. Serve.

Note: Frozen peas may be substituted here, but you will need to use vegetable stock in lieu of the stock (above) made with pea pods.

Taiim Falafel Shack

598 Warburton Avenue
Hastings-on-Hudson, NY 10706
(914) 478-0006
TAIIMFALAFELSHACK.COM
Owner: Zamir Iosepovici;
Chefs: Sean Carmody and Florencio Salazar

Falafel has had a hard time on these shores. What is (in Israel) a crunchy, satisfying, and juicy treat has become (in the United States) the dry and vaguely punitive fodder of broke college vegetarians who don't know enough about food to know what they are missing. Cue Taiim Falafel Shack, which hit Hastings-on-Hudson with a vengeance. Its mission: to bring authentic Israeli soul food to the banks of the Hudson River.

While this minuscule, cash-only "shack" is an actual bricks-and-mortar restaurant, Taiim offers no bathroom, no bar, and only twelve seats on-site. So what? None of this hinders Taiim's legion fans, who happily cram thigh-to-thigh for tangy, drippy falafel sandwiches, addictive hummus, and carnal *shawarmas*—all of which are paired with bright, clean salads like this one.

Taiim Falafel Shack's Quinoa Salad

(SERVES 4)

For the dressing:

2 teaspoons salt
2 teaspoons freshly ground black pepper
4 teaspoons sumac
¼ cup freshly squeezed lemon juice
½ cup extra-virgin olive oil

For the salad:

1 cup quinoa
Red pepper flakes to taste (optional)
½ cup dried chickpeas
1 small tomato, diced
2–3 scallions (white and light green parts only), chopped
½ red bell pepper, diced
½ green bell pepper, diced
Salt and pepper to taste
4 large romaine lettuce leaves

To make the dressing: Whisk the salt, pepper, sumac, lemon juice, and olive oil together and reserve.

To make the salad: Cook the quinoa according to package directions. If you'd like to use the red pepper flakes, add them to the boiling water in which you cook the quinoa. While the quinoa cooks, place the dried chickpeas in a small saucepan. Cover the chickpeas with water and bring to a boil. Reduce the heat to simmer and cook chickpeas for 30 minutes, or until tender. When the chickpeas and quinoa are fully cooked, drain and place in a large bowl. Add the tomato, scallions, peppers, and the dressing and gently toss the salad together. Season with salt and pepper to taste and serve on the romaine leaves.

X2O & the Dylan Lounge

71 Water Grant Street
Yonkers, NY 10701
(914) 965-1111
xaviars.com
Owner/Executive Chef: Peter X. Kelly;
Chef de Cuisine: Eric Diokno;
Xaviar's Restaurant Group Wine Director: Billy Rattner

If the Hudson River has a legendary figure, it's got to be Chef Peter Kelly. He practically rose, Poseidon-like, from the river itself. Kelly has spent his career on Hudson's banks creating some of the region's most beloved restaurants: X2O, Xaviar's, Freelance Cafe, and Restaurant X & Bully Boy Bar. None of this was given to him; Kelly is a self-made man. Unlike many of the chefs working in his echelon, Kelly's family could not bankroll the nascent chef's education in travel and fine dining, nor could it afford a costly Culinary Institute of America stamp of approval. Instead, Kelly's childhood was Dickensian. When Kelly was twelve, his father died. This left Kelly's mother, Harriet, a widow with twelve children (Peter was the tenth); the Kelly kids battled it out on some of the toughest streets in Yonkers.

Yet Kelly was hardworking, entrepreneurial, and enamored of the restaurant world. As children, Kelly and his brother, Ned (who still works with Peter), played imaginary restaurant games. Any spare money that Peter earned went toward dining out—and the juvenile Kelly was a tough customer: He sent his first steak back at the age of fourteen. By twenty-one Kelly had turned his high school, front-of-house job at the Plumbush Inn in Cold Spring into a captain position, and then he turned that into a shot in the Manhattan big time. At Laurent Restaurant, a fashionable frog pond on the Upper East Side, Kelly became the youngest captain in the restaurant's history. But by the time he hit twenty-three, Kelly had struck out on his own. His Xaviar's at Highlands Country Club in Garrison earned Kelly two stars from the *New York Times*.

Soon the new restaurants and accolades started to roll in. Four stars for Xaviar's in Piermont (1987), raves for Freelance Cafe & Wine Bar (1989), raves for Restaurant X & Bully Boy Bar (1997). But a new venture loomed that would dwarf all of Kelly's previous accomplishments. Lured by the city of Yonkers, Kelly took over the decrepit Yonkers recreation pier, which in 2006 jutted its rusting hulk into the Hudson from a scary, no-mans-land on the banks. Pouring millions into the historic pier, Kelly turned it into X2O, the glittering jewel in the Yonkers crown. It affords panoramic views of Manhattan to the south, the soaring Palisades to the west, and the glittering lights of the Tappan Zee to the north. It's magical.

Says Kelly, "X2O grew out of an idea to return to my roots in Yonkers. I mean, this restaurant would have been a whole lot easier to build in Chappaqua or Rye, but I wanted to be a part of the waterfront. I wanted to be a part of what this city could and will be."

Grilled Double Cut Cowboy Rib Eye with Brown Sugar Glaze & Caramelized Shallots

(SERVES 2–4 AS A MAIN DISH)

For the caramelized shallots:

¼ cup granulated sugar
10 peeled shallots
⅓ cup balsamic vinegar
½ cup brown stock or beef stock

For the steak:

1 (40-ounce) bone-in rib eye steak,
    cut 2½ inches thick
Salt and freshly cracked pepper
1 teaspoon cayenne pepper
3 tablespoons dark brown sugar

To caramelize the shallots: Preheat oven to 400°F. In an ovenproof casserole dish placed over medium heat, carefully melt the sugar and cook until it caramelizes. Do not burn the sugar. When the sugar is a dark amber color, quickly add the shallots, vinegar, and stock. Stir this mixture until the caramel is smooth, then reduce the liquid over high heat until it has thickened into a light syrup, about 3 minutes. Place the casserole in the preheated oven and roast the shallots until tender, about 20 minutes. Reserve.

To grill the rib eye: Sprinkle steak with salt and freshly cracked pepper. Rub the steak with cayenne pepper and brown sugar, then allow the steak to rest and absorb the seasoning for at least 3 hours. When ready to serve, heat an outdoor barbecue grill or indoor char grill. When it is hot, grill the steak for 3 minutes on each side until its exterior is nicely charred. Continue grilling the steak, turning often, for about 6 more minutes, aiming for medium rare. Allow the steak to rest for 10 minutes before slicing. Serve with caramelized shallots.

Bone Marrow & Alaskan Crabmeat, Garlic & Herbs, Salad of Hearts of Palm with Parsley & Frisée

(SERVES 6)

For the hearts of palm salad:

3 ounces sherry vinegar

1 tablespoon Dijon mustard

Pinch of sea salt and a few turns of freshly cracked white pepper to taste

1 cup extra-virgin olive oil

4 fresh hearts of palm, cut on a thin bias

2 bunches flat leaf parsley

1 cup frisée

Salt and freshly ground black pepper

For the bones:

3 beef marrow bones, cut into 8-inch lengths and split

Salt and freshly ground black pepper

18 ounces Alaskan king crab, shell and cartilage removed

3 cloves garlic

½ shallot

1 bunch flat leaf parsley

1 sprig tarragon

1 sprig thyme, stripped

1 tablespoon brandy

1 tablespoon Pernod

4 tablespoons unsalted butter, softened

Coarse sea salt

To make the salad: In a small bowl whisk together the vinegar, mustard, salt, and white pepper and then slowly whisk in the olive oil.

In a large bowl toss together the hearts of palm, parsley, and frisée. Season this with 4 tablespoons of the vinaigrette (reserve the remaining vinaigrette for another purpose). Season with salt and pepper to taste and set salad aside as you finish the dish.

To prepare the marrow bones: Preheat oven to 350°F. Season the marrow with salt and pepper and place the bones on a sheet pan. Pour a small amount of water on the bottom of the pan and wrap the pan in plastic wrap. Place the wrapped pan in the preheated oven and allow the marrow bones to steam in the oven for 5 minutes, or until their marrow is set. Remove the pan from the oven and allow the marrow to cool. Using a spoon, remove the marrow from each bone and slice it into five equal pieces.

Slice the crabmeat into small lengths and fill each bone with five pieces of crabmeat, pressing the crab sections into the hollow of each bone. Top the crabmeat with five slices of the bone marrow and set aside.

To make a compound butter: In the bowl of a food processor, place the garlic, shallot, parsley, tarragon, thyme, brandy, and Pernod and process into a smooth paste. Add the butter and cream the mixture together. Heat 6 tablespoons of this compound butter until it is just melted. Spoon 1 tablespoon of the butter over each crab and marrow bone. Place the bones back in the oven and warm just until heated through, about 5 minutes.

Toss the hearts of palm salad and plate alongside one hot marrow bone.

Savory Warm Corn Custard with Green Onion, Crab & Shaved Chorizo

(SERVES 6)

For the custard:

1 Thai chile

4 ears fresh corn

3 eggs

12 ounces heavy cream

Salt and white pepper to taste

For the crab and chorizo garnish:

2 tablespoons unsalted butter

3–4 ounces crabmeat

2 scallions, minced

Salt and pepper to taste

1 Spanish chorizo sausage (frozen solid)

To make the custard: Preheat oven to 325°F. Butter six 4-ounce ramekins and set aside. To a large pot of generously salted water, add the Thai chile and bring to a boil.

Using a heavy knife, cut the corn kernels from the cobs. Cook the corn kernels in the boiling water for 3 minutes, then use a fine mesh skimmer to remove the corn from the water. Drain the corn and discard the chile.

Fill a kettle with water and bring this to a boil while you prepare the rest of the dish. In a mixing bowl place the eggs and cream. Beat lightly, then add 1½ cups of the cooked corn (reserve the remainder of the corn for garnish). Into a blender pour the corn mixture and puree it until smooth. Season the corn mixture to taste with salt and white pepper, then pour the mixture into the prepared ramekins.

Place the ramekins in a roasting pan and pour boiling water from the kettle into the roasting pan until the water comes three-quarters of the way up the sides of the ramekins. Place the pan in the preheated oven and bake for approximately 50 minutes, or until custard is set. Remove the ramekins from the water bath and keep them warm as you finish the dish.

To plate: In a medium sauté pan placed over medium heat, melt the butter. Add crabmeat and minced scallions and heat through. Season crab mixture with salt and pepper to taste. Loosen custard from the ramekins and invert one ramekin onto the center of each serving plate. Spoon the crabmeat and scallion mixture around custard and, using a handheld micro grater, shave a fine dusting of chorizo over custard. Serve immediately.

SPAETZLE WITH MUSTARD SEED

(SERVES 6)

4 cups all-purpose flour
1 cup whole milk
4 eggs
1 teaspoon Dijon mustard
1 tablespoon mustard seeds
¼ teaspoon grated fresh nutmeg
Salt and pepper to taste
1 tablespoon unsalted butter

Place a large pot of salted water over high heat and bring to a boil. In the bowl of a stand mixer fitted with the paddle attachment, place flour and milk and mix on medium speed. Add eggs one at a time until the mixture is smooth and elastic.

Spoon in the mustard, mustard seeds, nutmeg, salt, and pepper and combine. Place a spaetzle maker (or colander) over the boiling water. Push the spaetzle batter through the spaetzle maker into the boiling water. Using a wire skimmer, remove the cooked spaetzle as it rises to the top. Allow the spaetzle to cool and set aside.

When you are ready to serve, place a nonstick pan over medium-high heat. Add the butter and heat until it is sizzling and light brown. Immediately add the spaetzle to the butter and sauté until it is lightly browned and puffed. Season to taste with salt and pepper and serve immediately.

Index

About the Author

Julia Sexton stepped into the role of restaurant critic for *Westchester Magazine* in 2007, after fifteen years cooking in professional kitchens. She has published articles in the *New York Times, Boston Globe,* and several magazines. Her food features, reviews, and recipe-based articles for *Westchester* regularly appear in the *New York Times* food blog *What We're Reading.* In 2009, Sexton's own blog, *Eat Drink Post,* won the CRMA Best Blog Award in all subjects. A Hudson Valley native, she's been a local editor of *Zagat's Westchester and Hudson Valley Restaurant Survey* since 2009.

About the Photographer

Andre Baranowski is a photographer best known for his beautiful and sensual still life, food, travel, interior, and landscape photography. His client list ranges from top American corporations like Benjamin Moore, Kellogg's, American Express, and Hearst to magazines like *Saveur, Better Homes and Gardens, Garden Design, Food & Wine, Men's Health, Shape, Departures, Country Gardens,* and many others. Andre has photographed a number of books including, *Mediterranean Fresh* by Joyce Goldstein, *Sustainably Delicious* by Michel Nischan, and *The Kimchi Chronicles* by Marja and Jean-Georges Vongerichten. He lives in Westchester County, New York. Visit him at andrebaranowskiphoto.com.

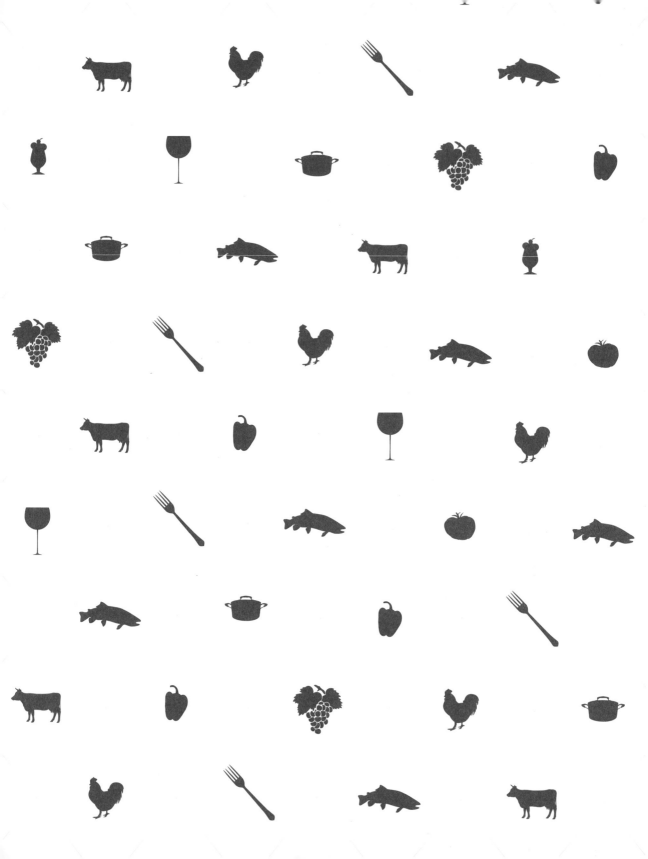